ASK WHAT
YOU
CANDO

Why local government
needs more technologists
and how you too can serve

David Doyle

First published by David Doyle 2020

Copyright © 2020 by David Doyle

ISBN: 978-0-578-66537-5

First edition.

Advisor: Jenny Richards
Cover art by Jennifer Fox
Editing by Lisa McCoy

And so, my fellow Americans: ask not what your country can do for you—ask what you can do for your country.
- President John F Kennedy, Inaugural Address, 20 January 1961

For my daughter, Chandler.

CONTENTS

PART I: THE "WHY"

PART II: THE "WHAT"

PART III: THE "HOW"

PART IV: OK, WHAT'S NEXT

ACKNOWLEDGEMENTS

I wish to express my profound appreciation to the many people who helped make this book a reality. Without their help in ways large and small, completing this book may not have been possible and their contributions helped make this book better.

Jenny Richards, who was an amazingly supportive partner in crime during my time at the city of Seattle, and who later stepped up to offer her considerable talents and help me get this book published. From regular breakfast and lunch meetings, creating a marketing and launch plan for the book, being the first person to read the full book and giving me incredibly valuable feedback, and holding me accountable. Words can properly express my thanks for her support, and belief in me and the value of this book. If I was the writer, then she was the producer.

Melanie Kitzan, with whom I shared my recent sabbatical adventure and who was a constant source of support and encouragement from the very beginning of this project. A gifted writer whose storytelling abilities I am in awe of; I'm looking forward to reading her first book before too long.

Kevin Merritt, who provided great encouragement, challenged my ambition with this book, and generously introduced me to potential advocates of this book from within his own network. As CEO of Socrata, he was very supportive of my work as Open Data Manager at the city of Seattle, and his continued support since then is greatly appreciated.

Lisa McCoy, who edited the book and helped make my multi-dialect English more legible! I thank her for her patience with my ever changing schedule and requirements as I walked through this process for the first time.

Jennifer Fox (Atomic Fox Design), who designed the book covers and other branding assets used in the book's website and social media content. She was able to take my initial concept and translate it into a book cover that truly captures the power of the words in the book's title.

To everyone who took time out of their busy schedules to both read and provide feedback on the book outline, all of which was really valuable and some of which fundamentally altered the content and structure of the book. All of you helped make this a much better book. Thank you to: Rachel Petzold, Melanie Kitzan, Selena Tonti, Steve Balo, Kevin Merritt, Wendy Cort, Nina Showell, Eloisa Renyault, Richard Todd, Kate Garman, Katrina Earnst, Ismaila Midadi, Jenny Richards, Sasha Anderson, Ron Murray, Bridget Quigg, Will Saunders, Gwen Goetz, Michael Mattmiller, Brittany Fiore-Gartland, and Tanner Barlow.

Professor Dan Jacoby at the University of Washington Bothell, my capstone advisor during my Policy Studies master's degree and who has continued to mentor me in the years since my graduation. His advice and insights have been hugely beneficial as I navigated both my time in public service and in the writing of this book.

To all of the wonderful staff at the Starbucks at Redmond Ridge near my home, where some of this book was written. Their support and camaraderie, as well as the endless supply of Tall Skinny Mochas that I consumed over countless hours working on this book, were always greatly appreciated.

The staff at the University of Washington Bothell library who helped me with research questions and for providing such a great space with extended opening hours. The bulk of the book was written here. UW Bothell holds a special place in my heart, it was where I began the journey that ultimately led me into public service and local government, and it seemed fitting to write the book there and avail of the extended writing hours when the Starbucks staff had had enough of me.

Public Servants: to all of my fellow public servants, those who served in the past and those who continue to serve until the present day, for providing me with the inspiration to serve in government myself. I would like to call out all of the amazing public servants who I had the honor to work with during my time at the city of Seattle, I learned an enormous amount from this amazing group of people and much of that learning informed the content in this book. A special word of thanks to my former open data colleague at the State of Washington, Will Saunders. He helped influence my decision to enter local government and was a tremendous support in pursuing regional open data initiatives, and provided me with great insights into how state government differs from municipal government. To my sister Niamh, who in her own right is a fine public servant as an elementary school teacher in Ireland, and ironically who was present when I first sketched out the idea for this book in a coffee shop in my home town of Gorey, Ireland in September 2018.

To all of my family back in Ireland, and especially my parents, Seamus and Kathleen, for their constant and unconditional support from afar as I navigate my unconventional career path and embark upon new adventures that may not always make sense initially.

Finally, to my beloved daughter Chandler, to whom I dedicate this book. Her presence is a constant reminder of the future, and of what's next. Watching how she and her Gen Z friends interact and use technology in every aspect of their lives gives me valuable insights into how this next generation to enter our workforce will think about connectivity, communication, online learning, digital services, and data privacy. They will demand much more from their government when it comes to technology, that much is clear to me. Believe me, Chandler and her generation will be asking what they can do.

INTRODUCTION

This book is a call to action.

The title of this book is a play on the challenge laid down in President Kennedy's inaugural address moments after being sworn in as the thirty-fifth president of the United States. His short presidency marks the high point of how government was perceived in largely favorable terms within the last century. Working in government in the early 1960s was considered to be one of the coolest things a new technology or science graduate could do. Top graduates from the best colleges were recruited into the federal government, the National Aeronautics and Space Administration (NASA), and the many contractors that supplied government programs with the cutting-edge technologies required to achieve their ambitious goals. The immense scale of government budgets and solid congressional support enabled them to drive the programs that resulted in the development of many of the technologies we take for granted today and helped humans set foot on the moon. It wasn't until the Obama administration, some forty-five years later, that we got close to having similar positive aspirations about serving in government.

A lot has changed since the Kennedy era in terms of technology and power structures. We are seeing the rise of powerful cities leading the way in terms of progressive policymaking, and the implementation of innovative technologies within our communities that are changing how we live, work, and play. One of the key differences between then and now is that these technology-focused initiatives are being almost solely driven by the private sector. These new paradigms have led to an array of complex challenges and many unintended consequences. It is no secret that local governments across the United States struggle to keep pace with increasingly disruptive technologies emerging with growing frequency. The gap between the public's experience when availing themselves of government services and what they enjoy in other aspects of their daily lives continues to widen. In an era where almost all other aspects of our lives have been disrupted to a greater or lesser extent by technology, local government remains stubbornly immune to the forces of cultural change wrought by technology.

As a technologist who had a long career in one of the world's leading software companies before serving in local government in a major U.S. city, I believe we are entering a period where a real technological transformation of local government could be at hand. The current political climate is leading to a renewed interest and engagement in public service in all its forms. The need for increased government regulation of powerful new technologies and platforms is resulting in an increased awareness of the need for government to play a key role in our society. The Millennial and Gen Z generations appear to be the most idealistic and mission-driven cohorts since the early 1960s and find the mission of government appealing. Some technologists in the private sector are questioning whether their work is having the kind of positive societal impact they originally envisioned. Many skilled technologists are asking the question "why can't government be better?" and volunteer their time and skills towards civic technology initiatives that aim to improve their local governments. The building blocks are available, and the conditions ripe, for a new wave of technologists to join the effort to build a new local government ecosystem. One that leverages the power of data and technology to efficiently and fairly deliver digital services to the public, positively increase social impact, and improve people's perceptions of their government. In a world where it feels like everything is being disrupted to some degree or another, now seems like the time to seriously ask why our government institutions are not better equipped to handle the current technological and data-driven disruptions we're experiencing. Better yet, why are they not better equipped to take advantage of these advances?

DISRUPTION

Disruption caused by technology has always been a fact of life. From the earliest inventions such as the wheel, to the invention of navigational aids and the printing press thousands of years later, to in more modern times the discovery of flight and the eventual leap into space and the development of computing, each new technology has resulted in humans making significant leaps in our ability to push the boundaries of knowledge and exploration.

Since the latter half of the eighteenth century, we have experienced three major industrial revolutions that have transformed our ability—both individually and as a society—to be productive, and we now appear to be firmly in the early stages of the fourth such revolution. The First Industrial Revolution began in Britain around 1760 with the development of the steam engine, which led to the development of the first factories. Building upon this technology, the Second Industrial Revolution came roughly one hundred years later, with the development of new industries based on steel, oil, and electricity powering mass production and building some of the great cities that we know and love today. The light bulb, communications technologies such as the telegraph and telephone, and the internal combustion engine were some of the major inventions of this era that completely transformed how humans traveled, communicated, and lived. Fast-forward roughly another century, and we enter the Third Industrial Revolution, powered by the creation of the semiconductor and the development of the Internet. This began the process of digitization. We are now in the Fourth Industrial Revolution, where new technologies powered by data and artificial intelligence are transforming our world and where the boundaries between the physical, biological, and digital spheres are blurred.

What is notable about the emergence of these new paradigms is that the time period between these technology-driven revolutions is shrinking. While there was roughly a one-hundred-year period between the first, second, and third industrial revolutions, the gap between the third and fourth has been reduced to about sixty years. As the power and capabilities of new technologies increase exponentially, we should expect the periods of time between major industrial changes powered by technology to continue to shrink. The implications of more rapid revolutionary changes powered by technology are not yet fully understood. Society is currently grappling with the unintended consequences of recent technological advances around smart phones, social media, and big data. Aside from government needing to play a more central role in understanding and regulating these powerful platforms and capabilities, government will also need to develop its capacity to better understand how to leverage and manage these technologies within the public sector itself.

THE FOURTH INDUSTRIAL
REVOLUTION AND GOVERNMENT

Disruption comes in many forms, not just technological. Over time we have experienced disruptions to our financial systems, major shifts in the makeup of our workforce, and societal changes driven by major political reforms. Sometimes the disruptions to existing systems and ways of life were initially welcomed, other times not so. Ultimately, society readjusted, and we became even more productive than before. One common element in all of these disruptive events is the central role that our government plays in them, either driving the disruption via new policies and laws or reacting to major political or economic disruptions through regulation and oversight. Recent rapid advances in technology continue to disrupt many industries and reshape our expectations about how we consume goods and services in almost real-time modes, be those goods physical or digital. How we interact, travel, shop, eat, and arrange our lives have altered in some dramatic ways over the last ten years. Our capacity to quickly adapt to these changes is remarkable.

Ironically, government itself has proven to be mostly immune to technological disruption on a massive scale. Why is this? In the private sector, when an industry or market gets disrupted, it usually means that the incumbent is usurped by a newcomer to the market. In some cases, the previous market leader goes out of business and quickly fades from the collective memory of society, take Netflix effectively putting Blockbuster out of business as an example. With government, it is not possible to completely replace all of the functions and services it provides with the emergence of a new startup or two. To do that kind of massive disruption similar to what we experience in the private sector, we would need to create an entirely new form of government. That is not an option that any of us truly want. This permanent nature of government is one of the reasons why it tends to be a technology laggard—it doesn't face any existential threats from the market.

However, in my view, it is inevitable that government, too, will be disrupted. What will this "disruption" of the government actually look like if it cannot be completely replaced? When people speak about disruption within government, they appear to be thinking more about how to enable government to function more efficiently and to provide digital services more akin to what the public enjoys in other aspects of their lives and less about the kinds of market disruption that we see in the private sector. Words and phrases like "enabling innovation" or "the digital transformation of government" tend to be used to describe how government will be disrupted, which doesn't suggest a massive upheaval. This lack of urgency about addressing these technological deficiencies in government runs the risk of leaving the public sector in a more precarious state in the future. Why?

One aspect of the disruptive age that we are now living through that doesn't command much attention is that we're still relatively early into this Fourth Industrial Revolution. If we think the issues we are grappling with today are complex, as we push further into this technological age, we will encounter profoundly more challenging questions caused by increasingly advanced technologies. Advances in the capabilities of systems powered by machine learning and artificial intelligence (AI) continue at a staggering pace. As technologies such as blockchain gain mainstream acceptance, we can expect new platforms to emerge that enable paradigm shifts in areas such as the emergence of mainstream digital currencies, a continued push towards voting in elections by using our phones, and a better ability to control access to and sharing of our personal data. Quantum computing systems will provide an exponential growth in computing power compared to what exists today and will require a new class of algorithms to be designed to take advantage of the probabilistic outputs of this new generation of super computers.[1] We can expect new breakthroughs in climate change research and drug development, fundamental changes to our encryption and cybersecurity infrastructure, and radical improvements in how we can solve difficult optimization problems (of which the government has many!). If government at all levels is struggling to come to terms with the technologies that exist today, then urgent action is required to develop the internal technical capacity to not only better handle the needs of today but also the emerging needs of the next decade or two.

RESEARCH & DEVELOPMENT VERSUS OPERATIONS

Apart from some rare exceptions at the federal government level, governments do not create new technologies. Contrast this with the tech sector, where companies will invest huge sums of money into research and development (R&D) with the explicit aim of inventing the technologies of the future and disrupting existing markets. Government, on the other hand, is primarily focused on operations such as deploying technology that can assist in its public service mission. This is an important distinction, and one that needs to be well understood by technologists and others who are attempting to build technology transfer pipelines between the public and private sectors. The DNA of a private-sector tech firm will not be easily transferrable to the public sector, and vice versa. There have been several efforts to build partnerships between the tech sector and the public sector, many of which are referenced in this book, and yet I have witnessed multiple instances where there is a fundamental disconnect between those two sectors, where invalid assumptions are being made and not corrected in time, and where too many initiatives fade away without having achieved their desired outcomes. How do we improve the chances of these worthy programs and initiatives succeeding? By expanding the flow of technical talent into government. By having more technologists within government with knowledge of the private-sector technology ecosystem, we can build up the capacity of government to more accurately translate the requirements and expectations of both parties when it comes to advancing the use of technology and data within government.

THE FLOW OF TALENT INTO THE PUBLIC SECTOR

My own journey into local government began when I read a paper commissioned by the Ford Foundation titled "A Future of Failure? The Flow of Technology Talent into Government and Society."[2] It was the first time that I had read a description of the journey I was attempting to make, and to have a framework and language with which to describe the pivot in my own career. That paper led me down many more paths of research, where I discovered the world of open government and open data and, ultimately, to an incredibly rewarding period of public service as open data manager for the city of Seattle

The reason that the "Future of Failure" report resonated so much with me was because it described a problem that I intuitively knew existed but had never seen laid bare in this manner. It "examines and aims to staunch the flow of technology talent away from the public sector and finds a severe shortage of individuals in civil society and government who have the skills necessary to develop, leverage, or understand technology" I also knew I was one of the individuals who was being referred to in that report and that I was now in a position in my career to be able to do something about it.

What also became clear to me during my public service is that while local government has yet to be disrupted to the same extent as other sectors in our society, there is pent-up demand to make significant changes happen. A range of efforts have been undertaken both inside and outside of government when it comes to "modernizing" government, mostly funded by private-sector actors. These include philanthropic efforts like Bloomberg Philanthropies "What Works Cities" program, and other initiatives supported by large technology companies and other actors that have a vested interest in helping government to modernize.[3] These programs have enabled some amazing work and continue to have demonstrable impact, some of which I saw firsthand during my own public service. These programs are designed to be temporary in nature and are relatively small in terms of the scale of the technological capacity they help build, with a focus on helping local governments maintain those efforts through their own budgets once the initial philanthropic funding has ended. This book is arguing for a related focus on building up the internal technological capacity within local government, to help amplify the impact of these efforts to drive the modernization of local government from the inside. This is where you, the aspiring public-sector technologist, comes in.

HOW I CAME TO WRITE THIS BOOK

The genesis of this book came exactly one year into my local government career, when I wrote an article on LinkedIn that described my journey from the private to the public sector.[4] I wrote that article because I had come to realize that the path that I had been following was not one that was well traveled. I knew this because of the number of questions and at times quizzical looks I got when I shared the news with my friends and colleagues that I was leaving Microsoft to go work in local municipal government at the city of Seattle. A couple of people were bold enough to directly ask me why I would contemplate making such a move—they had a hard time understanding my decision. In general, people were intrigued and wanted to know more. The overwhelmingly positive reaction to my article added to my suspicion that many people are possibly interested in working in government but simply don't have enough information on how to procced or are simply too scared to make the leap. I thought back to the reactions to my initial move into local government and some of the questions I had been asked, and I began to see some similarities in the reactions to the article.

After completing my service in local government, I reflected upon my own experience during that time, and I realized that there were few signposts along the way to help others navigate a similar journey. As a technologist, I had a deep understanding of the private-sector ecosystem, its compensation and incentive structures, work environments, culture, performance expectations and accountabilities, and emerging trends and systemic issues. Looking back, I realized I knew almost nothing about those things in the public sector while I was transitioning into local government. While every career transition process is unique, and my own personal journey into local government certainly fits that description, there are many aspects of moving from one domain to another that are not unique. This is certainly the case with moving from the private to the public sector, especially as a technologist making such a pivot. After I completed my public service, I took a sabbatical and thought about how best I could help fill this knowledge gap and inspire more technologists to serve in local government. This book is my attempt to create a roadmap for technologists and others who may join the flow of talent into the public sector.

WHY FOCUS ON LOCAL GOVERNMENT?

Aside from local government now being a domain I have a reasonable understanding of, another motivation to focus on local government was due to the focus of existing efforts to encourage technologists to serve in government being aimed primarily at the federal government level. For example, President Obama instituted the office of the United States Chief Technology Officer (CTO), who ran federal government technology policy efforts from within the Office of Science and Technology Policy (which existed prior to the Obama administration). These CTOs were eminent technologists hired from the private sector. Other agencies, such as the U.S. Digital Service, were created to drive the effort to attract talented young engineers and data scientists into the federal government. The Office of Technology and Policy at the White House coordinated efforts with these agencies. No such coordinating efforts exist at the state and local government levels, which is understandable, since there are no centralized structures to help coordinate efforts. As referenced earlier in this chapter, programs such as Bloomberg Philanthropies "What Works Cities" are helping to help address this by having their efforts be nationwide, with a focus on developing networks and sharing knowledge. By partnering with several other organizations and universities, these programs aid local governments in the development of policies that undergird the technological capacity-building elements of this work. These policies include open data and privacy policies.

As discussed in more detail later in the book, the huge variations in the sizes of local governments is also a consideration. Some local governments are quite large—for example, the municipal government of Seattle where I worked had about 12,000 staff at that time. Other local governments can be quite small, which leads to opportunities for regional approaches regarding technological capacity development. As a strong proponent of the policy diffusion model, and by extension an innovation diffusion model, I believe that enabling larger local governments to build up their internal capacity of technologists will lead to the development of regional hubs where both policy innovation and technological innovation best practices and know-how can be shared with smaller regional local governments, leading to improved outcomes on a broader scale. This book then acts as one more element that can be applied to programs such as these, as well as reaching other technologists who may not be aware of these programs to begin with.

Other questions related to technology at the local government level are worth exploring. Why do local governments build their own datacenters? Why does every local government, regardless of its size, have an internal IT department? If the public cloud enables the most successful companies in the world to successfully run and scale their businesses at a relatively low cost, why not local government? As secure government clouds are being developed, along with new security models such as FedRAMP, why are there still significant barriers to adoption at the local government level?[5] What efficiencies are being unrealized, and opportunity costs lost, by this reluctance to fully embrace cloud computing? How could machine learning and AI play a more central role in the management and provision of government services? How can local government use human-centered design and customer-first principles to create a delightful experience for residents when they access services? How can local government improve how it collects, stores, analyzes, and shares the vast amounts of data it possesses? Building up the internal capacity of technologists who have developed a deep understanding of cloud computing infrastructure and applications, machine learning and AI, data science and data governance, user experience (UX) design principles, and a customer-first focus can help accelerate the process of retooling our local governments so that they are better prepared for the current and emerging technological challenges ahead.

By itself, the need to attract more technical talent in these fields into local government isn't enough. An important, and often overlooked, aspect of capacity building is how to retain this talent for a period long enough for it to have significant impact. Leaving aside some of the known compensation differences between the public and private sectors, issues related to organizational culture and the ability to create centers of innovation within local government are a real challenge. Having enough technical expertise to form a center of gravity can propel the organization forward and drive the disruptive changes required.

DOES LOCAL GOVERNMENT ACTIVELY PURSUE TECHNOLOGICAL TALENT?

The answer to this question, in my opinion, is no. Of course, local government hires many people who work with technology on all kinds of levels, from entry-level application developers to chief technology officers, policy professionals to chief privacy officers, and data analysts to chief data officers. There is an enormous range of people who work with technology within local government. How it attracts these professionals, however, is quite passive when compared to the private-sector technology companies.

Earlier, I referred to some people being surprised at my move into local government. The reason why people would be surprised at such a pivot is an interesting question. I believe the reason is that the majority of people, technologists or otherwise, don't automatically think about government as an obvious place for technologists who could work at the Facebooks or Amazons of the world instead. Why could this be? In my view, part of this has to do with how local government thinks about itself as a technology enterprise being somewhat behind the curve and how this internal view is compounded by the same common perception in the public sphere. For want of a better description, it lacks the confidence to aggressively seek this talent. Private-sector technology companies spend an enormous amount of time and resources on seeking and hiring new talent. Significant budgets are allocated for intern programs each year, as this is one of the most important channels of talent acquisition. A large percentage of new hires in technology firms are those who initially worked there as interns. It is quite common for talented engineers to have a job waiting for them in the private sector before they start their final year of their undergrad program.

The competition is fierce. Local governments, even the largest municipal or county governments, do not even come close to the levels of proactive engagement with technology talent. Ask yourself, when was the last time you saw a local government actively recruiting at a technology fair, or had a recruiter send you a LinkedIn InMail, or had someone from your local government come to your company HQ to speak to employees about the work they are doing in government. The answer is likely to be rarely, if ever. Many technology professionals only become aware of their local government by attending a local hackathon that leverages government data or is focused on a specific social issue that volunteer technologists are trying to help solve with additional technology solutions in partnership with their government. By building up the capacity of technological talent within local government, more and more technologists will be attracted to join them as word spreads about the cool mission of government, the tough problems that technology and data can help solve, and the ability to have truly meaningful impact within their community. This virtuous flywheel effect will ensure a continuous flow of talent that will help our local governments handle the technology disruptions of the future with confidence.

WHO THIS BOOK IS FOR

In a word, technologists. What is the definition of a technologist? One definition describes this person as "an expert in a particular field of technology." For the purposes of this book, a technologist can refer to any role where expertise in a discrete technology is required or having expertise at any of the intersections of technology with science, data science, design, policy, law, ethics, and other social sciences.

While we usually think about technologists in terms of computing, the internet, and the applications we use every day, it is important to remember that local government provides an enormous range of services that require staff, often in the field, to have intensive interactions with technology and data. In government, not all technologists will spend all their time working in a cubical crunching data or deploying IT infrastructure. Often the role of a public-sector technologist isn't to build new technologies, it is to implement more modern technologies and to do better with the existing legacy technologies.

It is important to call out that when it comes to technology and the public sector, there are in fact several distinct groups of technologists with different areas of focus that have emerged in recent years. As it can get a little confusing, let's review how those groups operate and interact with government and how they differ from technologists working inside government.

PUBLIC INTEREST TECHNOLOGISTS

An emerging movement within the technology community that is focused on doing public good through technology is public interest technology. One of the leading proponents of this movement is the New America Foundation, who defines it as "a field dedicated to leveraging technology to support public interest organizations and the people they serve."[6] While organizations such as the New America Foundation focus primarily on building awareness of this movement and creating the conditions for new public interest technology projects and pipelines to develop, other organizations focus their public interest technology efforts on building technologies and incubating startups that are focused on solving specific problems. A good example is Giving Tech Labs, based in Seattle, whose model is to increase the number of startups focused on building sustainable public interest solutions and to help them scale.[7] Both of these examples highlight how public interest technologists usually operate *outside* of government, building technology solutions targeting specific social problems or gaps in service provision that can then be implemented in conjunction with government.

CIVIC TECHNOLOGISTS

Another group, albeit quite similar to public interest technologists in some ways, are what are commonly known as civic technologists. Civic technologists tend to operate in a volunteer capacity, and like public intertest technologists, do so outside of government. The largest and best-known organization that focuses on amplifying the impact of civic technologists is Code for America.[8] They describe their mission as using "the principles and practices of the digital age to improve how government serves the American public, and how the public improves government." Their model includes targeting specific national issues such as criminal justice and building technologies that can help alleviate problems in those sectors, as well as establishing volunteer brigades in cities where local private-sector technologists can volunteer their time and skills towards helping alleviate local civic issues and concerns. These groups usually meet monthly and are involved in creating hackathon events and other initiatives that focus their energies on attempting to develop solutions for local problems, such as homelessness or transit or improving the design of government services. Code for America brigades, along with other civic technology organizations such as data science for social good groups, play an important role in driving awareness of the critical role that technology can play in improving how government delivers its services to the public. During my own time in government, I regularly interacted with the local Code for America brigade in Seattle (known as "Open Seattle") and other civic technology organizations, as they were heavily reliant upon the open datasets that the city of Seattle published. As such, I considered them to be valuable partners in helping us as a local government amplify our impact within the community.

PUBLIC-SECTOR TECHNOLOGISTS

Finally, we have the group that I will refer to in the book as public-sector technologists. Basically, this refers to a technologist who chooses to serve *within* government itself, as I did. What this book is arguing is that in addition to building up the public interest and civic technologist sectors, we need more technologists on the inside of government to help create the capacity to interact with these outside efforts in an effective manner. We also need to develop the capacity of government's technical talent to help tackle a host of issues and opportunities and help build a local government ecosystem that truly meets the needs of everyone in our society. There are myriad opportunities for talented technologists to make a difference in local government—we simply need more technologists to join the public service in general and local government in particular.

NON-TECHNOLOGISTS

While this book is primarily focused on the role of technologists within local government and the development of that pipeline of talent into government, it will be of use to anyone who is interested in learning more about what it is like to work in local government, or perhaps how to serve in other capacities in the public sector.

PERSONAS

Not all technologists are alike, and not all may fit into one of the groups as described above. With this in mind, it may be helpful to filter down this broad description of technologists into some distinct personas. Personas are a method that technology companies frequently employ to help them better understand their customer base, backed up with data. The personas that I have constructed below will hopefully help readers to better understand how their skills and experiences can directly map into government service.

The first is a college student or young professional who may be considering public service during their career but may not see it as a viable option early in their career. This young technologist will soon graduate from college, or has about three to five years of professional experience in a technology firm. They could be a data scientist or a software engineer; a project manager or a designer; or any role central to the agile development of hardware, software, and online services. They are skilled in cloud-based technologies and environments, conditioned to use data as a key part of their decision-making processes, always starting with the customer experience. From an organizational culture perspective, they strive to continually learn and advance. The mission of the organization is very important to them, which makes the public service mission of government a potential great fit for them. This new wave of technologists is critical to the future of government in a cloud-first, mobile-first world.

The second is an experienced technologist who wishes to serve in local government after a significant career span in the private sector. This person will typically have about ten to fifteen years of professional experience in a variety of technology firms or organizations where technology and issues related to technology have played a key role in their work. They will initially have been trained in software tooling and techniques that have or will soon become obsolete and are familiar with upskilling to new technologies and transitioning into new roles caused by technological shifts. They are now at a point in their career where they are contemplating making a change and thinking about how to "give back." An opportunity to do some public service is a great way for them to leverage the broad range of skills they have developed during their career within a new domain (government). Their leadership experiences and skills will be highly valued within local government.

A third persona that may find this book valuable are non-technologists who may be thinking about serving in local government, or local government staff who may be considering a lateral career move into a more technology-focused role. From my own experiences speaking with people inside and outside of local government during my time there, there are many who potentially fit this description and who could benefit from the strategies and tactics I outline in the book.

On a personal note, I fit into the second persona. I first graduated from college and entered the technology sector in the late 1990s. Comparing the availability and power of computing to when I began studying computer science in 1992 with what is available today simply blows my mind. Using Windows for Workgroups 3.11 workstations connected to a Unix server where I had 2MB of disk storage for all my needs (the average size of a compiled program we would write was a whopping 35k), connecting to the internet before the World Wide Web was invented by manually opening a TCP/IP port, or saving files to 5¼-inch floppy disks that were inherently prone to data corruption—I feel like an historian when I explain those fun times to recent technology graduates. Throughout my career I have proactively sought opportunities to upskill and cross-train as the technology landscape around me shifted. As a result, I am a lifelong learner and place a huge value in paying it forward and sharing my knowledge and experiences with future leaders in forums such as this book. My recent pivot into the public sector provided me with the evidence that government, at all levels, needs new technologists and lots of them.

HOW WILL READERS BENEFIT
FROM THIS BOOK?

If you are a technologist who fits squarely into one of the personas described earlier, this book contains many useful insights and ideas for how you can have impact in a career in the public sector or for existing public-sector technologists who wish to amplify their impact. Even if you don't fit the description of a technologist, most of the suggestions for how to integrate into a local government environment will prove helpful. In short, anyone who is interested in serving in their local government should benefit from reading this book.

Readers will benefit in four main ways:

1. **Why**: You will gain a new understanding and appreciation of local government and the key role it plays in our society, insights into why more people with your skills and passion for public service are needed, and incentives for why you should seriously consider this as a future career option.

2. **What**: You will learn what local government is, its structures and funding models, and its roles and responsibilities within our society. You will learn about the specific needs that technologists can help address and what the future of work might look like within local government.

3. **How**: You will learn how to get started on your own journey into public service, how working in local government compares with the private sector, and discover strategies for how to succeed and have impact within your local government.

4. **Future**: Finally, you will gain some perspective into how "future of work" issues and emerging technologies will likely affect the way that local governments will provide public services in the next five to ten years. You'll also learn how government leaders can think differently about how to leverage the vast amounts of data they have, and how they could transform their approaches in using current and emerging technologies to build the next generation of local government. Finally, you'll learn about the role that inspiration can play when deciding whether to serve in government.

Outside of those technical cohorts, there is a wide range of people directly or indirectly involved with local government who could also benefit from this book:

*   **Government leaders and their executive teams**: One of the key challenges that this book addresses is the need for local

government to develop a more innovative culture. The level of culture change required will not happen without the full backing of the chief executive and their team. Words are not sufficient; culture change requires living those ideals and leading through example. Additionally, this book contains insights into the technology disruptions yet to come and how they may affect local government in the future.

- **Government department directors**: The people who run government departments are often those with the ability to have the most impact. Their control of departmental budgets and detailed domain knowledge, coupled with their understanding of their constituents, enables them to identify the right scenarios through which to drive improvements with technology. This book may provide new ideas for how to reimagine their department's ability to scale their impact.

- **Volunteers and civic technologists**: While this book is advocating for more technologists to serve within local government itself, there will continue to be many technologists for whom this is not feasible but yet wish to contribute through volunteering their skills. This book will provide these volunteers with valuable insights into how their local governments function, helping them focus their civic technology efforts in more effective ways. Similarly, the technologists building the software that government uses may gain new knowledge of the role of technology within local government that could lead to more tailored solutions for that market.

- **Residents**: Any resident of any city, county, or state who is interested in learning more about their local government will benefit from reading this book. Having the public be more informed about the role that technology plays in the delivery of local public services can help spur calls for innovation and improvements.

OK, WHAT'S NEXT?

This book aims to encourage and inspire technologists to serve in local government and to create meaningful positive social impact by doing so and provides a roadmap for them on how to build the next generation of local government. If you are reading this book, there is a high probability that public service is something that already appeals to you. I am hoping this book will help you go from considering public service as an option to making the decision to join the ranks of public-sector technologists. We need you. Read on, and ask what you can do for your government.

NOTES

1   "A Quantum Leap for Open Data?," David Doyle, last updated May 14, 2019, https://www.linkedin.com/pulse/quantum-leap-open-data-david-doyle/.

2   "A Future of Failure? The Flow of Technology Talent into Government and Society," Ford Foundation, accessed September 16, 2019, https://www.fordfoundation.org/library/reports-and-studies/a-future-of-failure-the-flow-of-technology-talent-into-government-and-society.

3   "About What Works Cities," Bloomberg Philanthropies, accessed September 15, 2019, https://whatworkscities.bloomberg.org/about/.

4   "Reflections on My Journey from the Private to the Public Sector," David Doyle, last updated September 7, 2017, https://www.linkedin.com/pulse/reflections-my-journey-from-private-public-sector-david-doyle/.

5   "FedRAMP—Home," General Services Administration, accessed November 16, 2019, https://www.fedramp.gov/.

6   "Public Interest Technology—About," New America, accessed September 15, 2019, https://www.newamerica.org/public-interest-technology/about.

7   "Giving Tech Labs—About Us," Giving Tech Labs, accessed September 15, 2019, https://giving.tech/about-us/.

8   "Code for America—Values," Code for America, accessed September 15, 2019, https://www.codeforamerica.org/values.

I

THE "WHY"

1

WHAT IS LOCAL GOVERNMENT, EXACTLY?

It might seem like a strange question, and an odd way to begin this book, but having a good understanding of what local government is and how it operates *before* you enter into your public service there is actually pretty important. I say this from personal experience, where I frequently found myself encountering situations at the beginning of my time at the city of Seattle where I wished I'd had a better understanding of some of the basic structures and power dynamics. Had I known some of these things in advance, I might have avoided some common pitfalls and handled certain situations differently. This was one of the key learnings I took away from my time in local government, and one of the main motivations for creating a guide for other technologists to follow when moving into the public sector. Having thought about why I knew so little about local government prior to joining it, I had two additional realizations.

The first was that as an immigrant to the United States, I had grown up under a very different form of government in my native Ireland and had to learn almost from scratch about how things get done in the U.S. form of local government. Ireland inherited its system of government from the British after it gained independence, like many former British colonies. One of the major differences between local governments in the United States versus Ireland lay in how much power local governments

25

in the United States have compared to their European counterparts. The ability of U.S. local governments to levy taxes; have their own police force, court system, and school districts; and directly elect executives who would run those jurisdictions stood in sharp contrast to the weak local government structures I had been used to, where the national government centrally managed all aspects of society. The other realization was that many technologists who work in the U.S. tech sector also immigrated here, and therefore many of them could also benefit from knowing more about the basics of U.S. local government when evaluating whether to work there.

Based on those insights, and before we discuss the practicalities of what transitioning into a local government role might look like, it is important to step back and review the national landscape that local governments operate within today and also to peek through the lens of history and learn how the local government system evolved over the lifetime of the United States. We need to learn from history so we can gain a better understanding of the forces that shape our governments today and how these might affect the kind of work you as technologists may wish to accomplish in the public sector. This chapter can be considered somewhat of a "101" for readers who may not have had much exposure to U.S. government studies. If you studied political science in college, you may be tempted to skip this chapter; however, I would encourage you to review the material here, as the machinations of state and local government can be quite different from those at the federal level.

DEFINITIONS OF GOVERNMENT

Before we delve into the history and machinations of government, let us pause for a moment and reflect on the actual definition of government itself. Government is an institution that everyone in our society is aware of, and affected by, and yet very few of us could accurately define what it actually is. Many variations of the definition are available, but one I like defines government as "the organization of power within a society, specifically how power is divided and used." I find this to be a useful definition because of its emphasis on *power*.

POWER

Most readers will be familiar with some concepts of power, such as notions of "hard power," which is the use of military force, and "soft power," which is defined as the ability of a country to persuade others to do what it wants without force or coercion, usually via diplomacy. If these notions of power are usually applicable to nation-states, then what does the application of power look like at the state and local government levels?

One way I like to think about this concept at the local level is through the profound ability of local governments to shape and then reshape our cities and regions. One of the reasons I love to look at photos of cities from decades ago is because it reminds me of how our cities and towns are living things, constantly changing and growing. The primary force driving these changes over the decades, and indeed centuries, is our local government. While the pace of change can appear slow in real time, the effects and impacts over time can be truly dramatic, and this is why looking back at the evolution of our cities and regions through the mists of time can be fascinating and even jarring. In addition to the massive infrastructure projects that shape our regions, power can be exercised by implementing new public policies and enacting new laws, which transform some of our social and cultural norms. Like our ever changing cities and towns, it can be both fascinating and jarring to look back at the social norms that were acceptable a generation or two ago that are anathema to us today.

While state and local governments are responsible for most of the decision-making in designing and implementing these changes, the public plays a vital role in this process. Some major changes are the direct result of grassroots pressure from the public, either lobbying their elected representatives or voting them out of office should they not be responsive to their needs. In some states, it is possible for the public to push special ballot initiatives into the voting cycles and have them become law should they gain an electoral majority. Similarly, some major changes that government wishes to bring forward require a vote of the people to approve, usually when these changes require new taxes to be enacted. The public possesses enormous power to shape our cities, environment, and quality-of-life standards, even if at times the process can appear messy and slow.

It wasn't until I served in local government that I began to get a true sense of what power actually was and how it could be yielded. I had worked within a large tech company for many years and worked with people who had a lot of internal power within the organization, and which ultimately may or may not have translated into effects that affected external customers. The thing that struck me about working in government was just how much external power it possesses. Even as a junior official in a major municipal government, I was surprised on occasion by how much weight the things I did and said in public forums had. A loose comment in a tweet that suddenly snowballed into a mini controversy. An idea for an event that quickly grew into a large multiday training exercise involving both public- and private-sector organizations, complete with city TV cameras documenting it. A single line item in an annual report that caused a reporter from a national government online news outlet to highlight how one city department was not in compliance with our program, when in fact we had greatly exceeded our initial participation goals for the year, causing me to field some uncomfortable phone calls. How speaking with reporters about your work could get misinterpreted in their articles and podcasts. Even with the miniscule amounts of power that I possessed as a technologist in local government, once I fully understood that how I represented my work and its impact in public was something I had to take incredibly seriously, it forced me to think very carefully about everything I said and did and how I went about getting my outreach activities more closely vetted. This was not done to obscure the truth—in fact, the opposite was true as my work almost completely revolved around helping the government be more transparent. Rather, it helped me develop the discipline to ensure that the core messages I was trying to get across to the public would not be obscured by an unforced error on my part. To paraphrase that well-known saying, even with little power comes great responsibility. Another realization was that there were sections of the public and press who really do pay close attention to the work of government, and this was something I was glad to see, and support where possible with interviews and comments for articles. For technologists entering government for the first time, it is crucial to understand these power dynamics in government and to learn that what worked well in the private sector in terms of communicating about your work may in fact have the opposite effect within government. This is especially true if your role in government requires outreach.

POLITICAL EFFICACY

Related to the idea of power and how to yield it, another important concept for technologists to understand when working in government is the idea of "political efficacy," that is "the belief that government listens to normal people and that participation can make a difference in government." Technologists within government are in a great position to help increase the chances of political efficacy occurring. How? By putting in place the mechanisms that greatly improve the ease with which the public can interact with their government, both in person and virtually. This can be as simple as providing the ability for the public to give feedback and interact with officials when public meetings are being streamed online, or improving the feedback loops when the public do provide feedback, either directly in public meetings or when submitting ideas or complaints directly to local government. The lack of acknowledgement can be one of the biggest sources of frustration for the public when they interact with the government, and technology can help alleviate some of these issues. Similarly, having more government services be available 24/7 through the use of interactive bots and other online tools can help people feel that government is available to them on their terms, not the government's terms. Reducing the experience gap between how the public avails itself of services provided by the private sector versus the public sector could result in a radical change in how the public perceives their government and their ability to affect its future direction. This notion of "representation" and how it affects communities of color and those who are traditionally underrepresented in local government is a critically important consideration for all government employees to have at the forefront of their thinking and decision-making. Technologists within government can play a crucial role in helping achieve a more equitable relationship between our governments and the public, especially in our major metropolitan areas.

A VERY BRIEF HISTORY OF LOCAL GOVERNMENT IN THE UNITED STATES

While the history of the federal government is well documented and generally well understood, the same cannot be said for state and local government. Perhaps one reason for this is that whereas the federal government is primarily centralized around the Washington, DC area, local government is quite fragmented and varies in size and shape on a state-by-state basis. While the slow establishment of the now fifty U.S. states continued throughout the eighteenth, nineteenth, and into mid-twentieth century, the development of the varied local government structures we know today happened quite organically and has resulted in many tens of thousands of local government entities.

Local governments have been in operation since the United States was founded, and in fact predated it. "The emergence of American local government coincided with the birth of American federal government under the United States Constitution in 1789. Even though American city government already existed in the British colonial era in the United States, early era local governments were not organized and did not provide municipal utilities or other services."[1] As the central federal and state governmental structures of the United States solidified over time, so, too, did those of local governments, beginning not with city (municipal) governments, but with the creation of charters that established the counties that most of us live in today. As the United States was primarily a rural society in the early years of its existence, "Early state constitutions originally created counties to serve as the administrative arms of state government, performing state-mandated duties, including property assessment and record keeping. Historically, counties were established without the consent of the voters, possessed no charter or legislative powers, performed no business or proprietary functions, and shared immunity with the state from suit." [2]

From the mid-eighteenth century into the early nineteenth century, as the industrial revolution began to attract more people from the land into the cities, the role of municipal governments became more important. A massive wave of immigrants added to this flow of people into the major cities and saw the establishment of powerful local government operations (i.e., the fabled Tammany Hall in New York). The end of World War II gave birth to modern suburbs as populations began to spill out of the major cities, thereby causing county government to again take on a significant role in the governance of key services within the state. This enabled county governments to generate larger revenues and gain more autonomy and accountability from the States. Fast-forward to the beginning of the twenty-first century, and we again see the rise of municipal government, as many of our major metropolitan areas have experienced a significant renaissance with populations again moving back into cities both large and small, fueled by younger generations attracted by significant opportunity in the tech sector.

While these major city/county shifts were happening within each state, a host of other local government form factors were also developing, some of which we are aware of without thinking of them as "local government," and some others that many of us are not aware of at all.

POWER STRUCTURES

Due to the fragmented nature of local governments across the United States, their power structures also vary state by state. While it's not feasible to list all of the various forms of structures in existence in the United States today, there are some commonalities that are useful to share. For those readers who wish to learn more about the power structures for local governments within their own state, the state government website is often the best place to begin, as the laws overseeing the establishment of local government entities will have emanated from the state government over many decades.

STATE GOVERNMENT

In March 1781, the Articles of Confederation, initially proposed by the Continental Congress in November 1777, were finally adopted and laid the foundation for the first governmental structure at the national and state levels. In essence, these articles were the United States' first constitution.[3] The articles created a weak central government structure and divested most of the power to the states under Article 2. These initial Articles of Confederation formed the basis of the current U.S. Constitution, which was enacted in 1789. Under the Tenth Amendment to the U.S. Constitution, "all powers not granted to the federal government are reserved for the states and the people."[4] All state governments are modeled after the federal government and consist of three branches: executive, legislative, and judicial. All states are led by a governor, who is directly elected, and that person leads the executive branch along with several other elected leaders, such as the lieutenant governor, the attorney general, and the secretary of state. All states, apart from Nebraska, have what is known as a "bicameral" legislature structure, with a smaller upper and larger lower chamber. The systems of checks and balances that exist at the federal level are typically mirrored in state government.

MUNICIPAL GOVERNMENT

Similar to state and federal government, municipal governments will typically follow the executive/legislative/judicial branch structure. For example, the mayor is the chief executive of the executive branch, which is responsible for running the day-to-day operations of government, including the implementation of policies and laws. The legislative branch consists of a council of elected members, which crafts legislation (in cities these laws are usually referred to as "ordinances") and provides oversight of the executive branch, including approval of all spending and budgets. The judicial branch runs the court system and evaluates local laws when issues arise, making sure they are not repugnant to the state constitution.

COUNTY GOVERNMENT

County government administers the areas outside of the main municipal government's span of control but within the state boundaries. All states have at least several counties. For example, my home state of Washington has thirty-nine counties. Like other forms of local government, the size and scope of counties can vary wildly—in Washington State, King County (where Seattle is located) has a population of 2.2 million people, whereas Garfield County in rural eastern Washington has a population of just 2,200 people. While the rules about how county governments are structured will vary from state to state, there are three basic types of county government in the United States:[5]

1. Commission system: "The most common form of county government in the US. Under this structure, an elected commission, which generally consists of a small number of commissioners, serves as the governing body within the county, performing all legislative and executive functions. These include adopting a budget, passing county resolutions, and hiring and firing county officials."

2. Council–administrator system: "The voters elect council members to serve for a specified period of time, and the council in turn appoints an administrator to oversee the operation of the government. The administrator serves at the directive of the council and can be terminated by the council."

3. Council–elected executive system: "The voters elect both the members of the council and the executive. The executive performs functions similar to those of the state governor. For instance, he or she can veto the actions of the council, draft a budget, and provide suggestions regarding public policy."

All county governments will list their own governance structures on their websites. Similarly, all other forms of local government (special districts, school districts, townships, etc.) will list their own governance structures on their websites, as well as any special relationships or partnerships they maintain with their respective regional county or municipal governments.

TYPES OF LOCAL GOVERNMENTS

As the United States has one of the most complex local government systems in the world, for the purposes of this book, will we use the U.S. Census Bureau's classification of government units to simplify things.

According to the U.S. Census Bureau, there are five basic types of local government:

1. County
2. Municipal
3. Township
4. School district
5. Special district

Rather than going into a detailed breakdown of each type of local government unit in this book, readers who are interested in learning more can check out the excellent high-level overview provided by the National League of Cities,[6] or in incredible detail via the U.S. Census Bureau "2017 Census of Governments" report.[7]

As referenced earlier, there are many other kinds of local government entities in existence, and they can vary broadly from state to state. These can include metropolitan planning organizations (MPOs), economic development districts (EDDs), port districts (e.g., the Port of Seattle), and Environmental Protection Agency (EPA) regions, to name but a few. Additionally, some major metropolitan areas have established metropolitan councils to help create more regionally focused government structures, typically operating across several metro areas and counties.[8] These forms of local and regional government can be unknown to, or overlooked by, the public when considering what public-sector organizations exist in their area. These organizations typically have broad mandates and make a significant impact towards the economic development of our major cities and counties and are well worth considering when thinking about how to contribute as a public interest technologist.

NUMBER OF LOCAL GOVERNMENTS

While there are fifty state governments in existence, plus the District of Washington, the number of local governments in existence in the United States is huge. According to the U.S. Census Bureau, the latest aggregated figures from the 2012 Census of Governments[9] are:

- 89,004 local governments existed in the United States, comprising...
- 3,031 counties
- 19,522 municipalities
- 16,364 townships

- 37,203 special districts
- 12,884 independent school districts

It is worth noting that these local government vary wildly in terms of their size. Whereas some county and municipal governments are responsible for millions of people and as a result have a staff in the thousands or even tens of thousands, the majority of local governments provide services for far smaller populations. Townships tend to be even smaller in scope. Special districts and school districts can also vary significantly in terms of the populations they serve and the level of power they wield. Special districts, sometimes officially called special-purpose districts, are limited-purpose local governments that are separate from a municipal or county government. Generally, they perform a single function, with some performing a limited number of functions. Examples include industrial development districts (ports), housing authorities, sewer districts, county rural library districts, public hospital districts, county airport districts, and so on. Each state will maintain a list of all special-purpose districts in their jurisdiction. School districts, which run the public K–12 schools, are in fact another kind of special-purpose district. They have the powers of taxation and eminent domain (in all states except Virginia). One common example of how school districts exercise their taxation power is through adding levies to local property taxes, usually requiring a vote of approval from the people. These levies then generate the revenues required to build new public schools and expand services such as new bus routes, hiring more teachers, buying new equipment, etc. School districts are one of the best-known forms of local government and play a critical role in how people who are raising a family decide where to live, as seeking an area that has good public schools is usually high on the list of priorities (I can speak to this as a parent myself). In fact, most online real estate services will list the relevant school district information in their housing listings, and real estate brokers will highlight this information in their marketing materials. Few people reflect on the fact that these school districts are in fact another form of local government.

One common need all local governments share is the ability to leverage technology in order to be able to manage their operations, provide services, collect revenues, analyze and share data, and communicate internally among staff and externally with the public. As technologists, we should consider using our expertise in all areas of local government and not just the major cities and counties. As you can see from the numbers, there are many places where our talents are needed.

FUNDING MODELS

Understanding how your local government is funded is an important aspect of working within government, as without funding, the government will simply not execute programs or implement new policies. You may be familiar with the expression "the power of the purse" in relation to the federal government and Congress, and the same is true of local government. While IT budgets within larger local governments can run into the hundreds of millions of dollars, this doesn't translate into funds being readily available for new technology initiatives. As mentioned elsewhere in this book, government budget cycles are long (typically biennial) and getting requests for additional funding can be arduous. Most of the IT budget is already tightly ring-fenced for long-term services, and generally there is little wiggle room. Even if the mayor suddenly decided that the entire city government needed to move to the cloud, that doesn't mean that the money will suddenly appear or be reallocated without a major fight, unlike what can happen in the private sector. It is, after all, taxpayers' money that is being spent. Therefore, understanding the budgetary parameters within which you as a technologist will have to operate will be important to your overall ability to be successful.

While most people are aware of the fact that state and local governments have the power of taxation and can raise significant resources in that manner, most local government funding comes from grant allocations from the federal government, sometimes referred to as "pass-through grants." One reason for this is to ensure that poorer areas of the country receive adequate levels of funding to ensure basic government services can be provided, such as health care, public education, housing, community development, child care, job training, transportation, and clean water. The amounts of money being allocated in this manner are staggering. According to the latest figures that have been made available, in 2016 these grants made up 31 percent of state budgets and 23 percent of state and local budgets combined.[10] In dollar terms, this amounted to $661 billion in 2016.[11] The effect of these grants can be seen in the following figure, where there is a clear gap between the revenues raised by state and local governments and what they appropriate (i.e., spend).

In addition to these federal grants, state and local governments raise substantial revenues through taxation. Of the $5.1 trillion raised by U.S. governments in 2016, 35.3 percent of that total was raised by state and local governments, or $1.8 trillion.

Figure 1-1: *Revenue and spending by level of government*

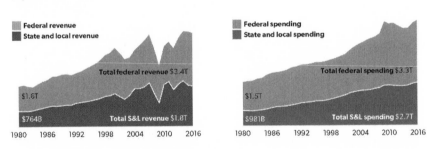

Revenue and spending by level of government
(Adjusted to 2017 dollars)

Source: https://annualreport.usafacts.org

If these figures seem surprisingly high, then it is quite likely that your local government has an annual budget of several billion dollars. For example, the city of Seattle's 2019–2020 proposed budget was approximately $5.9 billion per year, including about $1.3 billion in general fund spending per year.[12]

Taking this down from the macro to the micro level, it is important to understand how your local government's budget is structured. Usually, local governments will have a detailed breakdown of how the budget is structured on a departmental basis, and this should be publicly available. Depending on the government in question, they may provide even more granular information. This can be important information when serving in government, as knowing whether the technology and data programs and projects you will be engaged upon are adequately funded into the future or if it could provide the opportunity to request extra budget for new initiatives. Sometimes funding is linked to revenue sources that will shrink over time. For example, the open data program that I managed in Seattle had a "cable fund" as its primary funding source. This was a levy based on the number of people subscribing to cable TV, which was diminishing over time as more and more people opted to "cut the cord." While funding for the open data program wasn't in any immediate danger, it was something I had at the back of my mind when entering budget cycles, and I did initiate conversations with the budget team on this topic. I simply wanted to get ahead of any future funding crunch. In summary, while state and local governments are generally well funded, they are not immune to budget cuts in times of recession. Nor can we as technologists have unlimited funds to pursue technology-based initiatives—unlike what can happen in the private sector when a technology company decides to ramp up its research and development investments. Because of this, one of the key roles of data and technology in state and local government will be to drive efficiencies and seek optimizations that can result in cost recovery and other savings.

AREAS OF RESPONSIBILITY

The types of services that state and local governments provide also vary by domain. Over the many decades that our local government system has been evolving, a high-level set of roles and responsibilities has settled into place. While these may vary from state to state, it's possible to break these down into some common areas. Following is a great overview provided by Will Saunders, former open data manager for Washington State and someone with whom I partnered extensively during my local government service. It succinctly lays out the typical split of roles and responsibilities within state and local government in Washington State.[13]

Cities do:	Counties do:	States do:
- Public transportation - Utilities - Police - Culture	- Planning and land use - Courts and justice - Safety net	- Education - Human services - Natural resources - Highways

It is true that some services will cross over between jurisdictions. A key differentiator is who actually performs the work. For example, most cities of a certain size will have a human services department, but the bulk of their work may primarily be in providing funding and oversight to other (nonprofit) organizations who provide the services on the ground—whereas the state government is typically directly responsible for the provision of key health-related services.

Even with these advanced systems of government, there are instances where an intermediate body is required to help coordinate planning and policy development on a regional level within some states. Such agencies are usually known as regional councils. An example in my own region is the Puget Sound Regional Council, which provides a forum for the three most populous counties in Washington State with a combined population of 4 million people "to make decisions about transportation, growth management and economic development" in a coordinated fashion.[14] Regional councils may also form to focus on a single issue that is also considered to be a regional issue, for example, addressing homelessness.

SIZE AND DEMOGRAPHICS

Similar to the size of U.S. government budgets, the numbers of people working in government are also impressive. According to the latest data, 19.41 million people were employed in state and local government in 2016. As you can see from the following figure, this level of employment has remained quite steady, even during the recent recessionary period that began around 2008 and continued until 2013.

Figure 1-2: *Total number of full-time employees in state and local government 2009–2016*

Number of Employees	2008	2009	2010	2011	2012	2013	2014	2015	2016
+ Establish Justice and Ensure Domestic Tranquil...	2,684,166	2,647,124	2,614,021	2,593,426	2,546,364	2,536,142	2,544,106	2,553,098	2,564,570
+ Provide for the Common Defense	n/a	n/a	n/a	n/a	n/a	n/a	n/a	n/a	n/a
+ Promote the General Welfare	4,732,244	3,717,505	3,674,480	3,603,163	3,580,208	3,578,046	3,597,642	3,600,025	3,631,348
+ Secure the Blessings of Liberty to Ourselves a...	2,831,382	11,978,810	11,920,495	11,832,864	11,741,602	11,676,333	11,757,087	11,802,130	11,865,809
+ General Government and Other	2,445,013	1,345,639	1,317,717	1,272,135	1,320,464	1,316,581	1,330,483	1,337,338	1,344,627
Total Employees	2,692,805	19,689,078	19,526,713	19,301,588	19,188,638	19,107,102	19,229,318	19,292,591	19,406,354

Source: https://usafacts.org/data/topics/government-finances/employment/

One of the major issues facing this massive workforce has become known as the "Silver Tsunami." This refers to the large number of workers from the Baby Boomer generation that still make up a significant portion of the workforce and who are now retiring. While this affects both the private and public sectors, the effects are especially severe in government. Although the currently available data varies, in general, government at all levels is expecting that a significant portion of its workforce will retire during the next five years, on top of the many retirements that have already occurred. A 2014 General Accounting Office (GAO) report found that 31 percent of career federal employees were eligible for retirement by September 2017. The situation at the state government level appears to be worse, with some states reporting upwards of 30 to 40 percent of their employees being eligible for retirement.[15]

A separate but related demographic issue that government faces is that the next generations have been slow to enter government and help backfill these openings. Millennials currently account for 18 percent of the federal workforce, compared to 32 percent of the overall U.S. workforce.[16] With large numbers of government retirees not being quickly replaced by younger workers, governments are struggling to fill these gaps in their workforce. Some governments are using this as an opportunity to reevaluate their needs and the kinds of skills they will require in the future, including the role that technologists will play.

While there are over 19 million workers in state and local government, the vast majority of them work in education, both in public K–12 schools and in our public colleges and universities. In fact, the number of workers in state and local education is ten times larger than the next category.[17] This finding may be surprising to some readers, as usually when we think about local government, we visualize a city hall and departments being run by bureaucrats. This is a good reminder that public servants come in many forms and perform many vital services that we all enjoy daily and frequently take completely for granted.

UNION REPRESENTATION

An important aspect of how our governments function, rarely encountered by technologists in the private sector, is the role of labor unions within the government workforce. A 2019 report from the U.S. Bureau of Labor Statistics found that although overall union membership continued to decline, the rates of membership in the public sector far exceeded those in the private sector.[18] Some of the main findings included:

- In 2018, 7.2 million employees in the public sector belonged to a union, compared with 7.6 million workers in the private sector.
- The unionization rate in the private sector (6.4 percent) remained substantially below that for public-sector workers (33.9 percent).

- Within the public sector, the union membership rate was highest in local government (40.3 percent), which employs many workers in heavily unionized occupations, such as police officers, firefighters, and teachers.

To put this into some context for readers of this book, the same report states that union representation in the private sector for workers in "professional and technical services" was 1.5 percent. While no union representation of any meaningful scale exists in the tech sector, it has become a topic of discussion in recent years as employees in most large technology companies have begun to advocate for better conditions for temporary staff, as well as organizing around issues related to climate change and ethical uses of new technologies such as facial recognition by governments in the United States and around the world.

A separate 2018 report on unionization within the public sector highlighted important demographic facts about the makeup of those public-sector unions:[19]

- A majority (58 percent) of union workers (workers covered by a collective bargaining contract) in state and local government are women.
- African Americans, Latinos, and Asian Americans and Pacific Islanders make up one-third of unionized state and local government workers.

Unions play a powerful and critical role within state and local government and help ensure that our state and local public servants are made up of a diverse workforce that mirrors the community it serves. From a technologist's perspective, it is important to note that union representation will likely exist within state and local IT departments or other departments where technologists may be prevalent. We will cover this in more detail in Chapter 6.

FINALLY, THINK ABOUT SCALE

"State and local" governments are often lumped together when we speak about local government, and yet are hugely different in terms of their scale and the types of services they provide. While this book is primarily aimed at local governments such as municipal government, partially due to the author's experience in municipal government, many of the insights and suggestions outlined here will also be relevant for state government. One good way to understand the differences between the various layers of local government is to look at the hierarchy of local governments in your region, along with some metrics to help with identifying the scale. In my own case, I was working in the city of Seattle (municipal government), which is located in King County, which is part of Washington State. We can visualize the relationships in the following figure.

Figure 1-3: *Comparison of state, county, and local government in Washington state*

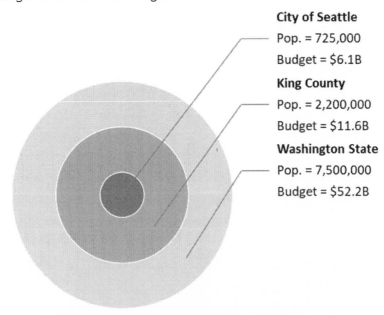

City of Seattle
Pop. = 725,000
Budget = $6.1B

King County
Pop. = 2,200,000
Budget = $11.6B

Washington State
Pop. = 7,500,000
Budget = $52.2B

Source: Population and budget data from the city of Seattle, King County, and State of Washington official websites

As you can see, there are significant differences in terms of scale, looking only at populations served and budgets. Earlier we referred to the breakdown in the respective areas of responsibility, and this can be applied to the nature and scale of the technology investments and data management needs. Depending on the scale of your own ambition as a technologist, and how you might apply your skills and passion in government, having a basic understanding of the scale of the challenges and opportunities can help you shape a clear path into one level of government before potentially moving to a larger scale of government.

CHAPTER 1: KEY TAKEAWAYS

- Having a good understanding of what local government is and how it operates *before* you enter into your public service is actually pretty important.
- Many technologists, like the author, are immigrants to the US and as such grew up under very different forms of local government.
- Therefore, step 1 is to make sure that we have a good understanding of the environment that we're trying to effect change within. This is also true for technologists who grew up in the US.
- To help build a solid understanding of state and local government, in this chapter we explore the following topics:
  - Definitions of government (power, political efficacy).
  - A very brief history of local government in the United States
  - Power structures in state, municipal and county government
  - The many types of local governments
  - The numbers of local governments – so many!
  - Funding models
  - Areas of responsibility
  - Size and demographics
  - Union representation
  - The scale of state and local government!

NOTES

1   "Local Governments in the United States," Oxford Bibliographies, accessed October 17, 2019, https://www.oxfordbibliographies.com/view/document/obo-9780199756223/obo-9780199756223-0070.xml.

2   "Local Governments in the United States," Oxford Bibliographies, accessed October 17, 2019, https://www.oxfordbibliographies.com/view/document/obo-9780199756223/obo-9780199756223-0070.xml.

3   "The Articles of Confederation," U.S. House of Representatives, accessed December 7, 2019, https://history.house.gov/Historical-Highlights/1700s/The-Articles-of-Confederation/.

4   "State & Local Government," The White House, accessed December 7, 2019, https://www.whitehouse.gov/about-the-white-house/state-local-government/.

5   Coppa, Frank J. "County Government: A Guide to Efficient and Accountable Government." (2000).

6   "Cities 101—Types of Local Governments," National League of Cities, accessed October 14, 2019, https://www.nlc.org/resource/cities-101-types-of-local-governments.

7   "Individual State Descriptions: 2017," U.S. Census Bureau, last modified April 2019, https://www.census.gov/content/dam/Census/library/publications/2017/econ/2017isd.pdf.

8   "Metropolitan Councils," National League of Cities, accessed October 17, 2019, https://www.nlc.org/metropolitan-councils.

9   "Census of Governments," U.S. Census Bureau, accessed October 17, 2019, https://www.census.gov/programs-surveys/cog.html.

10 "Federal Aid to State and Local Governments," Center on Budget and Policy Priorities, last updated April 19, 2018, https://www.cbpp.org/research/state-budget-and-tax/federal-aid-to-state-and-local-governments.

11 "2019 Annual Report," USAFacts, accessed November 6, 2019, https://annualreport.usafacts.org.

12 "2019-20 Proposed Budget," City of Seattle, accessed November 8, 2019, https://www.seattle.gov/city-budget/2019-20-proposed-budget.

13 "Understanding State Data—A Guide for Civic Technologists," State of Washington, accessed December 11, 2019, https://data.wa.gov/stories/s/tkg7-xxjz.

14 "PSRC—What We Do," Puget Sound Regional Council, accessed December 11, 2019, https://www.psrc.org/about/what-we-do.

15   "9 Stats About the 'Silver Tsunami,'" NeoGov, accessed December 17, 2019, https://blog.neogov.com/is-the-silver-tsunami-upon-us-9-stats-you-cant-ignore.

16   "The Public Sector's Millennial Opportunity," Deloitte Consulting, accessed December 11, 2019, https://www2.deloitte.com/us/en/pages/public-sector/articles/public-sector-millennial-leadership-report.html.

17   "Where Do State and Local Government Employees Work?," U.S. Census Bureau, accessed December 12, 2019, https://www.census.gov/content/dam/Census/library/visualizations/2015/econ/g13-aspep-visual.pdf.

18   "Union Members Summary." U.S. Bureau of Labor Statistics, last updated January 18, 2019, https://www.bls.gov/news.release/union2.nr0.htm.

19   "A Profile of Union Workers in State and Local Government," Economic Policy Institute, last updated June 7, 2018, https://www.epi.org/publication/a-profile-of-union-workers-in-state-and-local-government-key-facts-about-the-sector-for-followers-of-janus-v-afscme-council-31/.

2

THE IMPORTANCE
OF GOVERNMENT

On a bitterly cold day in January 1961, the newly sworn-in president of the United States uttered one of the most inspirational phrases about patriotism and public service ever. In his inaugural address John Fitzgerald Kennedy laid down a challenge to current and future generations when he declared, "My fellow Americans, ask not what your country can do for you, ask what you can do for your country."[1] At the time, those words were aimed primarily at the federal government level and were referring to a very different set of issues back in the early 1960s, when the United States was deeply engaged in a Cold War with the Soviet Union and was about to embark on the race to the moon. Big government was very much in vogue, and it was fashionable for young people to serve in government during that period.

INSPIRING FUTURE GENERATIONS

Less than two months into his term, President Kennedy issued an executive order to establish the Peace Corps, whose purpose was "to promote world peace and friendship through a Peace Corps, which shall make available to interested countries and areas men and women of the United States qualified for service abroad and willing to serve, under conditions of hardship if necessary, to help the peoples of such countries and areas in meeting their needs for trained manpower." To date over 220,000 Americans have served in the Peace Corps, working in over 140 countries.[2] In the decades that followed other programs inspired by the Peace Corps were established. Examples include the AmeriCorps program established by President Clinton in 1993 to provide renewed investment in community service[3] and nongovernmental programs such as Teach for America, which was established in 1989 with the aim of recruiting college graduates from top universities around the United States to serve as teachers.[4] In turn, the Teach for America model has inspired other volunteer efforts, including Code for America, which was established in 2009 to "organize a network of people who build technology to further local governments' priorities of creating healthy, prosperous, and safe communities." Code for America is of particular interest to technologists, as it is the largest and most impactful civic technology effort to emerge in the United States to date. Many of you reading this book may already be familiar with this organization and their work, and in fact some of you may even volunteer in your local Code for America brigade.

Organizations such as Code for America are typical of the initiatives that have been directly or indirectly influenced by Kennedy's words, with missions that inspire and encourage people to volunteer their time and skills in the service of their local community or communities worldwide. The wonderful thing about President Kennedy's words is that even though newer generations of Americans were not alive when he spoke them (including this author), they continue to resonate with people today and provide a North Star for us to follow. Before we dive deeper into the minutiae of local government and why more people with deep technical skills and a passion for public service are needed there, it is useful to first step back and spend some time thinking about the "why." Why government is so important in our society, the massive impact it has on our economy, and what can happen when the government services we take for granted are suddenly unavailable. Understanding the many ways that government plays a critical role in our society is an important step towards inspiring a new wave of mission-driven technologists to consider entering government and to improve how our government serves the people.

WORDS MATTER

In the intervening decades since the Kennedy administration (1961–1963), presidents from both parties have at times used very different language when it comes to the importance of government. President Regan in his first inaugural address used a phrase that became synonymous with how many people subsequently viewed government when he said: "In this present crisis, government is not the solution to our problem, government is the problem."[5] Some argue that this quote was taken out of context, so you can read the full text of the speech and form your own opinion. In his 1996 State of the Union address, President Bill Clinton stated that "the era of big government is over" in order to woo more fiscally conservative voters to support his reelection bid.[6] While there were specific reasons at the time for why both presidents made those negative statements about government, unfortunately, those phrases have remained stuck in the public lexicon and are often cited to this day by people who wish to portray government in a negative light. Unfortunately, these negative sentiments have also bled into the discourse around state and local government at times.

PERCEPTION ALSO MATTERS

Counteracting these viewpoints is challenging. Clear, easy-to-explain examples of the positive impacts and importance of government over time are difficult to find. Indeed, when it comes to the common perception of local government, the TV comedy show *Parks and Recreation* is what almost immediately springs to mind for many people. To say that it doesn't portray local government in the same reverential light as how *The West Wing* TV show portrays the executive branch of the federal government is a huge understatement. *Parks and Recreation*, while very funny and highly popular, also helped reinforce some cultural stereotypes about the disfunction within local government. Although there are many wonderful public servants and organizations that are working hard to change these perceptions, the *The West Wing* for city hall has yet to be created—a compelling narrative about the positives of local government that enters into the mainstream consciousness that help attract new talent.

EDUCATING THE PUBLIC

One useful way to begin that process is by educating the public on the sheer scale of the impact of government, and especially local government, upon their lives and their community. Another is to describe local government in terms that can be easily understood by the public, by using comparisons with things they are already familiar with. Helping the public, and indeed existing government employees, see their government in a different light can help with elevating some important discussions from the micro to the macro level. Seeing the bigger picture and where your government fits into overall societal and secular trends can make it easier to push for the kinds of institutional change that are required at the state and local government level. To develop some insights into the sheer scale of the importance of our government at all levels, let's examine it from the following perspectives:

1. The economic impact of government
2. An engine for technological breakthroughs
3. As a handbrake
4. You don't know what you have until it's gone
5. Government is a silent superhero
6. The rise of powerful cities

Developing a true understanding of the role of government in our society is a useful exercise for anyone considering public service. Upon serving in government and while you're in the middle of navigating this complex environment, being able to step back and gain a perspective on how the work you're doing fits into the overall grand scheme of your government's mission is a useful tool to have in your toolbox.

THE ECONOMIC IMPACT OF GOVERNMENT

On the face of it, trying to figure out how to measure the overall impact of government at all levels seems insurmountable. One of government's central roles is the provision of myriad services to the public, both physical and digital in nature. The sheer range of services government provides is mind-boggling, with much of that work hiding in plain sight. Even at a programmatic level within a single municipal government, this can prove to be difficult. In my role as open data manager in Seattle, trying to measure the impact of the data the city made freely available to the public was something we could never fully accomplish. As in any major enterprise or project, the key to knowing what success might look like is to establish some initial targets or goals and assess progress against them. Fortunately, when it came to the establishment of the federal government, the Founding Fathers understood this and included six initial goals into the Preamble to the United States Constitution:[7]

> We the People of the United States, in Order to form a more perfect Union, establish Justice, insure [sic] domestic Tranquility, provide for the common defense, promote the general Welfare, and secure the Blessings of Liberty to ourselves and our Posterity, do ordain and establish this Constitution for the United States of America.

If we break out the original goals in this statement, we get:

- to form a more perfect Union,
- establish Justice,
- ensure domestic Tranquility,

- provide for the common defense,
- promote the general Welfare, and
- secure the Blessings of Liberty to ourselves and our Posterity,

You'll notice that these goals don't have time limits or expiration dates. The first goal, to form a more perfect union, acts as the North Star for the whole country. It is why in every State of the Union speech the president will use the line "the state of our union is strong" and in other important speeches often use lines such as "in order to form a more perfect union." The subsequent five goals act as the methods through which this "more perfect union" will be pursued. It turns out that these goals set by the Founding Fathers are a useful way to measure the impact of our federal government in these current times. Thanks to some excellent work by USAFacts,[8] a not-for-profit, nonpartisan organization established to help the public answer questions about the impact of government in their lives, it is now possible to measure progress against these goals through their annual reports. Using their data, let's examine the impact of state and local government through two metrics: the total number of employees and the total amounts of spending and revenue collection by state and local governments.

EMPLOYEES

In 2016, the last year for which we have complete data at the time of writing, there were 19.41 million people employed in our state and local governments,[9] which represented 12.7 percent of the total U.S. employed workforce at that time (152.28 million people).[10] Note that this number includes both full-time and part-time employees. As you can see in Figure 2-1, the overall state and local government workforce levels appear to have remained stable while slowly recovering from the effects of the Great Recession. In 2008, state and local government employment peaked at 19.69 million before shrinking to 19.11 million in 2013. Once the data for subsequent years becomes available, we should expect to see the employment levels in state and local government have fully recovered to their pre-recession levels.

Figure 2-1: *Total government employees (state and local)*

Number of Employees	2008	2009	2010	2011	2012	2013	2014	2015	2016
+ Establish Justice and Ensure Domestic Tranquil...	,684,166	2,647,124	2,614,021	2,593,426	2,546,364	2,536,142	2,544,106	2,553,098	2,564,570
+ Provide for the Common Defense	n/a	n/a	n/a	n/a	n/a	n/a	n/a	n/a	n/a
+ Promote the General Welfare	,732,244	3,717,505	3,674,480	3,603,163	3,580,208	3,578,046	3,597,642	3,600,025	3,631,348
+ Secure the Blessings of Liberty to Ourselves a...	,831,382	11,978,810	11,920,495	11,832,864	11,741,602	11,676,333	11,757,087	11,802,130	11,865,809
+ General Government and Other	,445,013	1,345,639	1,317,717	1,272,135	1,320,464	1,316,581	1,330,483	1,337,338	1,344,627
Total Employees	692,805	19,689,078	19,526,713	19,301,588	19,188,638	19,107,102	19,229,318	19,292,591	19,406,354

Source: https://usafacts.org/data/topics/government-finances/employment/

Such a large population of workers is bound to have a large impact within their communities in terms of their wages earned being primarily spent in the locality. In 2015, total wages earned by state and local government employees totaled $944.872 billion, and it is quite likely that these figures have exceeded $1 trillion in subsequent years (Figure 2-2).

Figure 2-2: *Compensation – Wages (state and local)*

Compensation	5	2010	2011	2012	2013	2014	2015
− Wages & Salaries							
+ Federal Government	A	$328,524M	$331,668M	$327,651M	$320,404M	$324,003M	$329,664M
+ State and Local Government	A	$862,567M	$863,088M	$870,589M	$887,564M	$912,692M	$944,872M
Total Wages & Salaries	0	$1,191,091,000,000	$1,194,756,000,000	$1,198,240,000,000	$1,207,968,000,000	$1,236,695,000,000	$1,274,536,000,000

Source: https://usafacts.org/data/topics/government-finances/employment/

Note that these figures exclude other forms of compensation, such as pension contributions and payments toward benefits like health insurance. All told, state and local government employees inject massive amounts of money into our local economies through their wages, and as evidenced by the data, these wage levels remained relatively static even during the recent Great Recession. This wage data example helps highlight the incredible importance of local government spending during economic downturns, helping amplify the impact of federal government stimulus package funding during those times.

SPENDING

Another excellent way to gauge the importance of local governments is to examine how much money they inject into the overall economy. The 2019 Annual Report from USAFacts outlines some interesting metrics that highlight the scale of the impact of state and local government on the overall economy.

Statistic: 45% of all government spending is from state and local governments

According to the data, $2.7 trillion in total spending was attributable to state and local governments in 2016—an enormous sum of money. As shown in Figure 2-3 below, the levels of spending at the state and local government level are almost equivalent to the overall federal government spending. As previously noted, a significant amount of this money is spending of federal government grants and transfers—but leaving that aside, it is clear that state and local governments inject a tremendous amount of money into the overall economy.

Figure 2-3: *Federal spending versus state and local spending*

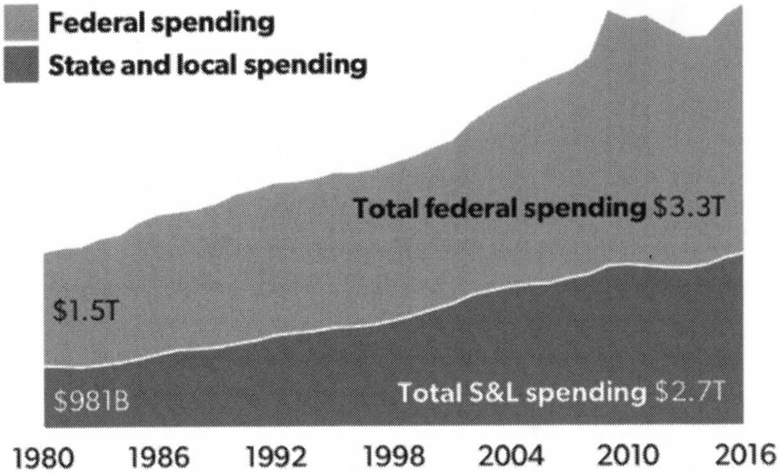

Source: https://annualreport.usafacts.org/articles/49-government-finances-fed
eral-government-transferred-661-billion-grants-state-local-governments-2016

If you wish to understand the exact impact of the spending in your own state and/or city or county, that data is also readily available. An annual survey of state and local spending is carried out by the Department of Commerce and the Census Bureau, and their findings are made available on the federal Open Data portal.[11] Each state and local government also publishes data on the state of their finances. Note that state governments (with the exception of New Hampshire) are required to balance their budgets, so their spending data may be complete and readily available than at the local government level. Local governments tend to publish their budgetary data, but not the actual breakdown of the "projections versus actuals" spending data. However, the budgetary data alone will provide you with a great sense of the scope and scale of that administration's spending priorities.

Statistic: The federal government transferred $661 billion in grants to state and local governments in 2016

As part of the overall state and local government spending totals, about 17.8 percent (or $661 billion) comes from the federal government according to the most recent data.[12] This funding is mostly in the form of food assistance and transportation grants. That state and local governments obtain a large portion of their overall funding from the federal government is a fact that the public can be largely unaware of until an issue arises where that funding is threatened and makes the news headlines.

REVENUES

When we think about governmental revenue collection, federal income taxes are often the first things that come to mind, since these are so significant in terms of the impact to our overall compensation and spending power. However, state and local governments have significant revenue generation powers of their own.

Statistic: State and local revenue make up just over one-third of all government revenue (35.3%)

As we see in Figure 2-4, state and local governments accounted for $1.8 trillion of all government revenue generated in 2016—more revenue than every country in the Organization for Economic Cooperation and Development (OECD) generates (apart from the United States).[13]

Figure 2-4: *Federal revenues versus state and local revenues*

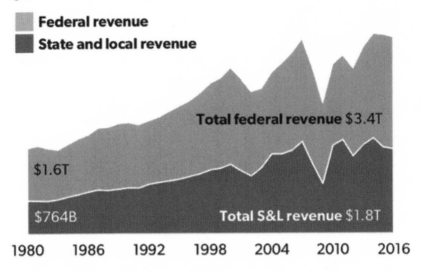

Federal revenue

State and local revenue

Total federal revenue $3.4T

$1.6T

$764B

Total S&L revenue $1.8T

1980   1986   1992   1998   2004   2010   2016

*Source: https://annualreport.usafacts.org/articles/49-government-finances-fed
eral-government-transferred-661-billion-grants-state-local-governments-2016*

It is also worth noting that most state governments have significant income tax revenue generation powers of their own, with only nine states not having an income tax on wages (Alaska, Florida, Nevada, New Hampshire, South Dakota, Tennessee, Texas, Washington, and Wyoming). In 2016, we see that states alone generated an additional $384 billion in income taxes, providing those states with significant revenues that help fund vital services (Figure 2-5).

Figure 2-5: *Federal income tax revenues versus state and local income tax revenues*

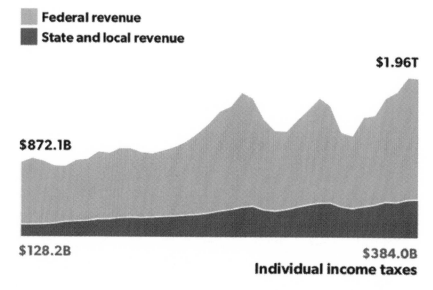

■ **Federal revenue**
■ **State and local revenue**

$1.96T

$872.1B

$128.2B

$384.0B
Individual income taxes

Source: https://annualreport.usafacts.org/articles/48-government-finances-state-local-revenue-make-just-onethird-35-3-government-revenue

Income taxes are seen as "progressive" taxes, where those who earn the most pay the most. There is also a set of "regressive" taxes that state and local governments employ to fund various initiatives and services. Chief among these would be sales taxes, where everyone pays the same amount regardless of their income. Another key source of revenue for state and local governments are property taxes, which are used to fund public schools in many jurisdictions. Both of these taxes generated more than $500 billion each in 2016, with sales and excise taxes generating $570.3 billion and property taxes bringing in $513.6 billion.[14] Again, when we compare these revenues against major OECD countries, we see that these state and local taxes surpass most countries' entire revenue collection. These figures help give a sense of the enormous economic power that our local governments wield.

AN ENGINE FOR TECHNOLOGICAL
BREAKTHROUGHS

We recently celebrated the fiftieth anniversary of the first moon landing, which occurred in July 1969. Over 400,000 people were directly employed in helping achieve this goal at a massive cost to the U.S. taxpayer. It is estimated that the entire cost of that project would be $640 billion in today's money, which is only $100 billion less than the annual U.S. defense budget. Only the federal government has the resources to mobilize and pursue projects and aims on such a scale. Private enterprise played a key role in supplying the technologies and know-how required to achieve the mission in the timeline required, but without the government's ability to direct and fund this work none of these missions would have been successful. Aside from the immense satisfaction and national pride in achieving such an incredible feat, not to mention the renewed focus on how we think about our humanity and the fragility of the planet Earth, these massive government-driven projects led to some incredible new technologies that continue to play key roles in our lives. For example, the incredible advances in multistage rockets used to propel humans to the moon accelerated the development and deployment of the hundreds of satellites we now rely on for everyday uses, such as global positioning system (GPS) navigation.

GPS is a wonderful example of how government-funded basic research can lead to the development of new technologies that affect every single person in the world. GPS came out of the Space Race, where both the Soviet Union and the United States developed methods for tracking the position of their spacecraft.[15] In the 1970s the U.S. Department of Defense (DoD) continued the development of GPS and later made a version of the positioning service available to the world, leading to the development of new space satellite industries and a service that we all take for granted when navigating to our destinations on a daily basis. An even more consequential example is the development of the Internet itself, which emerged from a research project led by the U.S. military's famed Defense Advanced Research Projects Agency (DARPA) agency beginning in the 1970s.[16] It is hard to think of a single technological breakthrough that has had such a consequential impact on our world. It is only through the government's ability to fund massive research projects and deploy resources at huge scale that some of the most fundamental technologies we depend on so much today actually exist.

While the previous examples speak to the development of technologies at the macro level and the federal government's role in that process, state and local government also plays an important role in helping spur technological innovation. One important way that is near and dear to my heart is through the release at scale of government data, better known as "open data." Governments at all levels and all sizes have one thing in common: they are sitting on vast amounts of data. By building platforms of open data, entrepreneurs and enterprises can use that data to develop services and applications that benefit the public and create economic opportunity. For example, one of the four goals of the Seattle Open Data program is to "encourage the development of innovative technology solutions that improve quality of life."[17] Useful apps can be developed at the local level, such as local transit applications, or the data can be consumed into larger research and development efforts at regional and national levels. Indeed, use cases involving open data are one of the most common ways that civic tech volunteer organizations and universities partner with their local governments.

AND A HANDBRAKE

While government may act as a large engine for the development of new technologies and systems, it also plays another critically important role on the other side of the equation. Government, and in particular Congress, also acts as a brake that helps to add checks and balances to the rapid development of disruptive technologies. Government has some powerful tools it can deploy in order to fulfil this role, including the oversight of industries and the institution of regulations if required. For example, regulations play a significant role in ensuring that our environment is kept clean, our food supply is not contaminated, and the medical drugs we consume are safe. When it comes to technology and its impact on our society, regulations are one important way that government can protect society from monopolies abusing their power and ensure that markets are not rigged so that true innovation can flourish. Well-known examples include the 1982 AT&T antitrust consent decree, which resulted in AT&T being broken up into several regional "Baby Bells," most of whom became hugely successful companies in their own right and are very familiar to us today. For example, Verizon resulted from a merger between one of the seven regional "Baby Bells" and GTE Corporation in 2000.

A more recent example was the Microsoft antitrust case begun in 1998 when the U.S. Department of Justice charged Microsoft with abusing its market dominance, particularly tied to the bundling of the Internet Explorer browser with the ubiquitous Windows operating system. While the initial ruling in 2000 decreed that Microsoft was to be broken up into two separate companies, one building the operating system (OS) and another building the software application that would run on the OS, a successful appeal by Microsoft resulted in a 2001 settlement being reached that allowed the company to remain intact and submit to several remedies, including the requirement to release its application programming interfaces (APIs) to third-party companies. While at the time this was seen as somewhat of a win for Microsoft, it did result in major changes at the company and the subsequent "lost decade" where Microsoft missed out on both the search and smart phone eras to a large extent. As someone who worked at Microsoft throughout this entire period, I can attest to the massive impact this antitrust case, along with the related European Union antitrust case, had on the company's ability to focus on emerging technology trends. In that period, companies such as Apple, Amazon, Google, and Facebook eclipsed Microsoft's market positions.

While these examples focus on the federal government's role in driving the creation and management of new technologies, it is important to note that local government also plays an important role in these areas, albeit at a much smaller scale. How? We are now entering a phase where increased government regulation of data privacy is likely. For example, while we await a federal law on data privacy, some state governments have begun to develop their own data privacy policies and laws in light of increasing public concern. Similarly, at the local government level, some major cities have instituted bans on new facial-recognition technologies being used by law enforcement. Policies being implemented at the local government level are now beginning to shape the national debate on these important technology policy issues.

YOU DON'T KNOW WHAT YOU HAVE UNTIL IT'S GONE

Government is one of those things in life that we take for granted. Every now and again, like a prolonged power outage, we get a stark reminder of just how much we actually depend on it. Thankfully rare, periods of time where our government stops fully functioning serve as reminders of the importance of these institutions in our lives and why our government functioning well is of critical importance to the future of our society. There are a few ways in which governments can suddenly, or indeed gradually, cease to function as expected. Some of these are politically motivated, such as federal government shutdowns. Others are caused by economic woes, such as in the Great Recession of 2008 and beyond. There is another growing class of shutdown caused by cybersecurity attacks, and this is most certainly an area where more technologists in local government can help shore up the defenses.

GOVERNMENT SHUTDOWNS

While there have been several federal government shutdowns in recent decades, the recent partial federal government shutdown beginning in December 2018 and ending in late January 2019 managed to sear itself into the public consciousness. Not because it was the most recent example, but because it was the longest government shutdown ever, lasting five weeks. This resulted in enormous hardship for hundreds of thousands of affected federal workers, with examples of dire personal circumstances being featured in the media. Images of the impacts to the public were heavily featured also, such as national parks having to close due to safety issues or the unavailability of background-check services affecting hiring at a time when the economy was adding a lot of jobs. Although the lingering impacts of this shutdown are still being assessed at the time of writing, available data suggests that the shutdown affected our economy in real terms. A report at the time from the Congressional Budget Office (CBO) showed that the shutdown cost the U.S. economy $11 billion, with $2.75 billion of that being permanently lost, and 0.4 percentage points being wiped off 2019 Q1 growth projections.[18] Another report from the CBO revealed that the 2019 Gross Domestic Product (GDP) projections were being reduced from 3.1 percent in 2018 to 2.3 percent in 2019, partially as a result of the shutdown.[19] Aside from the enormous impact inside of the federal government, the effects of government shutdowns at the federal level can quickly spread downstream to state and local governments, affecting the communities who are most dependent upon government services.[20]

FINANCIAL CRISES

Less recent in our collective memories are the gradual reductions in local government services caused by recessions and financial crises. The impacts to state and local government arising from the so-called "Great Recession" that began in December 2007 provide clear evidence of the upheaval a massive recession can have on the ability of our local governments to properly function. A 2016 study published in the *Journal of Urban Economics* found that forty-nine out of the top fifty metropolitan areas in the United States were hit by this recession, which was primarily driven by the collapse of the housing market.[21] As a result, revenues from property taxes dried up and forced many local governments across the country to reduce spending and curtail services. If we look at the trends nationally, we can see that these spending cuts were implemented in two main ways:

1. Cuts in personnel spending resulted in hiring freezes, furloughs, and layoffs (something quite unusual in government). Pay increases were also put on hold. Some staff were furloughed, which essentially means that they were required to take periods of unpaid leave. While these decisions to force pay freezes and incur periods of unpaid leave were very painful for the individuals involved, they were preferable to the alternative of being laid off permanently. These decisions had lingering effects well beyond the main period of the recession, which was from 2007 to 2013. When I joined the city of Seattle in 2016, I encountered some staff who had been furloughed during that period and were still recouping some of that lost time as extra paid vacation once the city budgets had stabilized. The impacts were not restricted to those currently employed in local government—in some cases, pension benefits had to be reduced, which would affect future retired government workers, who would be heavily reliant upon that income. According to the data, "the most common action taken by these cities was to put in place a hiring freeze (74 percent of cities did so in 2010), followed by salary/wage reductions or freezes (54 percent), and layoffs (35 percent)" and "the one notable exception to declining use of personnel cuts was the percentage of cities reducing pension benefits, which grew from 7 percent in 2010 to 22 percent in 2013."[22]

2. Cuts in general fund spending resulted in severe impacts to service provision on a broad scale. These cuts would have resulted in the changes most visible to the public during this time. While overall local government direct general expenditures declined 6.1 percent between FY09 and FY11, recent research by the Lincoln Institute of Land Policy highlights the main areas of impact, such as K–12 education and highway maintenance.[23] This variance in where the cuts landed give a sense of the kinds of tough decisions and trade-offs that local governments across the country had to make during this period.

As outlined earlier, the federal government is responsible for channeling vast sums of money into state and local governments. It is worth noting that as bad as those cuts in local government were, the impacts would likely have been more severe had it not been for emergency federal government economic stimulus packages being approved by Congress. The American Recovery and Reinvestment Act of 2009 poured hundreds of millions of dollars of financial aid into state and local governments, mostly in the form of grants that were directed at completing existing infrastructure projects or kick-starting new "shovel-ready" projects.[24]

INFRASTRUCTURE CRISES

A more recent threat to the availability of local government services has unfortunately become all too common. Local governments across the United States, and especially municipal governments, have been repeatedly targeted by so-called "ransomware attacks," where ransomware is defined as "a type of malicious software, or malware, designed to deny access to a computer system or data until a ransom is paid. Ransomware typically spreads through phishing emails or by unknowingly visiting an infected website."[25] These attacks have crippled multiple local governments at city and county levels, and even some state agencies.[26] Even the largest municipal governments are not immune. In 2018 the City of Atlanta was targeted, with the hackers demanding a ransom of $51,000 to be paid in bitcoin. The city refused, and instead spent millions of dollars attempting to restore affected services and harden its cybersecurity defenses. The total bill could be as high as $17 million.[27] More examples of millions of dollars of taxpayer money being spent on cleaning up the aftermath of these attacks have highlighted the urgent need for action to harden our local governments' critical technology infrastructure.

Cyberattacks are not the only Information Technology (IT) infrastructure threat faced by local governments that could result in an entire government being suddenly shut down. Aging and obsolete IT infrastructure also poses a real risk to local governments, as do the environments within which they are running. The local government within which I served provides a textbook case of how not proactively dealing with these scenarios can lead to bad consequences. Let's ignore for the moment the fact that the city's main datacenter was located on the twenty-sixth floor of a sixty-two-floor tower in the middle of downtown Seattle, a city at risk of experiencing a major earthquake. In late July 2012, a damaged busway in the datacenter resulted in the city having to essentially go offline for several days to make emergency repairs.[28] At the same time, $3 million was immediately allocated toward the creation of a "next-generation datacenter," which was completed in 2017. The location lesson had been learned, and the city now has two datacenters, both located outside of the city limits and in areas where there was a considerable datacenter infrastructure already in place. While the city was somewhat fortunate in that it was able to limit the scale of the shutdown to a few days over a holiday weekend, other local governments facing similar legacy infrastructure challenges may not be so lucky in the future.

GOVERNMENT IS A SILENT SUPERHERO

In his book, *The Fifth Risk*, author Michael Lewis outlines some potentially alarming consequences when the importance of our federal government is taken completely for granted, at best, or, at worst, deliberately sabotaged.[29] By examining three relatively obscure departments in the federal government, Lewis explains how some indispensable government functions, such as securing nuclear waste (Department of Energy), providing food safety and food security (Department of Agriculture), and developing accurate weather data (Department of Commerce), came under threat as a result of a poor presidential transition process. These examples highlight how the risks that a lack of knowledge or interest in the operations of massive government departments on the part of an incoming administration presents could potentially result in disastrous consequences. Most of what the federal government does, Lewis declares, only makes the news when disaster strikes. The same could be said of state and local government.

The everyday work of government at all levels, often unnoticed by the public, involves dealing with enormously complex challenges that can't be managed by the private sector. We're all familiar with some large federal government agencies, like the Federal Emergency Management Agency (FEMA), that come to the public's attention when natural disasters strike. Yet there are many examples of government agencies that operate silently in the background, doing incredibly important work, that perhaps never come to the public's attention. While some agencies prefer to operate quietly behind the scenes, other agencies could benefit from having the story of their amazing impact on our lives more widely known.

If we think about these scenarios at the local level, it becomes clear that we have also conditioned ourselves to take basic services for granted and assume things will always just work. Take, for example, our utilities; when we experience power, water, or Internet outages, they are almost shocking to us. We suddenly realize just how many everyday things we do completely depend upon these services. Prolonged outages can make us rethink our preparedness for future outages and instill a renewed appreciation for the government and/or utility companies that provide these basic services. Yet as normality returns, we typically revert back to our usual state of unpreparedness and operate under the assumption of a continual, uninterrupted supply of these basic services and utilities.

Aside from those outage events, when was the last time you stopped to think about all of the work that your local government does on your behalf? Think of all of the public infrastructure provided by local government we use each and every day. The roads we drive on, the traffic lights that guide us, the sidewalks we walk on, the bike lanes we cycle in, the street lights that provide safety, the libraries and community centers that connect our communities, the parks we enjoy in fine weather, and the countless other public services we enjoy that are hidden in plain sight. Now think about the staff that maintain these services. From the first responders who arrive so quickly when needed, to the staff who maintain the public parks and spaces we all enjoy. Without these services, and the people that keep them running every hour of every day, our society would be a much less pleasant place to live in. Now think about the role that technology plays in ensuring that all of these services get delivered or that emergencies are responded to in a matter of seconds or minutes. To help get a sense of the breadth and scale of the services that your local government offers and the role that technology plays, visit their home page and review the list of services and drill into each specific area. Even the smallest of local governments provides an amazing array of services, all powered to a greater or lesser extent by technology and data. As you read this book, take a peek behind the curtain of your local government and think about the ways your skills as a technologist could be used to build upon the work that has already been done.

THE RISE OF POWERFUL CITIES

Over the centuries, from the ancient to the medieval worlds, powerful city-states were commonplace. Well-known ancient examples include Rome,

Athens, Sparta, and the ancient Phoenician city-state of Carthage. In the fifteenth century, city-states such as Venice were among the most powerful trading and military powers in the world. Over time these centers of power consolidated into the modern European, North African, and Middle Eastern countries we all know today. These city-states wielded enormous power, in some cases created vast empires, and left behind important legacies that still shape our world today—such as the architecture of our capitol buildings, teachings on philosophy and logic, and the core democratic principles that shaped our constitutions and systems of government. Although some modern-day city-states exist, mostly in the Middle East and Southeast Asia, the notion of a city-state is a foreign concept to us in the United States today.

In the United States, a different system of government unfolded where the first colonies were established, before becoming quasi-independent states regulated by a powerful new federal government. As the United States expanded in the eighteenth and nineteenth centuries and developed into the fifty-state Union we have today, the loci of power struggles were around the idea of "states' rights" and the role of Congress and the U.S. Supreme Court to regulate and curtail those rights where necessary. Fast-forward to current times, and we are begging to see a shift in the national political dynamic. Major U.S. cities and their surrounding metropolitan regions have grown considerably in terms of their power and influence, both economically and politically.

ECONOMIC POWER

A widely known fact is that if the state of California was a country in its own right, it would be the fifth largest economy in the world with an output of $2.7 trillion, greater than that of the United Kingdom.[30] As staggering a factoid as this is, even more remarkable is the fact that the economies of some major U.S. metropolitan areas also exceed those of some major countries, as illustrated in Figure 2-6.[31]

Figure 2-6: *Top twenty U.S. metro areas compared to countries*

Source: http://www.aei.org/publication/understandin
g-americas-ridiculously-large-19-5t-economy-by-comparin
g-the-gdp-of-us-metro-areas-to-entire-countries-2

While these metropolitan areas typically consist of a major city at the center with some surrounding counties and regional cities, it is a useful way for us to reframe our thinking when it comes to the incredible impact that local governments have through creating the conditions for such amazing socioeconomic outcomes to occur. Other recent studies highlight the growing economic power that the top U.S. cities will wield, such as a recent McKinsey report that states "In the next 15 years, the 259 large US cities are expected to generate more than 10 percent of global GDP growth."[32] These reports highlight the need for local government to play an ever increasing and important role in how our major metropolitan areas can continue to develop in an equitable and responsible way.

With more technology firms choosing to locate within city downtown areas, led by companies such as Amazon, this is leading to new trends in how people live, commute, and work in our major cities. Within these major metropolitan areas, much work is being done to improve mass transit options both within the cities themselves and from the surrounding suburbs into those downtown areas, with light rail being a common solution. Within the cities themselves, "last mile" transit options have included ride-hailing services such as Uber and Lyft and an explosion in the availability of bike sharing programs and electric scooters. These have proved to be wildly popular with the public, and at times local governments have struggled to keep pace with the desire to roll out these services when little or no regulation exists. The end result is that it is an exciting time to be involved in technology and public policy within local government.

As these major metropolitan centers of economic power continue to grow, efforts are underway to improve the physical connections between these cities. A prime example is the proposals to develop high-speed rail links between some major metropolitan areas. In the Pacific Northwest, studies into the feasibility of a high-speed rail link between Vancouver B.C.; Seattle, Washington; and Portland, Oregon, as part of a "Cascadia Innovation Corridor" initiative have been completed. A 2018 report estimated that such a system could result in an extra $335 billion in economic growth in the region.[33] What is worth noting about these proposals is that these efforts are being explored in conjunction with major technology firms, who are seeking to make it easier to create new technology centers outside of their traditional headquarters and increase their ability to hire top talent. For example, in the Cascadia Innovation Corridor example, Microsoft is a key stakeholder in these discussions and would likely contribute to the overall costs of the project—a form of public-private partnership.

POLITICAL POWER

Another manifestation of the growth in importance and perception of U.S. cities at the national level can be seen in the number of current and former city mayors who decided to run in the 2020 U.S. presidential election. In recent history, being governor of a U.S. state was often seen as a necessary prerequisite when running for president. In the last sixty years, most U.S. presidents were former governors and as such had extensive executive experience. Presidents Kennedy and Obama were elected while members of the U.S. Senate and as such had limited legislative experience and no major executive experience, which was seen as a disadvantage at the time. Running a major U.S. city is now being seen—by the candidates themselves at least—as proper executive experience similar in stature to that of a governor of a U.S. state. In fact, in the case of one candidate, being mayor of a mid-sized U.S. city with a population slightly greater than 100,000 is deemed to be sufficient.

This rise in political power is becoming apparent in other aspects of current national political debates. For example, city governments have been at the forefront of the immigration crisis, with several cities declaring themselves to be "sanctuary cities" and where these mayors being interviewed on national news shows is a common occurrence. Note that the designation is typically "sanctuary cities" and not "sanctuary states." Similarly, as a result of the U.S. government announcing that it would withdraw from the Paris Climate Change Accords in 2017, many U.S. cities and states have stepped into the breach. Over 2,700 states, cities, and businesses committed to adhering to the Paris Agreement under the banner "We Are Still In," with the goal being to greatly limit the impact of policy decisions made at the federal government level.[34] These are just some of the ways in which local governments, and in particular major municipal governments, are having significant impact on the development of policies of national concern. It is through this visibility on issues of national importance that propels some mayors to seek higher office at the federal level (as noted earlier).

POLICY INNOVATION

Related to their rise in political power, some major U.S. cities have been at the forefront of policy innovation efforts. Policies, including some that affect emerging technologies, being implemented at the municipal level are now affecting the national debate. This is resulting in policies diffusing up from the municipal government level into the state and federal government levels, whereas historically, policies would diffuse in the opposite direction.

On April 1, 2015, the city of Seattle instituted the Seattle Minimum Wage Ordinance, which mandated a $15.00 per hour minimum wage. The law has since been updated to reflect inflation and the rising cost of living expenses, such that in 2019 the minimum wage for all large employers (employing more than 500 workers worldwide) will be $16.00 per hour, with small employers (with 500 or fewer employees) paying at least $15.00 per hour.[35] The law made national headlines when it was first introduced and continues to affect the debate around "living wages," both within the private sector and at the municipal, state, and federal government levels.

The city of San Francisco has been at the forefront of efforts to curtail the adoption of some emerging technologies, such as facial recognition, whose unintended consequences we are just beginning to understand. In May 2019, San Francisco's Board of Supervisors voted to ban the use of facial-recognition technology by the city's police department and other agencies, sparking similar actions by local governments in California and other U.S. states.[36] Regulations such as these are reactions to the nascent consequences of a new breed of emerging technologies driven by Artificial Intelligence (AI) and machine learning that have yet to be regulated by the federal government, such as facial recognition, and also related to the expanding deployment of Internet of Things (IoT) devices as part of "Smart Cities" technology implementations and the impending deployment of 5G cellular networks. We will discuss topics like "Smart Cities" and 5G in more detail later in the book, but these scenarios are good examples of the types of policy innovation that are being driven at the local level, leading to pressure to enact similar legislation at the state and national levels.

WHY THIS SHOULD MATTER TO TECHNOLOGISTS

These perspectives into the importance of government in our society also help highlight the critically important role that state and local governments will continue to play in shaping the future of our economy and improving our quality of life. As more young people move into our major cities seeking opportunity and continue to drive the engines of metropolitan economic growth, they will bring with them an almost unquenchable thirst for change in how people will live in, and traverse through, our cities. State and local governments are now taking the lead in driving major public policy changes, such as regulating the so-called gig economy, implementing progressive living-wage laws, expanding the availability of new mobility services such as electric scooters, and introducing regulations to mitigate potential harms to the public from rapid advances in the power of new technologies driven by AI. As technology and data will continue to play a central role in the socioeconomic changes to come in our cities and counties, the need for more technologists to help lead and manage some of these efforts within local government will continue to grow. The often-hidden nature of the work at the state and local government level can mask its true importance and impact, yet many opportunities exist to showcase the incredible impact that technology and data can play in the creation of a next-generation local government. Technologists can play a leading role in amplifying these positive social impacts of government in our society.

CHAPTER 2: KEY TAKEAWAYS

- Actions within government to create programs to do good can lead to future generations being inspired to use those program models and build new organizations that inspire others to use their skills for the common good. Code for America is a great example of such an organization inspired by previous efforts.

- Words matter, as do perceptions. Technologists can play a leading role in helping reshape the narratives around state and local government.
- By better understanding the true importance of government, technologists can play a crucial role in amplifying the importance of our government to the public.
- The importance of government at all levels in our society is profound:
  - It is well understood that the economic impact of government in our overall economy is massive, yet the sheer scale and impact of state and local government are less well understood.
  - Government can act as an engine for technological breakthroughs that affect all of society for generations.
  - Government also acts as a handbrake in the form of introducing regulations to help mitigate the bad and/or unintended consequences of technological breakthroughs.
  - You don't know what you have until it's gone—it is only when our government fails to function as normal that we begin to get a sense of its true importance.
  - Government is a silent superhero—often the most critical work performed by government happens quietly and behind the scenes.
  - The rise of powerful cities—some large municipal governments are leading the way in driving the creation and implementation of progressive public policies that are later adopted at the national level. Municipal regions also possess tremendous economic power.

NOTES

1   "Inaugural Address, 20 January 1961," John F. Kennedy Presidential Library and Museum, accessed December 31, 2019, https://www.jfklibrary.org/Research/ Research-Aids/Ready-Reference/JFK-Quotations/Inaugural-Address.aspx.

2   "History: Peace Corps," Peace Corps, accessed December 19, 2019, https://www. peacecorps.gov/about/history/

3   "AmeriCorps," National and Community Service, accessed December 11, 2019, https://www.nationalservice.gov/programs/americorps/.

4   "The History of Teach for America," Teach for America, accessed December 31, 2019, https://www.teachforamerica.org/about-us/our-work/our-history/.

5   "Inaugural Address, 20 January 1981," President Ronald Reagan, The American Presidency Project, accessed December 31, 2019, https://www.presidency.ucsb. edu/documents/inaugural-address-11/.

6   "State of the Union Address, 23 January 1996," President William Jefferson Clinton, accessed December 31, 2019, https://clintonwhitehouse2.archives.gov/ WH/New/other/sotu.html.

7   "The Constitution of the United States," National Archives, accessed October 14, 2019, https://www.archives.gov/founding-docs/constitution.

8   "About Us," USAFacts, accessed October 12, 2019, https://usafacts.org/about.

9   "US Government Employment," USAFacts, accessed October 12, 2019, https://usafacts.org/government-finances/employment/ number-of-employees?gov_type=state_local&regions=US.

10 "Current Employment Statistics - CES (National)," U.S. Bureau of Labor Statistics, accessed December 31, 2019, https://www.bls.gov/ces/.

11 "Annual Survey of State and Local Government Finances," Data.gov, accessed December 31, 2019, https://catalog.data.gov/dataset/annual-survey-of-state-an d-local-government-finances.

12 "USAFacts 2019 Annual Report," USAFacts, accessed December 31, 2019, https://annualreport.usafacts.org/articles/49-government-finances-federal- government-transferred-661-billion-grants-state-local-governments-2016.

13 "Tax revenue," OECD, accessed December 31, 2019, https://data.oecd.org/tax/ tax-revenue.htm.

14 "USAFacts 2019 Annual Report," USAFacts, accessed December 31, 2019, https://annualreport.usafacts.org/articles/48-government-finances-state-lo cal-revenue-make-just-onethird-35-3-government-revenue.

15 "Global Positioning System History," NASA, accessed November 15, 2019, https://www.nasa.gov/directorates/heo/scan/communications/policy/GPS_History.html.

16 "A Brief History of the Internet & Related Networks," Internet Association, accessed October 11, 2019, https://www.internetsociety.org/internet/history-internet/brief-history-internet-related-networks.

17 "Open Data Policy," City of Seattle, accessed October 21, 2019, https://www.seattle.gov/Documents/Departments/SeattleGovPortals/CityServices/OpenDataPolicyV1.pdf.

18 "The Effects of the Partial Shutdown Ending in January 2019," Congressional Budget Office, accessed October 21, 2019, https://www.cbo.gov/system/files?file=2019-01/54937-PartialShutdownEffects.pdf.

19 "An Update to the Budget and Economic Outlook: 2019 to 2029," Congressional Budget Office, accessed October 21, 2019, https://www.cbo.gov/publication/55551.

20 "The Risk of Another Government Shutdown Is Increasing," CitiesSpeak, last updated November 19, 2019, https://citiesspeak.org/2019/11/19/the-risk-of-another-government-shutdown-is-increasing.

21 "Metro Business Cycles," *Journal of Urban Economics*, Volume 94, July 2016, Pages 90-108, https://www.sciencedirect.com/science/article/pii/S009411901630016X.

22 "Local Government Finances During and After the Great Recession," Lincoln Institute of Land Policy, accessed October 22, 2019, https://www.lincolninst.edu/sites/default/files/pubfiles/2443_1789_Langley%20WP14AL1.pdf.

23 "Local Government Finances During and After the Great Recession," Lincoln Institute of Land Policy, accessed October 22, 2019, https://www.lincolninst.edu/sites/default/files/pubfiles/local-government-finances-great-recession-full_0.pdf, Figure 6.5, p.184.

24 "H.R.1 - American Recovery and Reinvestment Act of 2009," U.S. Congress, last updated February 17, 2009, https://www.congress.gov/bill/111th-congress/house-bill/1/.

25 "Ransomware," The Cybersecurity and Infrastructure Security Agency, accessed October 15, 2019, https://www.us-cert.gov/Ransomware.

26 "Report: Two-Thirds of Ransomware Attacks in 2019 Targeted State and Local Governments," StateScoop, last updated August 28, 2019, https://statescoop.com/report-70-percent-of-ransomware-attacks-in-2019-hit-state-and-local-governments.

27 "Atlanta's Cyber Attack Could Cost Taxpayers $17 Million," The Atlanta Journal-Constitution, accessed October 15, 2019, https://www.ajc.com/news/confidential-report-atlanta-cyber-attack-could-hit-million/GAljmndAF3EQdVWlMcXS0K.

28 "City of Seattle Partial Data Center Shutdown," City of Seattle, last modified August 31, 2012, https://alert.seattle.gov/2012/08/23/city-of-seattle-partial-data-center-shutdown-anticipated-impacts-to-online-applications/.

29 "The Fifth Risk," Michael Lewis, accessed October 22, 2019, https://www.penguinrandomhouse.ca/books/602174/the-fifth-risk-by-michael-lewis/9781324002642.

30 "California's Economy Is Now Bigger Than All of the U.K.," Fortune, last modified May 5, 2018, https://fortune.com/2018/05/05/california-fifth-bigges t-economy-passes-united-kingdom.

31 http://www.aei.org/publication/understanding-americas-ridiculously-large-19-5t-economy-by-comparing-the-gdp-of-us-metro-areas-to-entire-countries-2

32 "Urban America: US Cities in the Global Economy," McKinsey & Company, accessed October 17, 2019, https://www.mckinsey.com/featured-insights/urbanization/us-cities-in-the-global-economy.

33 "Ultra High-Speed Ground Transportation Study," McKinsey & Company, accessed October 22, 2019, https://www.wsdot.wa.gov/publications/fulltext/LegReports/17-19/UltraHighSpeedGroundTransportation_FINAL.pdf.

34 "Trump Tried to Kill the Paris Agreement, But the Effect Has Been the Opposite," Brookings Institute, last updated
June 1, 2018, https://www.brookings.edu/blog/planetpolicy/2018/06/01/trump-tried-to-kill-the-paris-agreement-but-the-effect-has-been-the-opposite.

35 "Minimum Wage Ordinance," City of Seattle Office of Labor Standards, accessed October 15, 2019, http://www.seattle.gov/laborstandards/ordinances/minimum-wage.

36 "Administrative Code - Acquisition of Surveillance Technology," City of San Francisco, accessed October 15, 2019, https://www.eff.org/files/2019/05/07/leg_ver3.pdf.

3

WHY YOU SHOULD CONSIDER PUBLIC SERVICE

When assessing opportunities to serve in the public sector, one of the obvious questions you will ask yourself is "why?" It's a great question to ask when making any big decision, and especially important when considering making a pivot to a new domain, such as government. There are many reasons why someone might want to make such a change at any point in their career. Some reasons are fairly common, such as moving to a role where you make more money or gain a new title with expanded responsibilities, or to learn a new set of skills. Others can be specific to the domain itself, and pivoting into local government from the private sector is one of those.

Often we are inspired to do something like committing to public service. Later in this book I write about some personal inspirations and how they helped influence my decision to serve in local government after a long career in the private sector. If you are reading this book, it is probably a fair assumption that you have some of your own personal inspirations that are nudging you to think about setting off on your own governmental career journey. Inspirations aside, other motivations exist that could play a large role in your own thought process.

In this chapter we will explore some factors that may play a role in your decision-making process. Some of the motivations I list here are generic in nature, some are more personal, but all will be useful for you to think about as you set out on your own journey and will hopefully help you to uncover your own unique motivations and spur you to action. Clearly understanding your own motivations for wanting to work in government is a very important first step in ensuring that you will end up in a place where you can truly have impact and that will help you identify exciting personal and professional growth opportunities during your time in government.

THE NOBILITY OF SERVICE

As I reflected upon my own tenure in local government and considered the next steps in my own career, one question I kept pondering was whether to return to the private sector or to continue serving within government itself. One scenario I often thought about is whether I could continue to have impact and influence on the public sector from within the private sector, using my newly acquired knowledge of, and insights into, local government. Yet there is a constant nagging voice in my head that compels me to consider serving in government again, albeit at a different level (county, or state, or federal) or within a different part of public sector (e.g., teaching in a public college). Having thought about this for some considerable time, I came to a clear realization about why I find it so difficult to move on from public service.

There is a nobility in serving others.

It wasn't until I had stepped away from my first foray into public service that I truly understood what it had meant to serve others. For the first time, I had an inkling of the deep emotional bonds that connect those who serve in the military or as first responders. Similarly, I began to see teachers and other public servants in a totally new light; to finally understand what inspired some people to pursue lifelong vocations in the service of others, often forgoing better financial opportunities in the private sector. I know of several former colleagues within local government

81

who could easily find higher-paying roles in the private sector yet choose to stay directly connected to the public service mission.

Before we delve into the details of what local government is and how it operates, I think it is useful for anyone who is thinking about working in local government, either as a recent graduate or as an experienced professional, to reflect on your reasons for wanting to make this step in your career. This isn't just so you can have a ready answer for those people who will inevitably be intrigued by your decision and will wish to learn more; rather, it will also be very useful for you to have a clear understanding ahead of time about what you hope to achieve in your government career and perhaps even where it might lead you further down the road.

EULOGY VIRTUES, NOT RÉSUMÉ VIRTUES

In his recent book *The Road to Character*, author David Brooks writes about the idea of moving from "résumé virtues to eulogy virtues."[1] As he explains it, the basic principle is that résumé virtues are the skills you bring to the marketplace, whereas eulogy virtues are the ones that are talked about after you have passed away. In other words, how would you like to be remembered? While Brooks uses this concept to think about building inner character, I believe this is another useful construct with which to think about adding time in public service to your career portfolio and builds nicely upon the idea of the nobility of serving others. Many companies today speak to the ideals of "having social impact" and typically have slick presentations and websites that highlight the work that they accomplish in this space. Private-sector companies can have a wonderful impact through their philanthropic work, yet it is sometimes difficult for the average technologist in the private sector to feel like they are truly having the kind of impact that they desire. Hence, we see a lot of technologists volunteering their time outside of their company's social impact programs, something we will discuss later in this book. If building those "eulogy virtues" is something that is really important to you also, then this is another reason to strongly consider joining your local government.

THE MISSION OF GOVERNMENT APPEALS TO YOU

Another common motivation for people to join public service is because the central mission and purpose of government are appealing and can be rooted in the desire to "give back," or indeed, to "pay it forward." Members of the Millennial and Gen Z cohorts appear to place a lot of value on the mission of the organization and its ability to do good in the world that they have inherited. Studies indicate that Millennials experience widespread dissatisfaction with their sense of purpose, partially stemming from how to connect their work to other aspects of their lives. A recent Gallup report, "How Millennials Want to Work and Live," found that about a third of Millennial workers strongly agree that the mission or purpose of their organization makes them feel their job is important and that just 40 percent of Millennials feel strongly connected to their company's mission.[2] If young technologists early into their careers are looking for that true sense of purpose, then I can think of few other organizations with more challenging and fulfilling missions than government. Where can you find the mission statement for your government? If we think about the federal government, the preamble of the U.S. Constitution is essentially the mission statement of the United States:

> We the people of the United States, in order to form a more perfect union, establish justice, insure domestic tranquility, provide for the common defense, promote the general welfare, and secure the blessings of liberty to ourselves and our posterity, do ordain and establish this Constitution for the United States of America.

The key statement here is "to form a more perfect union." In theory, everything that every American citizen does, whether they work in government or not, can be aligned in some way toward achieving that overarching goal. For example, the simple act of voting is one way that a citizen can contribute to the establishment of a more perfect union. This statement acts as a North Star for the nation, an idea that everyone can relate to, and yet we as a people will never achieve a state of perfection. In some ways, it is "mission impossible," but then all great mission statements should reflect this ongoing desire to continually improve and reach for an even higher level of achievement.

While the federal government does have a mission statement, it is notable that state and local governments for the most part do not. Instead, it is more common to see individual departments have their own specific mission statements, related to their individual departmental goals. For example, my home state of Washington does not have a central mission statement listed on its main website.[3] However, some of the many state agencies do have mission statements listed in their "About Us" sections, such as the Office of Cybersecurity, which lists its mission simply as "to keep the state's data safe and secure."[4] Personally, I think this is a real gap in the development of an overall culture of achievement and accountability at the state and local government level, something we will discuss in more detail later in the book. I am a huge proponent of having clear mission statements with associated strategies and tactics that will ensure success for any project, large or small, and I made sure these were included in our public-facing strategic plans. As a technologist in your local government, advocating for clearer mission statements that reflect the true nature of your work is something I would strongly encourage.

MOVE BEYOND VOLUNTEERING

One of the most interesting aspects of working in a technology-focused role in local government were my interactions with the local civic technology volunteers. Although I was somewhat aware of these civic tech (as they were more commonly referred to) organizations and programs before I joined the city of Seattle, I found myself surprised by the commitment and scale of the efforts of these highly skilled technology professionals. I had the opportunity to speak at some of their events, as these organizations were huge proponents of using our open data to develop new ways of providing public good, and remember being amazed that dozens of people would give up an entire Saturday or weekend to focus on a volunteer effort directly related to the mission of local government.

A key takeaway from those interactions was the realization that they were also frustrated that their efforts were not having a more direct impact within their local government. I fully understood this frustration, being able to have both a private-sector and public-sector perspective on those issues. I came to realize that they didn't fully understand how their local government functioned, and so some of their initial assumptions were incorrect, and I tried hard to educate these groups on the limitations of the local government system to absorb the tools and services they were building. This was one of several realizations I had during my public service that convinced me that we need to build up the capacity of technologists in local government itself in order to be able to take advantage of these opportunities and to develop robust technology transfer protocols between those two worlds, and indeed more empathy. Code for America is probably the organization that is closest to solving some of these technology transfer, integration, and sustaining issues. Yet there remains a scarcity of motivated technologists within local government itself who are equipped and empowered to take full advantage of the tremendous potential for civic technology volunteer groups to help amplify their social impact.

A useful way to think about this potential for impact is through the lens of political capital versus social capital. The term "social capital" became widely known as a result of a bestselling book by Robert Putnam titled *Bowling Alone: The Collapse and Revival of American Community*."[5] One definition of the term, "networks together with shared norms, values and understandings that facilitate co-operation within or among groups," captures its essence.[6] I view these communities of civic tech volunteers as groups attempting to build social capital in order to create social impact. As a technologist working within local government, you will have the power to help translate some of that social capital into political capital by enabling some of these projects and ideas to take effect as official government-supported efforts.

It is important to point out that this civic tech movement involves more than just the volunteers and organizations such as Code for America. It can also encompass the cluster of startups and enterprise software companies that build software solutions primarily for the public sector. Whereas civic tech can be defined as "technology used to inform, engage and connect residents with government and one another to advance civic outcomes," there exists a class of technology company, usually referred to as GovTech, that create "technology designed with government as the intended customer or user."[7] It is not unusual to have some connections between civic tech organizations and GovTech companies. For example, some GovTech firms may host local civic tech meetings, and it is a great way for staff and volunteers to network and develop new insights into the challenges their local governments are facing. A 2017 report commissioned by the Knight Foundation titled "Scaling Civic Tech, Paths to a Sustainable Future" outlines the challenges these volunteer organizations and GovTech firms alike face in sustaining their efforts and the huge opportunities to scale their impact.[8] Working at one of these companies is another great way for technologists to align with the mission of improving the public sector, and I have personally gotten to know dozens of highly passionate and skilled technologists working at these companies. Serving in government, either before or after working at one of these companies, would be a fantastic way to create a rounded set of public-sector experiences.

ADD TO THE FLOW OF TALENT
INTO THE PUBLIC SECTOR

In the introduction to this book, I outlined how recent studies into the flow of talent into the public sector were the catalyst for my own decision to serve in that arena. The need to increase the flow of technical talent is real, as initially outlined in the 2013 report "A Future of Failure? The Flow of Technology Talent into Government and Society."[9] A follow-up report in 2016 titled "A Pivotal Moment: Developing a New Generation of Technologists for the Public Interest" included strategies aimed at helping build out that pipeline of talent.[10] If you are seeking extra research materials outside of this book about the technology talent pipeline into government, I would highly recommend beginning with these two reports and their sources.

At the federal level, there have been efforts to increase the flow of technical talent into government. Two major programs were established during the Obama administration. The first is the U.S. Digital Service, based within the White House, which directly engages with departments and agencies across the federal government to "partner leading technologists with dedicated public servants to improve the usability and reliability of our government's most important digital services."[11] The second is 18F, an agency located within the General Services Administration (GSA), that "collaborates with other agencies to fix technical problems, build products, and improve how government serves the public through technology."[12] Additionally, 18F has created solutions that federal agencies can leverage to accelerate their transition to using cloud services, such as their Platform as a Service offering "cloud.gov." The U.S. Chief Technology Officer helps coordinate and direct these efforts in the most effective way. While the establishment of these initiatives at the federal government level is exciting and very welcomed, their success in scaling these efforts depends heavily on the ability of the various government departments they partner with to develop their own internal technical expertise.

Unlike at the federal government level, there are no centralized efforts to develop such a pipeline of talent for the local government sector. This is primarily due to the fragmented nature of the sector and huge variations in the size and capabilities of smaller local governments. Whereas some larger state and municipal governments have built internal programs that deploy some elements of those federal programs, the local government sector relies almost exclusively on solutions provided by third-party software vendors, often in conjunction with support from technical consultants. This heavy reliance on outsourcing of expertise is required due to the lack of the internal technical capacity within local government.

This is where you as a technologist can have clear and sustained impact. As more technologists join the local government service with these ideals in mind, regional and national networks of like-minded people will organically form, and it is through these connections that ideas for how to develop a robust pipeline of talent can emerge. Some networks already exist, but without the explicit goal of developing the flow of technical talent, so it could be possible to build on top of those existing efforts to develop new capacities within local government. With support from the various philanthropic programs and federal government grants, new initiatives could be developed to build upon the ideas championed by the U.S. Digital Service and/or 18F programs.

CAREER GROWTH OPPORTUNITIES

On a more personal level, completing a tour of duty in your local government will enrich your career in many ways, some of which may not become apparent until you after you have left government. Some of the experiences I had would be difficult to replicate in the private sector. In local government, interacting with the public is expected, and I find it hard to think of a public servant that I worked with who didn't engage either directly or indirectly with the public on a regular basis.

If you are a technologist who enjoys the customer engagement aspect of your work, then local government has probably some of the most rewarding and likely most challenging customer engagement scenarios you can think of. In local government, you are close to the people who are availing of your services, sometimes uncomfortably so. If people are upset about a service you're providing, you will hear about it, and often in person. These encounters mostly occur in public meetings and settings where government-sponsored events are being held, but sometimes people will visit a central service desk and you may end up fielding a specific complaint. This is a huge contrast from the private sector, where such personal interactions with individual end users are basically zero. These encounters will provide clear insights into what matters to the public, and their feedback and advocacy will help shape the future direction of the service provision you're responsible for. For the most part, the conversations I had with various members of the public helped improve my knowledge and reduced the risk of developing biases in how we approached our work. This is invaluable when developing services for the public using data and technology.

One aspect of public service that I didn't truly appreciate until after I had been there for about six months was the way in which my professional network dramatically increased. It is a fantastic way to build your network, with amazing opportunities to connect with other local governments, academia, other state and local agencies, philanthropic programs, and GovTech companies, to name but a few. Taking advantage of opportunities to attend and/or speak at national conferences, panels, guest lectures, and so on will lead to many people wanting to connect with you. Depending on your role, you may also have opportunities to engage with the public via social media, government blogs, webinars, and press interviews.

Earlier in my career, as I was building my own professional network, I did most of the outreach and I slowly built up my network. As I was working inside a private-sector company with little exposure to the outside world, my network was quite limited. It was mostly people in my existing company and connections from college. Once I began serving in government and sharing more about myself and the work that we were doing, that process inverted. At the peak of my government outreach activities and public speaking, I was fielding LinkedIn connection requests on an almost daily basis. As a technologist working in local government, these new connections and the new knowledge of a whole host of organizations doing amazing work in areas you may otherwise have not been aware of can lead to new ideas for future career paths, both within government and back in the private sector.

MASTER A NEW DOMAIN

One reason why you might be interested in working in government is because you're interested in exploring a whole new sector. This is especially true of experienced professionals, like me, who spent the entirety of their career to that point in the private sector. Making the leap into a whole new world can be quite challenging and indeed scary, so it is important to be clear on how to position yourself to have the best chance of success once you make such a transition.

As a result of thinking about this problem when I first began to seriously consider making a pivot in my career, I spoke with several trusted mentors in my network who could perhaps provide me with some useful advice and insights into navigating this challenge. One of the best pieces of advice I got was that when considering a pretty significant shift in your career, it was better to change either your "discipline" or your "domain," but not both together. By "discipline," I mean the type of work you do—in my case, it was as a manager of software engineering and data analytics teams. If you are not sure how to accurately describe yourself, job search websites often have useful taxonomies for describing professions and job types. By "domain," I mean the sector within which you perform your function. In my case, I equated "domain" to be either the private sector or public sector. Other ways to describe changing your domain could be moving from marketing into sales or from engineering into finance.

Let's use my own case as an example. After a long career at Microsoft where I had been managing software engineering and later data analytics teams, I decided that I wished to pivot away from that work and into a career that was more focused on the intersection of technology and policy, as I realized there was a real need for more people who could effectively operate within that niche. Since I knew next to nothing about policy and how it was formulated, implemented, and evaluated, I knew I had to acquire that knowledge. Making that decision was my real starting point, and it allowed me to research programs that might be able to provide me with the training that I needed. Fortunately, there was a program in my area that was specifically tailored to working professionals, and after establishing that it could be a great fit for me, I applied and was accepted. While working full-time at Microsoft, I earned a master's degree in public policy (Master of Arts in Policy Studies at the Interdisciplinary School of Arts and Sciences at the University of Washington, Bothell). It was during my studies that I focused upon the intersection of advancing positive policy outcomes through data as my area of expertise, and specifically in the area of open data at the governmental level. I knew my next role would involve working with open data within government itself, or in a company whose mission aligned with helping governments to do more with data, and especially open data.

I now had a new "domain" to target—the public sector. Less clear was what my new discipline would be, since I had zero professional policy experience at that time. Based on the advice I had received about changing either your discipline or your domain, but not both together, I knew I needed to find a role within government where I could use my existing skillsets to create the space within which I could quickly learn all about the new domain within which I was operating. Fortunately for me, about one year after graduating from my master's program, the city of Seattle was seeking to hire a manager for their Open Data program, and I was fortunate enough to be hired. The job entailed managing a small team of engineers, developing the operational capabilities of the program, and growing their existing platform of data. These were things that I already knew how to do. This allowed me to have impact early in my tenure, establish some credibility, and create the space to learn as much as I could about how municipal government worked and how to operate effectively within it. Later, having had time to learn how to have impact within a new domain, I could then think about how to develop additional skillsets (or disciplines) within the two domains that I now have experience with: the private sector and public sector. This is a really important aspect of public service for technologists to consider. Those skills and experiences gained in government are highly valuable in both the private and public sectors, and a new set of opportunities opened up as a result. Serving in government is a great way to expand your long-term career opportunities.

TOUR OF DUTY

There is a stereotype that working in government means a job for life or that taking a position in government means that you are expected to spend a considerable length of time working there. It is true that many people who work in local government, whether in administrative or field roles, do so for considerable periods. During my service, I encountered many people who had been in local government for at least twenty years, and in some cases more than thirty years. This appears to be a pretty common scenario across the country. I knew of several staff with long public service careers who split their tenure between state and local government or between county and municipal government. While working for more than twenty years in one private-sector technology company is less common, there are plenty of examples. Some of the senior leadership at Amazon have been at the company for more than twenty years, and I know of many ex-colleagues at Microsoft who have spent more than twenty years there. I myself worked at Microsoft for eighteen years. Another stereotype that has emerged in recent years is that the Millennial generation are job-hopping at a rate far higher than previous generations. The data appears to show that is also not correct—in fact, based on comparisons with those of us from the Gen X generation, the rate of change is basically equivalent.[13]

As with all stereotypes, there is an element of truth to them, but the data reveals the actual state of affairs. You might be surprised to learn that the average tenure of a public-sector worker in the United States in 2018 was just 6.8 years. As we can see from the data highlighted in Figure 3-1, it appears that the average tenure across federal, state, and local government has been falling in recent years. It is possible that this drop coincides with the rate at which government employees are retiring, as part of the "Silver Tsunami" that we referred to in Chapter 1.

Figure 3-1: *Median years of tenure with current employer for employed wage and salary workers by industry, selected years, 2008–2018*

Industry	2008	2010	2012	2014	2016	2018
Public sector	7.2	7.2	7.8	7.8	7.7	6.8
Federal government	9.9	7.9	9.5	8.5	8.8	8.3
State government	6.5	6.4	6.4	7.4	5.8	5.9
Local government	7.1	7.5	8.1	7.9	8.3	6.9

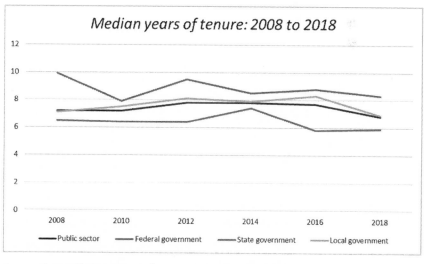

Source: https://www.bls.gov/news.release/tenure.t05.htm

Now that we have established that these old stereotypes mostly ring hollow, we can reframe the discussion about the expected length of public service for younger technologists in particular. It is quite common to describe working in the public service as a "tour of duty," and I would certainly encourage technologists to approach their thinking about serving in local government in this regard. After all, in technology companies it is common for staff to be encouraged and incentivized to think about changing their roles every eighteen to twenty-four months. This thinking is based on research into the so-called "plateau effect" that suggests that engineers typically require six to twelve months to get fully up to speed on a new project and reach their peak performance at about the eighteen-month mark before seeing their performance begin to plateau. Based on my own experiences in local government, I would say a two- to three-year period is sufficient to have impact before seeking a new or related challenge. This is why establishing a well-stocked pipeline of technical talent is vital to enable local governments to build upon the work of these predecessors. In this way, the process of innovation can be embedded into the culture of the organization. By performing a "tour of duty" in your local government, you can help with establishing that pipeline of talent in your own region.

MOVING FROM "WHY" TO "WHAT"

In the first three chapters of this book, we have discussed some of the main reasons why talented technologists may wish to consider serving in government, and especially within their state and local government. By first understanding what state and local government is, how those structures came to be, and how they operate in present times, we can gain a better perspective for the permanent nature of government. In the face of ever more rapid changes in our society, often driven by technological advances, this is an important consideration. Next, we reviewed the importance of government in our society through a number of lenses, including its sheer size and scale. Technologists love thinking about scale and solving big problems. I can think of few challenges greater than helping build the next generation of local government. Finally, we reflected on the personal reasons why we as technologists may wish to consider public service, and especially in the form of a tour of duty in state and local government. Now that we have taken the time to reflect on all the reasons why, let's move onto the "what." What are the reasons why we need to increase the number of technologists moving into the public sector, what are the challenges that technologists can help solve in local government, and what are the key differences between the private and public sectors that may affect, positively or negatively, your ability to have real impact?

CHAPTER 3: KEY TAKEAWAYS

- There is a nobility in serving others.
- Create eulogy virtues, not résumé virtues. In other words, will you regret it later in your career and/or life if you didn't serve in government?
- When thinking about the missions of organizations that you may wish to join and whether they appeal strongly to you, your values, and your desire to do good in the world, make sure to include local government in that mix.
- Move beyond volunteering—if you're already volunteering your time, energy, and skills in helping local government through civic tech programs, consider taking the next step and serving within local government itself.
- If you move from volunteering into public service, you'll be adding to the flow of technical talent into the public sector, where it is badly needed.
- Local government can provide some fantastic career growth opportunities, both within government itself and back in the private sector after your public service has ended.

- Serving in local government can give you an amazing opportunity to master a new domain: the public sector.

- Working in the public sector doesn't necessarily mean that you need to commit a large part of your career to that work. It is quite common for technologists and others to complete a "tour of duty" before returning to the private sector.

NOTES

1   David Brooks, *The Road to Character* (New York: Random House, 2015).

2   "Millennials Not Connecting With Their Company's Mission," Gallup, last updated November 15, 2016, https://www.gallup.com/workplace/236342/millennials-not-connecting-company-mission.aspx.

3   "Access Washington—Home," State of Washington, accessed November 17, 2019, https://access.wa.gov.

4   "WaTech's State Office of Cybersecurity," State of Washington, accessed November 17, 2019, https://cybersecurity.wa.gov/about-us.

5   Robert D. Putnam, *Bowling Alone* (New York: Simon & Schuster, 2000).

6   "What Is Social Capital?," OECD, accessed November 17, 2019, https://www.oecd.org/insights/37966934.pdf.

7   "Scaling Civic Tech," Knight Foundation, accessed November 17, 2019, https://knightfoundation.org/reports/scaling-civic-tech.

8   "Scaling Civic Tech," Knight Foundation, accessed November 17, 2019, https://knightfoundation.org/reports/scaling-civic-tech.

9   "A Future of Failure? The Flow of Technology Talent into Government and Society," Ford Foundation, accessed September 15, 2019, https://www.fordfoundation.org/work/learning/research-reports/a-future-of-failure-the-flow-of-technology-talent-into-government-and-society/.

10 "A Pivotal Moment," Freedman Consulting LLC, accessed November 17, 2019, http://tfreedmanconsulting.com/wp-content/uploads/2016/05/pivotalmoment.pdf.

11 "U.S. Digital Service—Our Mission," U.S. Digital Service, accessed January 21, 2020, https://www.usds.gov/mission.

12 "18F—About," General Services Administration, accessed January 21, 2020, https://18f.gsa.gov/about.

13 "Millennials Aren't Job-Hopping Any Faster Than Generation X Sid," Pew Research Center, last updated April 17, 2017, https://www.pewresearch.org/fact-tank/2017/04/19/millennials-arent-job-hopping-any-faster-than-generation-x-did/.

II

THE "WHAT"

4

TECHNOLOGICAL DISRUPTION AND LOCAL GOVERNMENT

It is no secret that government, and particularly local municipal government, is ill-equipped to tackle the challenges and opportunities presented by these technological disruptions. In their book, *A New City O/S: The Power of Open, Collaborative and Distributed Governance*, Stephen Goldsmith and Neil Kleiman provide a detailed and accessible synthesis of the structural, cultural, and technological issues facing local government, coupled with suggested solutions and approaches local governments can consider enacting to address these deficiencies.[1] The authors describe a new operating system (O/S) for a distributed, open local government:

> Decades into the computer age, cities simply haven't modernized enough. Although this book is not about technology, it recognizes that technological changes force, enable, and power the transformation to distributed governance and a new O/S. Amazing tools now provide promise to frustrated citizens and civil servants, mobile and cloud computing, GPS, data mining, digital platforms, and more could be harnessed to create radical

new ways of delivering municipal services and running
city government, if only we would let them.

As someone who worked for a significant period within the Windows
O/S division at Microsoft, I agree that the concept of government as
an operating system provides us with a useful framework for thinking
of government as a system of systems. Goldsmith and Kleiman build
upon the analogy to distinguish between the legacy O/S model (i.e., a
version of the O/S that is developed in isolation and rarely updated) versus
the new, distributed version of the O/S that is continually being refined
through feedback and data. With the advent of cloud computing, how
modern operating systems are built, deployed, and serviced has completely
transformed, and we are now in the era of "O/S as a Service." The key
to this transformation is the cloud. None of these capabilities would be
possible without the ability to connect the remote storage and computation
opportunities that the cloud enables.

Going back to my Microsoft experiences, I remain fascinated at how
the Windows O/S went from being at the center of everything the company
did to essentially being a product and service (referred to as "Windows as
a Service") orbiting around the new center of the Microsoft universe,
the Microsoft Azure cloud computing platform.[2] This paradigm shift in
how the Windows O/S is now perceived as part of a much larger cloud
ecosystem is a useful metaphor when we think about how local government
can reimagine its own O/S.

Regardless of the operating systems we use on our multitude of devices,
we're all familiar with regular updates being pushed to those devices, often
silently. Once or twice a year, new experiences designed to take advantage
of additional capabilities being added to the core O/S itself, along with
additional support for accessibility and over 100 languages that improve
access and equity outcomes, get released to hundreds of millions of
customers, often without a hitch. The technologists building the O/S then
use data collected from their customers during the development, testing,
and deployment processes to continually improve their experiences with

the O/S, service, or application in question. We are used to technology adding more convenience to our lives, admittedly with a few hiccups along the way to remind us that technology isn't perfect and is built by humans. The end result is that our expectations about how we consume services has changed, and this is why it can feel so jarring whenever we interact with services provided by the legacy government O/S.

Similar to the Microsoft example, let's reimagine how our current local government O/S could become a service of the larger cloud-based ecosystem. What would a "Government as a Service" digital platform look like? What opportunities exist to manage the provision of digital services to the public in new and exciting ways? What new regional government partnerships could be enabled? How could we positively change the general perception of government in the public's mind? In order to think about these and other fascinating questions, and to accelerate this effort to develop a new local government O/S, we simply need more technologists to enter public service and help with accelerating the cultural and structural changes required. The argument here isn't to use technology for technology's sake; rather, it is to inject fresh thinking, agile principles, and a desire to disrupt inefficient systems providing poor customer experiences and help reimagine this legacy O/S. As a public-sector technologist, you could play a key role in developing this new O/S for local government.

Fortunately, several major initiatives are engaged in tackling some of these challenges and helping to address some of the limitations in local government. Philanthropic efforts such as Bloomberg Philanthropies' What Works Cities program have been providing resources to build capacity and fund innovation teams within local governments across the United States and helping establish a culture of using data to make more informed operational and policy-making decisions.[3] Other efforts focus on building partnerships between public interest organizations, such as local governments and nonprofits, and expert technologists (known as public interest technologists) to help improve the delivery of services to the public—for example, the work being driven by the New America Foundation.[4] While these and many other worthy efforts have been making progress in addressing some of the deficiencies, their impact has been limited to a fraction of the local governments that require this assistance. For example, the What Works Cities program has joined forces with 100 mid-sized U.S. cities to help them use data more effectively.[5] These are challenges that every single local government in the United States is facing, from the largest municipal government to the smallest county or regional agency. How else might the expansion of these capabilities be achieved? How could this problem be solved without attracting more technical talent into local government itself?

It was during my public service that I became aware of the acute need for more technologists to serve within local government itself, and particularly those who have firsthand experience working in the kind of agile, distributed systems that this new government O/S should aspire to. Serving within the IT department of a major U.S. municipal government, I experienced firsthand the challenges that these rapid technological changes were bringing and how local government was struggling to keep pace, from the leadership on down through the organization. If Seattle, located in a region with one of the largest pools of world-class software development and data science talent outside of Silicon Valley, was struggling to attract more technologists directly into its local government, then what of other cities and regions without such pools of technological talent on their doorstep? While we will explore each of these topics in more detail later in the book, here are some key ways in which this need for more technologists to serve in local government currently manifests, or will increasingly do so in the coming five to ten years.

ACCELERATE THE DIGITAL TRANSFORMATION

While many industries are at advanced stages of the process of digitization or digitalization, local government remains a laggard in this regard. If local governments have websites and provide certain levels of online service, doesn't this mean that they are at an advanced stage of their digital transformation? I would argue, no. The need to further advance these capabilities has resulted in the emergence of digital services efforts as one major growth area within government at all levels, where the goal is for government to deliver information and services to the public anytime, anywhere, and on any platform or device. Initially, this involved the sharing of essential information or data in static form via websites, with some content quickly becoming stale. Open data portals were one of the first methods through which local governments provided data and information in a proactive way to the public, with many governments attempting to ensure the data was updated on a regular basis. More recent digital services efforts have focused on expanding the provision of basic services. Local governments routinely rely on Software as a Service (SaaS) applications provided by third-party vendors, where residents can pay utility bills, parking fines, or apply for permits online. There remain many services that have yet to be fully migrated online, as evidenced by the number of times a resident may need to call or visit their local city hall in order to fulfill certain tasks.

HUMAN-CENTERED DESIGN

Simply migrating a service to online mode isn't enough in itself. The experience of the resident (customer!) needs to be placed at the center of every decision. Sadly, this is one area where government digital services are generally found lacking. Readers who have availed of a government online service recently will likely understand this sentiment. Thankfully, this is a known issue. One initiative slowly taking shape within local government is the push to use human-centered design principles when building out new digital services or updating existing versions.[6] To help accelerate the adoption of these principles some civic user testing (CUT) groups have begun to partner with local governments in order to identify opportunities where these human-centered design principles can be applied to technology projects.[7] Creating the capacity to integrate these practices into all aspects of local government digital services work is another way a public-sector technologist can have real and lasting impact.

ACCESSIBILITY

Another emerging design consideration when developing digital services in local government is accessibility. Ensuring the product, process, or service being designed is fully accessible by everyone, regardless of their abilities, is fundamental to providing a good user experience. Similar to human-centered design, this is another aspect of service provision that is only beginning to truly get on the radar of local government. One reason much remains to be done is due to the lack of a common standards framework to ensure accessibility compliance across state and local governments. While Title II of the Americans with Disabilities Act (ADA) applies to state and local government entities, prohibiting discrimination on the basis of disability in access to the services, programs, and activities they offer, there isn't a mandated compliance structure that local governments must follow.[8] Rather, it is left to the public to report complaints whenever they encounter accessibility issues—for example, with local government websites that are not fully accessible. This is not the case at the federal government level, where accessibility design is regulated by Section 508 of the Rehabilitation Act of 1973 and a set of compliance standards and regulations have been developed.[9] Although this is a federal government mandate, the compliance standards for Section 508 have been adopted by several state and local governments as their standard; however, there is no legal requirement for this policy diffusion to spread to all state and local governments. Another standard some local governments attempt to adhere to is the Web Content Accessibility Guidelines (WCAG), developed through the World Wide Web Consortium (W3C) process.[10] Again, this is not a requirement for local governments to adhere to. All this is to say that an infusion of technologists with significant accessibility experience in product and service design could help construct a standards framework that could be adopted by all local governments, focusing on all aspects of the digital transformation process already underway.

One important point to call out here is that accessibility frameworks need not be isolated to the user-experience design of a digital service. If we think about the integration of technology into our cities, for example, it is clear that accessibility design needs to play a vital role in the built environment that enables these new and emerging technologies to function more easily. Take, for example, the recent growth in the availability of scooters in many U.S. cities. These new mobility solutions have caught people's imagination, and because of a lack of dedicated bike lanes in most U.S. cities, people often use them on sidewalks. Most U.S. cities have updated their sidewalks with "curb cuts," where a section of the sidewalk at intersections has been turned into a ramp to enable people using mobility-assisting methods such as wheelchairs to safely access crosswalks. One of the most powerful aspects of accessibility design isn't that it only positively affects those who have disabilities; rather, it helps the entire population. Those curb cuts also make it easier for parents to push their strollers onto and off of sidewalks, help delivery workers with hand trucks full of packages, people using bicycles, and, of course, those people riding scooters. This is a great example of how technologists with accessibility design experience can take a holistic view of the built environment when designing digital services with their local government. Initiatives such as these are merely the beginning of how local governments are thinking about the analog-to-digital transformation.

DIVERSITY AND INCLUSION

One important concern to address when pushing these digital transformations within local government is the question of who is doing the innovating and for whom? When it comes to new technologies and products being created, these are primarily developed outside of government. In the case of the federal government, agencies such as DARPA play a leading role in the development of cutting-edge technologies, but there are no real equivalents at the state and local government levels. These technology companies are then very eager to sell their products and services into local governments of all shapes and sizes, or in other words, push these innovations into the hands of local government customers—usually via the IT department. There have been some recent examples where technologies have been procured and implemented by local governments without sufficient scrutiny or transparency, leading to some undesirable, unintended consequences. Surveillance technologies, like street cameras and automated license plate readers, are examples.

One day, a colleague at the city of Seattle spoke with me about the question of vulnerable communities "being innovated upon," and that insight forced me to think about how the technologies we implement within government and the service provision they enable can have unintended consequences even when our intentions were good. One way to address this issue is to take an approach similar to what the city of Seattle instituted in 2017, with the implementation of their Surveillance Ordinance.[11] This law required that a master list of all technologies currently operational or in the process of being procured that fit the definition of a surveillance technology per the ordinance be compiled and reviewed by the city council. Aside from regulation and legislation such as Seattle's Surveillance Ordinance, these questions also highlight the need for more technologists from diverse backgrounds to serve in local government, and having more technologists from underserved communities serve in our local governments could have a huge impact and help educate all stakeholders about potential harms before in-house technology development and/or deployments proceed beyond the planning phase.

The digital transformation of local government is an exciting phase in the development of a more modern and optimized local government, and while much has been done, there remain many opportunities to accomplish real and lasting change. A larger number of technologists are needed on the ground inside of government who can push those initiatives forward. Technologists with diverse backgrounds and expertise in software engineering, data science, policy, privacy, and ethics are needed to ensure that local government and the public's needs are put first when deploying new technologies and services.

EVERYTHING THAT CAN BE AUTOMATED, WILL BE AUTOMATED

While much of the focus of the digitization of local government remains focused on the aspects of digital services that we discussed earlier, a far greater disruptive force is quickly emerging. The automation of rote tasks is already underway in some local governments, as evidenced by the increasing usage of chat bots to handle some simple customer service tasks or manage some routine workflows within local government IT departments, such as password resets. This steady implementation of automation over the next five to ten years will likely result in the most visible changes to how local government operates, both internally and externally.

ROUTINE TASKS WILL BE AUTOMATED

There has been much debate, complete with dire warnings, about the impact of automation and AI in the workplace over the next several decades. A 2013 paper titled "The Future of Employment: How Susceptible Are Jobs to Computerisation?" was one of several key pieces of research that triggered much of the speculation about the long-term impacts of automation.[12] The research found that "around 47 percent of total US employment is in the high risk category. We refer to these as jobs at risk—i.e. jobs we expect could be automated relatively soon, perhaps over the next decade or two." The easiest way to assess whether or not a modern-day profession is susceptible to automation is through the lens of task categorization, where workplace tasks can be categorized as either routine or nonroutine tasks and as manual (physical) or cognitive (knowledge) tasks. Routine tasks are those that are most at risk of automation, since they are usually repeatable. Similarly, tasks that are manual are also at high risk of automation. However, as outlined in their paper, "algorithms for big data are now rapidly entering domains reliant upon pattern recognition and can readily substitute for labour in a wide range of non-routine cognitive tasks." Note the reference to "non-routine" tasks—this is a key indicator of the role that machine learning plays in this equation, where tasks that were initially considered to be at less risk of automation are now becoming more susceptible.

What does this all mean for local government? Governments typically have many tasks that are routine and/or manual, as evidenced by the complex processes and mountains of paperwork we're often forced to deal with—either as a civil servant working within the government or as a member of the public trying to access services. Therefore, we could assess that the risk of automation displacing lower-level administrative jobs within local government is likely to be high. On the other hand, the public have ever-increasing expectations for 24/7 access to information and digital services. After all, this is what they enjoy when consuming products and services through the apps on their phones, for example. The expectation that people need to be physically present during daytime hours to avail of essential government services is no longer acceptable or viable. Virtual access to government is now an absolute necessity, and automation will play a central role in making this a reality.

Instead of looking upon the automation of many noncognitive tasks as an existential threat to the careers of many public servants in local government, I would argue that we should embrace these challenges head-on, and as public-sector technologists lead inclusive efforts to help all staff understand the nature and scale of the impending changes and to involve them in the work to implement new automated systems. Similarly, include the public in transparent efforts when rolling out new automated process and service delivery mechanisms and ensure their voices are heard during the design stages.

In the conclusions to their seminal paper, Frey and Osborne share an important insight that provides a helpful starting point for local government leaders to consider when thinking through these challenges" "Our findings thus imply that as technology races ahead, low-skill workers will reallocate to tasks that are non-susceptible to computerisation—i.e., tasks requiring creative and social intelligence. For workers to win the race, however, they will have to acquire creative and social skills." In other words, more staff time in local government could be spent on other aspects of public service as more automation is deployed, such as focusing on more personalized customer service engagements, reviewing data related to their area of focus and making better decisions on where to target their efforts, and having more time to focus on the strategic rather than the tactical. Automation can thus be seen as a tool through which meaningful productivity gains are possible, allowing public servants to derive more satisfaction from their work as a result of having to deal with fewer rote tasks, and likely resulting in less frustration and a more positive public perception of local government.

UNDERSTANDING AUTOMATED PROCESS DEVELOPMENT

A key rationale for more public-sector technologists lies in their understanding of this new paradigm and helping assess the organization's maturity level with respect to the automation of tasks and processes. There are several business process automation (BPA) frameworks that local governments can leverage to help with this work—sometimes these are referred to as "information technology process automation" frameworks. For the purposes of this discussion, we will use a useful framework from Smartsheet, a successful technology startup focused on business process automation and workplace productivity.[13]

This framework describes four types of automation, increasing in complexity:

- **Basic Automation:** *Basic automation centers are the simple jobs in your organization, giving a centralized place to store all related information. For example, using a centralized messaging tool for a topic or group allows transparency in communication, instead of hiding information in various email accounts.* [Author's note: Slack[14] would be an example of such a technology.]

- **Process Automation:** *This documents and manages your business processes for task consistency and transparency. It is more powerful than basic automation and can be controlled by dedicated software and apps.* [Author's note: As most local governments are running the Microsoft enterprise stack, their flow process automation platform would be an option.[15] Other options include "If This Then That" (IFTTT) apps.[16]]

- **Integration Automation:** *More complex than process automation, integration automation enables machines to observe the way that humans perform tasks and repeat those actions. Humans must define the rules, however.* [Author's note: The deployment of chat bots into customer support systems that process Frequently Asked Questions (FAQs) or automatically open tickets for humans to later process would be an example of an integrated automation approach.]

- **Artificial Intelligence (AI) Automation:** *Adding AI to integration software enables decision-making where your technological support is humanlike. The system would make decisions on what to do with the data, based on what it has learned and constantly analyzed.* [Author's note: In local government, the real-time analysis of data from IoT devices can help develop models for automating certain tasks, such as automatically regulating traffic-light patterns according to known usage patterns developed over time.]

This work is important, as using frameworks such as these can enable local governments to assess their organization's automation maturity level and use the findings to proactively develop a long-term strategy, understand the possible impact to future staffing levels, develop training programs for affected staff, initiate conversations with staff and the public about some of these impending changes, and come up with innovate programs that allow management and staff to work together to begin experimenting with these technologies and looking for those win-wins.

DEVELOPING AND DEPLOYING ALGORITHMS

One such opportunity lies in the development and deployment of algorithms. For scenarios where it makes sense to integrate algorithms into an automated decision-making process, having the staff who currently manage those manual processes help with designing those automated processes can be enormously beneficial. They know the existing systems inside out and should be able to call out obvious instances where bias can occur. They could also gain a better sense of how the new systems will function and the potential impact to their current roles and responsibilities, giving them more time to prepare for those changes.

Developing the capacity of technology staff who can help the entire organization navigate these inevitable changes will only grow in importance in the coming years. This includes technologists who specialize in ethics, issues related to bias, and human-centered design. Systemic changes wrought by powerful technologies will require a holistic, humanistic approach. Thankfully, awareness of the issues of bias being amplified by the use of algorithms is growing, and more excellent resources and supports are being made available to help governments navigate these important questions. A great example is the 2016 book *Weapons of Math Destruction*, by Cathy O'Neil, which describes the social impact of algorithms designed without adequate forethought and emotional intelligence being applied.[17]

THE IMPENDING ARRIVAL OF 5G

Of the new technologies that will be widely deployed over the next five to ten years, 5G is perhaps the most likely to profoundly affect local government. Why could this be? Many of the "smart cities" scenarios that have been envisioned for some time will be truly feasible once this new network is fully deployed. While no uniform definition exists, a "smart city" is essentially "a designation given to a city that incorporates information and communication technologies (ICT) to enhance the quality and performance of urban services such as energy, transportation and utilities in order to reduce resource consumption, wastage and overall costs."[18] The deployment of a "smart city" infrastructure is a topic that has garnered a great deal of interest within the local government community over the past five to ten years, and it is anticipated that this interest will continue to grow with the impending rollout of the 5G network. 5G, which stands for the 5th Generation of cellular technology, promises improved connection speeds up to ten times faster than the current 4G Long-Term Evolution (LTE) networks offer, and network latency is reduced to milliseconds. These faster speeds and reduced network delays will likely result in increased deployments of IoT (Internet of Things) devices across our cities and counties and will enable the collection of higher-quality data from the existing IoT infrastructure already deployed.

Up until now the discussion has mainly focused on retrofitting existing city infrastructure with IoT technologies, such as sensors that measure air quality or the volumes of traffic flowing through an area. Local governments can then use the data from these sensors to make decisions and help design solutions to improve the quality of life in the city. More recently, a new front has opened up in the smart city debate. As major cities experience increased development, resulting from population shifts into cities and increasing numbers of technology firms locating their headquarters in cities rather than in more suburban areas, whole sections of major U.S. cities are currently being redeveloped. This is providing opportunities for large-scale projects that can help us to reimagine what a city could and should look like in the future. A good example of what such a future "smart city" might look like is a project currently underway in Toronto, Canada. In a collaboration with Sidewalk Labs,[19] a part of the Alphabet family of companies, an entire section of the city could be developed from the ground up using "smart city" principles.[20] The scale of this project is immense, and if successful, could provide a template for other cities to follow. This project has not been without controversy, and concerns about data privacy have come to the fore. At the time of writing, these issues remain unresolved, but they also provide a fascinating insight into the kinds of issues that all local governments are beginning to grapple with as the explosion of new technologies making their way into our built environments continues.

As a technologist working within local government, you could be in a prime position to help create a thoughtful strategy for how to manage the integration of an expanded IoT infrastructure in conjunction with the rollout of 5G networks, help educate your government leadership on these issues and influence policy formulation, and provide guidance on what data analysis opportunities will exist when many more elements of our environment can be sensed and measured.

THE GROWING NEED FOR ADVANCED DATA ANALYTICS

Possibly the largest area of focus with respect to technological improvement within local government in recent years has centered on the need for government at all levels to radically improve how they use data to make decisions, manage operations, and create evidence-based policy. Local governments are sitting on vast quantities of data, much of it of significant historic value. One thing local government does seem to be really good at is collecting more data than it likely needs, holding onto that data basically forever, and not using much of it for useful internal or external purposes. Thankfully, efforts are well underway to change this dynamic. Much of the philanthropic effort we reference elsewhere in this book has been focused on this very issue, and great progress continues to be made. As important as these advances have been, I believe we're only starting to scratch the surface of the actual needs, and indeed the opportunities, that exist.

INVESTMENTS VERSUS COSTS

Let's step back for a moment and think about the need for the USAFacts Annual Report that we referenced earlier in this book. What does it say about our government's culture at all levels that that it took a philanthropic nonprofit organization to attempt to fix this gap in how we as taxpayers can easily access the annual report on how our government is spending our money? Other questions arise, like how does government hold itself accountable, or make key decisions? This was a question I frequently asked myself when I was serving in local government, when I had gained insights into the data analysis capabilities in place there versus the amazing levels of real-time information we had at our fingertips in the tech sector. This is not to disparage the people doing this work in local government—I think they are doing heroic work with few resources and in some cases almost zero executive support. It became clear to me that getting to an optimal situation where such annual reports could be readily produced by all levels of government was going to require a massive growth in investment. I use the word "investment" deliberately, as it also became clear to me during my public service that government needs to look at data analytics capacity building as an investment and not a cost. Whenever my colleagues and I advocated for the opportunity to do some innovative data analytics work using existing sources of data, we frequently were given an answer that made me realize that (a) the leadership typically viewed data analytics work as an IT project that would cost a lot of money and take a lot of time and (b) didn't understand that a small number of data scientists using open-source tools could do some amazing things in a matter of weeks using existing resources. Government departments tend to be quite guarded when it comes to granting access to their data, in most cases for very good reasons—yet there were many opportunities to break data out of its silos and enable collaboration and the development of powerful insights that went begging. Part of this was cultural, as I explained earlier, but part of it was also that the necessary infrastructure to quickly allow this kind of collaboration in a secure environment wasn't available. Some local governments have begun to address that infrastructure deficit with cloud-based solutions that allow for sharing of datasets across agencies in a highly secure environment, but this deficiency has barely begun to be addressed.

It's not all doom and gloom, however. There are exciting efforts to address this deficit in some local governments by attempting to digitize old analog records in order to make them machine readable and more accessible for data analysis. Additionally, local governments have embraced the open data movement and have been steadily sharing some amazingly rich datasets with the public. One of my favorite examples from my time as open data manager at the city of Seattle came from the Seattle Public Library, where they released a dataset containing a record of each physical checkout from their library system since April 2005.[21] This dataset, containing over 100 million rows of data and counting, provides deep insights into the borrowing habits of the public in Seattle over an extended period and could be layered with other datasets to perform valuable research into the intentions of the public as socioeconomic conditions change. There are many other examples of datasets such as this on government open data portals across the United States. However, much of the data collected by local government remains untapped.

In addition to these massive troves of mostly unliberated data, the increasing deployment of "smart city" technologies will likely accelerate the collection of data, much of it in real time. How much IoT data to collect, where to store it, how long to keep it, how to analyze it and leverage it, and how much of this data should be made available as open data are all important questions that require more experienced technologists, information management experts, technology policy professionals, and data scientists to help local government answer. Based on my own experiences, some of the most complex and interesting technology issues that local governments will face in the coming years will be in this space.

CHIEF DATA OFFICERS

When we think about the collection, storage, analysis, and sharing of data at this scale, we acknowledge the need for a new class of senior leader in local government who is responsible for overall data management and data governance. Enter the chief data officer (CDO). In January 2019 Congress passed the Open, Public, Electronic and Necessary, (OPEN) Government Data Act as part of the Foundations for Evidence-Based Policymaking Act.[22] This new law mandated each federal government department to appoint or designate a qualified CDO without regard to political affiliation. Some state governments have followed suit and have begun to enact laws or policies requiring CDOs.[23]

Although no such legal requirements exist at the local government level, local governments are also increasingly creating these roles, particularly at the municipal government level. The Ash Center for Democratic Governance and Innovation at Harvard Kennedy School has been working to establish and support a national peer network of urban CDOs.[24] I was honored to get to know some of these urban CDO pioneers during my time in local government and saw firsthand the transformational effect their work had on how their local governments used data in the management of their cities, from the mayor's office on down.

While the deployment of chief data officers into state and local government may appear be somewhat slow at the time of writing, the efforts to date illustrate both the progress that has been made and, more importantly, the extent of the opportunity that still exists. There are many states without a single CDO at either the state or local level. This is a huge gap, in my opinion, and one that urgently needs to be addressed. In the coming years, CDOs will continue to play a central role in building the next generation of local government that has data at the core of everything it does. We just need many, many more of them, supported by many more data architects, data scientists, and data analysts.

CULTURE CHANGE

After I left Microsoft in the fall of 2016 and began my local government service, I began to think a lot about culture change and why the culture of government appeared to be so different from what I had experienced in the tech sector. Toward the end of my time at Microsoft, I had been witness to a massive cultural revolution that was initiated by the new CEO, Satya Nadella. I couldn't help but think that if an organization as massive as Microsoft could completely transform itself, then why not government? Both are massive bureaucracies with many silos, both had to deal with internal and external politics, and both had entrenched cultures that didn't allow for the kinds of innovation that the coming wave of technologies required. Having thought about this for some time, I published an article on how government could learn from this example and outlined some reasons why a cultural change within local government is required:[25]

- Local governments are under increasing pressure to modernize their service delivery to align more closely with the online experiences that people are used to in their daily lives.
- We're entering a phase where most governments are experiencing, or will soon experience, renewed budgetary pressures and the need to use data to aid in proactively managing that challenge.
- Due to the large wave of retirements happening as a result of the "Silver Tsunami," the demographics of the government workforce are changing. New government employees have different expectations about what working in government should entail. Required changes include updating the rewards system to one not focused solely on long-term pension contributions, providing telecommuting options, more collaborative physical

work environments, and more flexibility regarding the use of "nonstandard" technologies that align better with those used by the public.

- Recent literature on how local government can make better use of data and analytics also speaks to the need for a major culture change to help unlock the value of data.

- In general, governments appear to lack a unified vision or mission statements. A clear vision/mission statement provides the entire organization with a "North Star" to follow, can inspire people to want to do more, and can help in attracting new talent into your organization. Incoming generations of workers place a high value on the mission of the organization.

Of course, we can't simply take that example or other examples of successful culture changes in the private sector and simply overlay them onto a complex environment such as government and expect it to be a perfect fit. While the mission of government is the polar opposite of private enterprise in one key aspect, which is the aim of achieving profits, I believe that both sectors can learn from each other when it comes to developing healthy cultures that enable socially responsible innovation and service delivery. Culture change is inherently difficult to make happen and is difficult to measure, and yet it is absolutely fundamental to the success of every organization on the planet. The sheer scale of the challenge in local government cannot be underestimated, but I believe that with the right leadership and desire to change, a transformation similar to the Microsoft example is possible.

How does having more technologists working in government help with making these kinds of changes happen? We will discuss this important issue later in the book, but while the real key to a successful organizational culture change comes from the CEO, technology plays a critical role in providing the tools to enable some of those changes to happen. Technologists are used to working in environments where their work aligns with a clear vision and where that vision becomes a mantra that feeds into everything the organization does. Disruption is a concept that all technologists are comfortable with, as disrupting a market is the *raison d'être* for most technology companies. As outlined in the introduction of this book, disruption in government has a different meaning and desired outcome than in the tech sector; yet this desire to optimize large systems using both established and emerging technologies coupled with agile methodologies can have a powerful impact on the culture of a local government organization. The ability to empower existing government employees with new and exciting ways of doing their jobs in more rewarding ways will provide the organization as a whole with case studies on how they, too, could optimize their workflows and reduce the need for them to spend large amounts of their time on less rewarding tasks. Based upon my own experiences in the public sector, local governments are more than ready for new leaders to help drive these kinds of cultural changes, with technology at its core.

CREATE A VIRTUOUS CYCLE

A good way to think about the nature of disruption is to think of it as a cycle. The tech sector frequently uses the idea of a "virtuous cycle" to describe the positive, cyclical effects of the technologies they develop. These cyclical effects are also referred to as "positive flywheel effects." The important thing to note is the positive nature of these effects, hence the use of words "virtuous" and "positive." We can apply the same concept to local government, like in Figure 4-1, and use that model to help government leaders and staff, as well as the public, better understand the positive intent of changes being driven or facilitated by improved uses of technology.

Figure 4-1: *Virtuous cycle caused by technologists entering and leaving government*

For example, if we think about the movement of technologists into and out of government as a virtuous cycle, we can visualize a system where local government veterans returning to the private sector can inculcate their new understanding of government back into the tech sector, where they can lead the way in helping to build better products and services for local government and other public-sector customers. During my time in local government, I had the opportunity to engage with many employees in technology companies dedicated to building solutions directly only for the public sector, or companies whose mainstream platforms and services included versions tailored for government customers. While all of these employees were passionate about their mission of building software for government, I noticed how many of them had never served in government. Government customers, like myself, who were eager to directly engage with them and share feedback and ideas were highly valued by these companies, partially because of this internal knowledge deficit. Having a larger number of employees with direct government experience can provide such companies with a competitive advantage in the lucrative government software vertical.

BUILD EMPATHY

Aside from the insights into how local government functions that would help them validate assumptions they make in their product and service designs, these employees would also bring with them a network of local government contacts that could prove invaluable in terms of gathering more feedback, sales leads, generating content for blogs and conferences, and so on. These networks and relationships help build empathy between the public and private sectors—something that is critical to making collaborative partnerships function more effectively. As someone who had a deep understanding of the tech sector before working in local government, I was able to act as a translator between those two worlds when opportunities arose to collaborate, or whether we needed to update an existing SaaS product or service. Both my private-sector and public-sector experiences gave me credibility on both sides and allowed us to get to the optimal outcome more quickly. Building empathy has additional benefits as we enter a period where government is struggling to regulate new technologies and services, including at the municipal level. Recent examples include some major municipal governments leading efforts to regulate the usage of emerging technologies, such as facial recognition. These policies then diffuse upward through state and federal government levels. Having increased levels of understanding and mutual respect between the public and private sectors will be valuable in the coming years as our society grapples with these complex issues.

CIVIC LEAVE PROGRAMS

An additional way to build empathy and increase the institutional knowledge of local government is through programs that enable tech-sector employees to spend time working in government in either a volunteer capacity or via a sabbatical arrangement. These programs, usually known as civic leave programs, can provide an excellent way for tech-sector employees to take a leave of absence and explore serving in government without having to commit to a major career pivot, and it allows for governments and major technology companies to develop policies to help grow these programs and incentivize more employees to think strongly about public service and what they can do for their government.

DISRUPTION INTO OPPORTUNITY

Now that we have some understanding of what disruption within local government means and the kinds of internal and external forces that will shape its digital transformation, let's examine some of the specific challenges and opportunities that technologists can help local government to embrace in the coming years.

CHAPTER 4: KEY TAKEAWAYS

- As governments accelerate their digital transformations, major changes to how government services are designed, built, and deployed will occur. Best practices related to human-centered design, accessibility, and ensuring that diversity and inclusion considerations are foremost in planning efforts will become central to how local governments deliver digital services.
- Everything that can be automated, will be automated. Local government will not be immune from the forces that are already disrupting the private sector. More and more routine tasks will be automated as automated process development takes a deeper hold in IT departments.
- Developing and deploying algorithms to aid with decision-making are becoming more common in local government, yet they are ill equipped to manage these complex scenarios.

- The impending arrival of 5G networks will unleash a host of new capabilities, in particular, the expanded use of IoT devices and sensors in our cities and communities. Local governments will be flooded with even more data as a result.

- Culture change is needed to drive positive disruptions into the local government ecosystem through more effective use of technology and data. More technologists serving in local government can help inculcate these kinds of changes from within.

- By thinking of disruption in terms of a virtuous cycle, technologists have a model that can explain the positive nature of their work, both within local government and back in the tech sector after their public service is complete.

NOTES

1   Stephen Goldsmith and Neil Kleiman, *A New City O/S: The Power of Open, Collaborative, and Distributed Governance* (Washington, D.C.: Brookings Institution Press, 2017), 6-7.

2   "Overview of Windows as a Service," Microsoft, last updated December 26, 2019, https://docs.microsoft.com/en-us/windows/deployment/update/waas-overview.

3   "What Works Cities—Home," Bloomberg Philanthropies, accessed December 14, 2019, https://whatworkscities.bloomberg.org.

4   "New America—About," New America, accessed December 14, 2019, https://www.newamerica.org/public-interest-technology/about/.

5   "Annual Report 2019," Bloomberg Philanthropies, accessed December 14, 2019, https://annualreport.bloomberg.org/government.

6   "Human-Centered Design—Field Guide," IDEO.org, accessed December 14, 2019, http://www.designkit.org.

7   "Seattle Civic User Testing Group—About," Seattle Civic User Testing Group, accessed December 15, 2019, https://openseattle.org/cutgroup.

8   "Americans with Disabilities Act—State and Local Governments (Title II)," U.S. Department of Justice Civil Rights Division, accessed December 15, 2019, https://www.ada.gov/ada_title_II.htm.

9   "IT Accessibility Laws and Policies," U.S. General Services Administration, accessed December 15, 2019, https://www.section508.gov/manage/laws-and-policies.

10   "Web Content Accessibility Guidelines (WCAG) Overview," World Wide Web Consortium (W3C), accessed December 15, 2019, https://www.w3.org/WAI/standards-guidelines/wcag.

11   "About Surveillance—The Surveillance Ordinance," City of Seattle, accessed December 12, 2019, https://www.seattle.gov/tech/initiatives/privacy/surveillance-technologies/about-surveillance-ordinance.

12   Carl Benedikt Frey, Michael A. Osborne, "The Future of Employment: How Susceptible Are Jobs to Computerisation?," Oxford Martin Programme on Technology and Employment (September 2013): 44, https://www.oxfordmartin.ox.ac.uk/downloads/academic/future-of-employment.pdf

13   "Everything You Need to Know About Business Process Automation," Smartsheet, accessed November 21, 2019, https://www.smartsheet.com/understanding-evolution-and-importance-business-process-automation.

14   "Why Slack—Features," Slack, accessed November 21, 2019, https://slack.com/features.

15   "Power Automate," Microsoft, accessed November 21, 2019, https://flow.microsoft.com/en-us.

16   "IFTTT—Home," IFTTT, accessed November 21, 2019, https://ifttt.com.

17   Cathy O'Neil, *Weapons of Math Destruction: How Big Data Increases Inequality and Threatens Democracy* (New York: Crown Random House, 2016).

18   "Smart City Definitions," Digi.City, accessed December 30, 2019, https://www.digi.city/smart-city-definitions.

19   "Sidewalk Labs—Home," Sidewalk Labs, accessed December 30, 2019, https://www.sidewalklabs.com.

20   "Sidewalk Toronto—Home," Sidewalk Toronto, accessed December 30, 2019, https://www.sidewalktoronto.ca.

21   "Seattle Public Library — Checkouts by Title," City of Seattle, accessed January 2, 2020, https://data.seattle.gov/Community/Checkouts-by-Title/tmmm-ytt6.

22   "H.R.4174 - Foundations for Evidence-Based Policymaking Act of 2018," U.S. Congress, accessed January 2, 2020, https://www.congress.gov/bill/115th-congress/house-bill/4174/text.

23   "What Do State Chief Data Officers Do? " Kil Huh & Sallyann Bergh, last updated March 21, 2018, https://www.pewtrusts.org/en/research-and-analysis/articles/2018/03/21/what-do-state-chief-data-officers-do.

24 "About the Civic Analytics Network," Ash Center for Democratic Governance and Innovation at Harvard Kennedy School, accessed November 12, 2019, https://datasmart.ash.harvard.edu/news/article/about-the-civic-analytics-network-826.

25 "What Government Can Learn from Microsoft's Cultural Transformation," David Doyle, last updated August 21, 2018, https://www.linkedin.com/pulse/what-government-can-learn-from-microsofts-cultural-david-doyle.

5

CURRENT AND FUTURE CHALLENGES IN LOCAL GOVERNMENT

Unlike most technology companies that have a relatively discrete set of problems they are attempting to solve, government has a vast range of challenges it needs to address. Unlike the private sector, it can't just pivot away from these problems if market conditions change—it needs to provide these services and solutions for the long term, meaning several decades and beyond. In addition to providing these services and supporting IT systems for prolonged periods, governments need to grapple with the constantly changing technology landscape and how best to implement the latest technologies in ways that will provide the most benefit for their residents while also ensuring their privacy, safety, and security are protected. The breadth of technology, data, and policy challenges local governments are tackling is amazing. For example, at the municipal level, the National League of Cities lists the top technology topics it considers as follows: [1]

1. Broadband
2. Cybersecurity
3. Data Management
4. Driverless Cars

5. Fiber-Optic
6. Innovation
7. Internet
8. Internet of Things
9. Opportunity Zones
10. Privacy
11. Smart Cities
12. Telecommunications

Similarly, at the state level, the National Association of State CIOs (NASCIO) lists the "Top 10 Priorities for 2020 Strategies, Policy Issues and Management Processes" as: [2]

1. Cybersecurity and Risk Management
2. Digital Government
3. Cloud Services
4. Consolidation/Optimization
5. Customer Relationship Management
6. Budget, Cost Control, Fiscal Management
7. Legacy Modernization
8. Data Management and Analytics
9. Broadband/Wireless Connectivity
10. Innovation and Transformation Through Technology

And its "Top 10 Priorities for 2020 Technologies, Applications and Tools" as:

1. Cloud Solutions
2. Legacy Application Modernization/Renovation
3. Data Analytics
4. Security Enhancement Tools
5. Identity and Access Management
6. Collaboration Technologies

7. Artificial Intelligence/Robotic Process Automation
8. Data Management
9. Enterprise Resource Planning (ERP)
10. Public Safety Radio Network

These lists are by no means static or definitive, and these priorities could easily change in response to emerging technology trends that were not visible when these lists were agreed upon. Each priority has many subtopics and areas of concern. As we can see from these sets of priorities, depending on the level of government, the nature and scale of issues it will face will differ greatly, and many may not be obvious to the casual observer of government affairs or indeed to the public at large. In fact, the issues that technologists may be interested in helping government solve through their volunteer work, such as using data more effectively or improving the design of online services, may not even be close to the top of the government's own priority list. A good example of this disconnect can be seen in the issues that municipal governments have publicly stated are their top priorities. In their "State of the Cities 2019" report, the National League of Cities reviewed over 150 speeches given by mayors of U.S. cities between January and April 2019.[3] Their analysis highlighted the top ten issues that mayors spoke in significant terms about during that time (Figure 5-1). Some readers may be surprised to learn that they spoke about technology and data only 11 percent of the time, ranking it only as the tenth most important issue. This finding mirrors the results for the previous several years that this analysis has been performed.

Figure 5-1: *Top ten issues in speeches given by U.S. mayors in 2019*

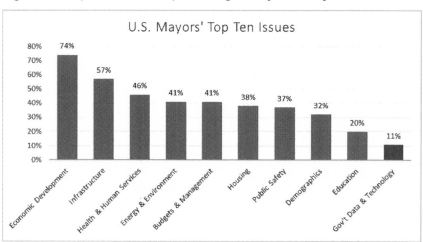

When we examine the subtopics of the speeches that did include technology and data, we see another interesting set of results (see Figure 5-2). The topic of "smart cities" is one of the most frequently discussed at government-related conferences and on public-sector podcasts, blogs, and social media channels. Yet it rarely made it into those speeches, at least explicitly. It is likely that concepts related to smart cities were wrapped up in other topics related to data and efficiency. Open data, something most civic technology advocates and volunteers like to champion and use (and something very near and dear to this author), also ranked lowly. Again, it is possible the topic of open data could have been included in the thinking for performance management or efficiency and effectiveness topics, but the lack of explicit mentions is telling.

Figure 5-2: *Top five subtopics re: data and technology in speeches given by U.S. mayors in 2019*

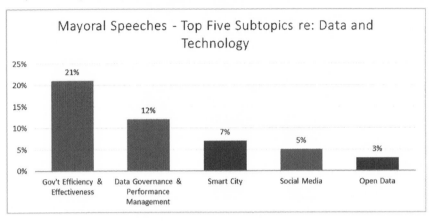

That government efficiency and performance management initiatives are seemingly the most widely discussed by city mayors at least makes sense, as most state and local governments have programs in place that focus on driving improvements across their workforces. A great example at the state level is the "Results WA" program, which runs out of the governor's office and has been successful at driving measurable performance improvements across a government workforce of more than 65,000 people.[4] Performance improvement and government efficiency programs tend to have very broad mandates, so it is possible to drill down even further into these areas and discover interesting problems that we as technologists can help solve.

What does this apparent disconnect between what technologists may think are the most important issues versus what senior government leaders typically speak about in public tell us? If technology is at the heart of everything that the government does and governments are attempting to become more data driven, then why aren't these topics higher up the priority list? One explanation could be that these activities tend to be more "behind the scenes," whereas issues related to public safety and infrastructure are highly visible to the public on a daily basis and tend to have a more immediate impact within our communities. Technology usually enters the public consciousness only when there is an outage of some kind with an app or online service they depend upon, or when there is a major privacy or data breach involving government data. Another explanation could be that government leaders are more comfortable talking about policies related to the economy, public safety, infrastrucutre, and so on. Most elected officials do not have a background in technology and often struggle to grasp complicated technical issues, as we have seen in recent congressional hearings related to social media and data privacy concerns. The same is true of data, where elected leaders tend to focus on improving their use of data in relation to topics that they are more familiar with, such as "evidence-based policy making" or improving local government operations (both highly desirable outcomes in their own right). As public-sector technologists, there are many opportunities to elevate these important topics and help educate our elected leaders and other senior policy makers. Following are just some of the current and future challenges that technologists can help address in government at all levels, shapes, and sizes.

CHALLENGES AND OPPORTUNITIES

With this apparent disconnect between what issues are top of mind for government leaders and what's seemingly important to the civic technology community, let's delve into some specifics and examine some areas where public-sector technologists could have measurable impact and enable our government leaders to bring these advances to the attention of the tax-paying public on a more regular basis and with more confidence. I discuss these challenges within these main areas.

- Building resilience
- Cybersecurity
- Service delivery
- Operations
- Project management

- Data analytics
- Customer focus
- Technology policy
- Culture change
- Education

While these topics are covered at a fairly high level and are not meant to be an exhaustive list of target areas for technologists, they provide a broad range of examples of the types of problems that governments are grappling with now and into the future.

BUILDING RESILIENCE

Over the past few years, we've seen several instances of where local governments have been almost completely taken offline. Later in this chapter I reference examples of these situations, from the ransomware attacks that continue to afflict local governments to earlier examples of major infrastructure failures that caused most online operations to go offline, such as the event that occurred at the city of Seattle. The fear of having a major infrastructure outage is not unique to government—these nightmare scenarios keep Chief Information Officers (CIOs) and Chief Technology Officers (CTOs) awake at night in all sectors and industries.

There are two main aspects to building resilience in any technology organization. The first is to ensure that attacks from bad actors are always repulsed, which is primarily the focus of cybersecurity efforts. The second is developing the ability to quickly, and fully, recover from any such attack or other event that disables either part or all of the organization's technology capabilities. The first part of that equation, cybersecurity, gets the lion's share of attention and focus primarily due to very serious ransomware incidents and concerns about election security. Less focus is given to how ready governments are to recover in the event of a major disaster, natural or otherwise.

A former colleague of mine was once given the job of building up the resilience of their organization in the event of a natural disaster occurring. In the Pacific Northwest, the threat of a major earthquake occurring in our lifetime is a very real possibility, and so it makes sense for technology companies to plan for these eventualities. The goal was simple: if a disaster of any kind took the current facility completely offline, they had to develop the protocols to get everything back up and running no later than twenty-four hours after the event, most likely at a completely separate location. By reverse-engineering all of their existing operational protocols, systems, and processes, they were quickly able to identify issues that would prevent them from reaching this goal. For example, they discovered that if they needed to reset a particular master admin password for a particular system, that reset required a twenty-four-hour window of time before the new password would come into effect. Basically, that one password reset security protocol ate up the entire twenty-four hours. Not good. Fast-forward to my time in local government, and based on my experiences there and from what I learned about other governments, I am fairly confident that few local governments have completed similar exercises *before* they have been forced to in the event of a major disaster hitting them. In my view, this is a major gap that more technologists with expertise in these areas can help quickly address.

There are many benefits of performing such exercises. Aside from building out an accurate blueprint for your IT systems, up-to-date information on who is responsible for what, and keeping security best practices top of mind for the organization, it can help identify what servers, applications, and databases would be ideal candidates to move from on-premises datacenters to the public cloud. Part of any resilience-building program should be the intent to identify and transition vulnerable applications to the cloud. Similarly, in the event of budget cuts and/or government shutdowns, a robust resilience plan can be used to better understand the implications of forced IT service reductions and help mitigate their impacts.

This leads us to the question, why do so many state and local governments have their own datacenters? Earlier in the book I referenced the issues that the city of Seattle encountered with their own datacenter in a high-rise tower in the middle of downtown Seattle, forcing them to move their infrastructure into two separate datacenters to ensure redundancy, with both facilities being located outside of the city limits. Another example from the Pacific Northwest was the decision by Washington state government to build its own datacenter right on its main campus. Not only did the facility cost hundreds of millions of dollars, they initially had no tenants, and a political fight erupted over who should cover the longer-term costs.[5] With the advent of a secure government cloud infrastructure being developed and scaled by leaders in cloud computing, such as Amazon, Microsoft, Google, IBM, and Oracle, it can be argued that it no longer makes sense for state and local governments to invest in their own massive on-premises cloud infrastructure. If all of the major companies in the world are primarily running their IT infrastructure and online service delivery via the public cloud, then why can't government? We are beginning to see a major shift in recent times, with some major government cloud deals happening, such as the so-called Joint Enterprise Defense Infrastructure (JEDI) contract from the Pentagon to move a huge portion of their computing infrastructure to the government public cloud, a contract worth up to $10 billion.[6] Since government's core competency is not building or running datacenters, it would make sense for government to accelerate their own push toward the public cloud and to avail themselves of the enhanced security features, as well as building their resilience in the event of the unthinkable actually occurring.

CYBERSECURITY

As previously noted, persistent ransomware attacks have highlighted just how unprepared local governments in the United States are regarding cyber threats. Since 2013, there have been over 250 ransomware attacks in the United States alone, with at least one attack in each state.[7] Six years is an eon in the technology world, and yet local governments seem unable to learn from these attacks and take the urgent steps necessary to prevent their local government from becoming the next victim. While governments are increasingly hiring Chief Information Security Officers (CISOs) at all levels, more investment in acquiring cybersecurity talent is required to help shore up local government defenses, both internally and leveraging outside experts where necessary.

What sets local governments apart is their seeming inability to adequately update and secure their IT systems to prevent themselves from succumbing to ransomware attacks. Private-sector organizations seem less at risk for these relatively unsophisticated attacks that have been plaguing local governments. Why is this?

While the major issue at the local government level appears to be these ongoing ransomware attacks, at the state government level, one of the most pressing issues from the public's perspective appears to be ongoing concerns about election security. Some funding from the federal government has been made available to help the states tackle this problem, yet many issues remain. One is the lack of a unified system for voting in the United States. Some states have so-called "early voting," where citizens have the ability to vote by mail ahead of the actual election day. Washington state, where I live, is one of those states. As someone who became a naturalized U.S. citizen in recent years and who has also voted in a different country (Ireland, where I grew up) using a different system where I had to go to a polling station to vote, I really appreciate and value the ability to vote at my convenience, as well as having more time to review the literature about the issues and candidates. These mail-in ballots also provide for a nice mix of paper records supplemented by technology—I have the ability to track the counting progress related to my ballot online. These measures help provide me with extra piece of mind when it comes to election security. In other U.S. states, people primarily vote using electronic voting machines, and here is where some of the issues arise. Innovative ideas such as "mobile voting"[8] are being proposed and debated, and the role that technologies such as blockchain and smart phones will play in how hundreds of millions of Americans will vote in the coming years and decades is still unclear—and therefore provides enormous opportunities for public interest technologists to play a vital role in shaping this critical aspect of our democracy.

Cybersecurity concerns span many more areas of government, however, and in all forms of government. These range from ensuring the physical and virtual security of government facilities and staff to helping protect the public infrastructure that we all depend upon and take for granted. For example, the authorities that run our major ports and airports are also part of the local government family, and being the chief information security officer of a major port system is a role with a huge responsibility and a need to coordinate with local, state, and federal government agencies.

In addition to the wide range of areas that require robust cybersecurity systems and protocols to be enacted, technologists who serve in this capacity in local government play a vital role in the development of a holistic resilience strategy. From accessing the risks involved when moving key infrastructure into the public cloud to thinking through disaster recovery scenarios, cybersecurity experts can help government leaders better understand current and emerging threats in ways that will engender trust. This building of trust in government is vital, as it will help government leaders speed up the migration of local government technology infrastructure into the cloud, while building trust and confidence with the public that their government services and interactions with the government are safe and secure.

SERVICE DELIVERY

The delivery of public services is the government's core responsibility and its core competency. The sheer range of services that need to be delivered by governments is mind boggling. To get a sense of the scale of the efforts involved, simply go to the home page of any local government and review the list of services that the government provides. For example, the city of Seattle where I worked listed the services it provides in the following twenty categories (Figure 5-3).

Figure 5-3: *Categories of services provided by the city of Seattle*

Services

Affordability	Animals and Pets	Arts and Culture	Building and Construction
Business and Economic Development	City Administration	City Employment	City Planning and Development
Court Services	Education, Schools and Learning	Environment and Sustainability	Grants and Funding
Housing, Health and Human Services	Neighborhood Services	Parks, Recreation and Attractions	Police, Fire and Public Safety
Transportation	Technology	Utilities	Volunteering and Participating

Source: http://www.seattle.gov

Each high-level service area usually contains a multitude of individual services, some of which are digital and some of which are analog and in person. No matter what the service is, technology plays a role in enabling the government to deliver it. At the local government level, the scale of service delivery will vary based on the size of the municipality or agency, and the biggest municipal government will pale in comparison to the scale of service delivery at the state government level.

Another way to gauge the scale of service provision efforts within local government, and to better understand the opportunities to drive improvements via technology, is to review the products and services provided by the "GovTech" sector that state and local governments deploy. Larger GovTech companies provide a broad range of solutions, both on-premises and cloud offerings, while smaller companies may focus primarily on providing one service or experience, such as solutions related to public safety or managing public record requests.[9] All state and local governments deploy technologies from third-party vendors, whether they are generic solutions from major technology firms like Microsoft (e.g., Office 365) or specialized solutions from the GovTech sector. Even though some of these solutions are specifically tailored for state and local government, the development of a government's technical capability can enable more value to be extracted from these technologies and solutions, improving the service delivery experience for government staff and public alike.

- *Reduce the dependency on consultants*: Governments at all levels have a huge dependency on IT consultants. Some of this dependency could be reduced by building up the internal expertise of technologists who can perform some of the key functions that governments would normally rely upon consultants to do, as well as facilitate deeper engagements with consulting and GovTech firms that result in better outcomes for taxpayers.

- *Accelerate the transition to the cloud*: According to recent research, 97 percent of the $3.7 trillion IT market is still on-premises, in corporate servers and datacenters, and not yet in the cloud.[10] This includes both the private and public sectors. What this suggests is that the real push toward moving government enterprise systems into the public cloud (otherwise known as Infrastructure as a Platform [IaaS]) has yet to happen and that more technologists within government can help accelerate this important transition that government at all levels will make in the coming five to ten years.

- *Innovating on top of the government O/S*: As we have been referring to government in terms of an operating system (O/S), there are two important aspects of the operating system life cycle that we can apply to government. First, we need to support and sustain the O/S. Once a public service needs to be delivered and has technology underpinning it, it needs to be in place for the long term. Life cycles of a minimum of ten to fifteen years are not uncommon for enterprise IT systems in government and elsewhere. This is why the Microsoft Windows O/S has a ten-year "free" support life cycle, along with an option to pay for support beyond that period. Most enterprise software vendors offer long-term service contracts for their implementations, be they on-premises, in the cloud, or via a hybrid solution. Similarly, any technology developed internally should also have the long-term sustainability requirements being clearly understood up-front. Second, there is not a huge incentive to innovate on top of the public service delivery technology platform. If we are to truly think about local governments as an O/S, then more technologists can help change this way of thinking and encourage the development of innovative applications and services, while ensuring that these apps and services continue to function as the underlying O/S gets updated over time. The user experience (UX) should relegate the underlying O/S into the background, where the public are blissfully unaware of it. After all, when we have a great user experience with an app and/ or online service on our phones, we never stop to think about the version of the O/S running on our phone. The public should be able to enjoy great local government service delivery powered by technology, without even thinking about the system underneath it. Unfortunately, too often they are exposed to these underlying systems. This can be fixed.

OPERATIONS

Separate from but closely related to the delivery of public services is the operational efficiency of government. Local governments of all sizes have complex operations systems that support the delivery of the vast array of services that were referenced previously. As the populations in our cities continue to rise and the scale of service delivery expands as a result, local governments are attempting to keep up with these demands, while being constrained by the realities of their ability to grow their budgets in a responsible manner. Increasing pressure on budgets typically requires raising new revenues or expanding existing revenue streams. New or expanded taxes are the most common way to generate new revenues, but these efforts are generally difficult to accomplish in a timely manner and can be unpopular with the public. Helping offset some of these revenue needs while also improving the level of services delivered would help improve people's perception of government and perhaps make them more willing to meet government halfway for future tax increases.

Additionally, and somewhat oxymoronically, governments should spend more when the economy is bad and less so when the economy is good. Why? In times of recession, government is usually the only entity that has the resources to stimulate the economy at a time when the overall economy is in contraction. The stimulus packages enacted by the Obama administration during the 2008–2013 recessionary period are good examples of this kind of emergency spending. A quick review of most local government budgets over the past several years will show that most major municipal government budgets have grown considerably during that time, and yet their ability to weather future economic storms without having to make at least some drastic cuts in service delivery or headcount remain doubtful. This is where more effective usage of technology and data can play an increasing role in helping develop efficiencies under good budgetary and spending conditions, thereby creating opportunities for more vital local government services to remain available to the public in times of crises. Here are some examples of how technology and data can play a leading role in optimizing the operational excellence of government:

- *Customer feedback data*: Through better analysis of customer feedback data (such as 311 calls/texts/emails, complaints, etc.) aligned with data provided from local government staff in the field, it will be possible to identify opportunities to optimize internal processes, as well as streamlining how services are provided to the public while simultaneously improving quality and responsiveness. This is probably the best way for technologists and data scientists to have immediate and large-scale impact within local government presently.

- *Automation as a Service*: With consolidated IT departments comes the opportunity to automate and streamline business processes, both within the IT department itself and other departments. By offering this capability as a service, the IT department can recoup the costs of the work while encouraging other departments to think about how investing in automation can be a positive and lead to good Return on Investment (ROI) outcomes.

- *Open-source software*: Having more technologists with open-source experience can enable local governments to lessen their dependence on third-party vendor technology solutions with high recurring costs. Additionally, using open-source solutions for some public-facing applications can lead to opportunities for more effective civic technology partnerships, for example, partnering with local government by adding features to an open-source open data portal.
- *Share and reuse*: Local governments in general are quite good about sharing their know-how, and increasingly their source code for open-source applications that some have developed. One of the barriers to greater adoption of local government open-source solutions is the lack of technical know-how in many local governments.

PROJECT MANAGEMENT

One thing local government does a lot of is IT project management. In his recent book, *The Fifth Risk*, author Michael Lewis highlights the risks when the project management of vast, complex federal government bureaucracies and critical systems are taken for granted and not carefully nurtured and developed.[11] Outside of the federal government, all small, medium, and large local governments have their own IT departments (a model that is ripe for disruption in my opinion) and usually need to manage multiple IT projects. In larger local and state governments, there has been a movement toward consolidation of IT resources into a single department, which then procures and manages the delivery of all IT systems to the entire organization. Such a consolidation process was in its final stages when I joined the city of Seattle in 2016,[12] and a similar effort was undertaken at the Washington State government level.[13] It is likely that similar consolidation efforts have been undertaken in local government jurisdictions all across the United States. With these consolidations of IT staff into single departments, the relationships between these new IT departments and the other departments (basically, the "clients" of the IT department) require careful management. As a result, project management has become quite important as a function within government IT departments. Titles like "client service directors" are becoming more prevalent, highlighting this need. "IT projects" usually consist of a tender being issued for a software solution for specific requirements, usually called a "request for proposals" (RFP). Vendors who wish to respond have a limited window of time within which to do so, and after a review of these proposals, some leading candidates will usually be offered the opportunity to provide a demonstration to project management, after which a winning bidder will be chosen, and the contract awarded. Then the implementation process begins. Note that at no stage of this process is the government itself involved in any product development work; instead, the government is a consumer of existing technology solutions. There are several other aspects to this process that I am glossing over here for the sake of brevity, but for readers who may be curious to learn more about the IT procurement and implementation processes, there are many great resources online.

While local government does a lot of IT project management, this doesn't mean that it doesn't have room for improvement. Unfortunately, government is somewhat notorious in the minds of the public for missing deadlines and exceeding budgets when delivering major projects. There are many instances where the opposite is true, but alas, the negative stereotype appears to have stuck. More technologists with broad experience in project management are needed to serve in government, both to help with current projects and to develop the organizational capacity to deliver projects on time, within budget, every time. Even though project management is a very broad discipline, with many different job descriptions that can fit into this area of work, a core set of principles or activities apply equally in either the public or private sector when it comes to managing large-scale technology projects. Here are some ways that more experienced technologists can help transform local government project management:

- *Planning*: Improving how government develops the initial project estimates, such as timelines, dependencies, testing and feedback, long-term sustaining costs and activities, staff training, future upgrade roadmap, etc., is the first step toward building that organizational rigor.
- *Agile Methodologies*: Encouraging the use of agile software development frameworks (Scrum, etc.) for project management activities, including those that don't involve software engineering—such as data science or analytics deliverables, IT implementations, and so on.
- *Tenets*: For large-scale projects, breaking them down into a core set of "tenets" is a useful way for technologists and project managers to ensure that no critical areas get overlooked and that the load is more evenly spread across the team. For example, a set of tenets for a major local government IT project could be cybersecurity, privacy, performance, sustainability, and interoperability. Each tenet has a designated owner who is responsible for driving all activities related to achieving key metrics and goals and ensuring the work is completed on time. These tenet owners then roll up their data to the overall project manager, who ultimately will have to make the decision on whether the project is complete or not. Local governments could benefit from being able to apply this type of "mission control" project management to their IT projects.
- *Data, data, data*: Local government's ability to leverage data requires investment and improvement in general, and this also applies to project management. Too often, there is no capacity for local government to gather test data prior to launching a new IT service, and this is a critical gap that technologists can help address.

145

- *Integration*: Another weakness in local government IT project management is in the area of integration testing. Ensuring that new applications and services integrate well with existing and/or dependent applications and services is a critical part of avoiding "go live" launch failures, which can be quite embarrassing and feed into the negative public narrative about local government's ability to deliver projects successfully.

- *Knowing when not to do something*: A key skill that is often overlooked, knowing when *not* to do something, is a way that experienced technologists can help local government develop. At times, political pressure may be applied to either fast-track or delay IT projects. Improving the capability of local government to anticipate these pressures, as well as improving the ability to clearly articulate the short-, medium-, and long-term consequences of those decisions would be valuable.

- *Evaluating and learning*: One thing I did repeatedly when working as a technologist in the private sector was to take part in project "postmortems" and evaluate what we did well and what we could have done better or anticipated but didn't and apply those lessons to future or concurrent projects. That was a time of "waterfall" project management with long development cycles. In a world of continuous development cycles driven by customer data, daily releases enabled by DevOps, and agile project management, it can be more difficult to perform such audits after the fact. Evaluating projects needs to adapt to those cycles, so that after each project sprint cycle an evaluation workflow is built into the backlog. As more local governments embrace more complex IT project and data analytics initiatives, evaluating the management and delivery of applications and services becomes more critical and improves the overall organizational learning.

DATA ANALYTICS

The establishment of a dedicated, and well-resourced, data analytics unit is a must for most local governments, and yet it appears to be a huge organizational hurdle for government to cross. Most local governments continue to rely heavily upon grants from philanthropic organizations to fund major portions of their data analytics (or "innovation") teams. A huge cultural shift around data is required, and this is probably the number one challenge that more experienced technologists and data scientists can help with within local government. How?

- *Act as chief data officers*:
  Local government needs to appoint many more chief data officers (CDOs). These executives set the strategic direction for the collection, storage, analysis, and sharing of data across the government, and beyond. They should not be a part of the IT department, but rather act as a peer to the CIO or CTO and manage up to the city council and mayor's office. They can also engage with other CDOs across the country and bring learnings back to their own government. There is a fantastic network of urban CDOs, known as the Civic Analytics Network, based out of the Ash Center for Democratic Governance and Innovation at Harvard Kennedy School.[14] Similarly, a new network with similar aims for CDOs at the state level has recently been established at the Beeck Center for Social Impact & Innovation at Georgetown University.[15]

- *Build overarching strategic data plans*:
  In addition to the lack of official CDOs, most local governments do not have a strategic data plan. Borrowing from other local governments and from the private sector, such as the excellent Tableau Blueprint guide for building a data-driven organization, is one way technologists and data scientists can help lead from

within and realize tremendous value from the troves of data local governments possess.[16]

- *Viewing data analytics as an investment:*
  Governments tend to view data analytics as an expense, rather than an investment. Having more experienced technologists with proven experience in building data-driven teams and using data to drive efficiencies and understand the customer's needs can help leaders in government shift their view on the power and positive impact that data analytics provides.

CUSTOMER FOCUS

My own experiences in interacting with local government services both as a citizen and as a public servant observing how a major local government deals with internal and external customers have led me to believe that "customer focus" is a skill that government still has some way to go in terms of mastering. Industry standards such as Net Promoter Score (NPS) and other metrics to help gauge the public's sentiment are generally not employed in local government. Even as the digital transformation of government is well underway, with more apps and online services becoming available, the collection and analysis of customer feedback and sentiment are largely being unrealized. This is a huge opportunity to drive improvements that is being lost.

Government has a tendency not to start every change and project from the perspective of the customer and work backwards, but rather to think about how to achieve the objective (i.e., release a new online service) while causing the minimal amount of change to existing processes and legacy systems, as well as disruption to staff. While some of this is due to the culture within government, as well as resistance by unions to major changes in staff working conditions and responsibilities, there is space for improvement that could be quickly achieved.

"Meeting people where they are" is also an important concept that government has been slow to embrace. We are now in a mobile-first, cloud-first world. People are spending less time on large screens and perform the bulk of their tasks via their phones and mobile apps. More apps and services provided by government need to be developed with this philosophy in mind. Similarly, accessibility needs to be a core aspect of all design decisions. More local governments are beginning to embrace the principles of human-centered design, sometimes in conjunction with civic technology partnerships, and bringing accessibility to the fore. However, local government has only begun to scratch the surface.

One of the largest growth employment areas in private-sector technology companies is for a discipline known as "customer success," where a process of continual engagement with the customer after they have bought your product or service is created. This is done to ensure that (a) the customer gets the most value from the product or service and (b) that the chances of selling them additional features or services or getting them to renew a subscription is improved. Government could also apply these principles to the provision of public services by investing more in these types of customer outreach activities, creating feedback loops where none exist, and checking in with their local residents on a regular basis on how these services are being received and what could be better. Most "high-touch" services will have formal or informal feedback loops due to the in-person nature of these activities. For digital services, governments have an unrealized opportunity to develop systems and processes that enable their residents to feel more connected to their public servants and to engender more trust and confidence in local government.

TECHNOLOGY POLICY

The proliferation of advanced technologies into our cities and counties is rapidly increasing, and with them comes a slew of complex policy issues and ethical questions. As a result, state and local governments need more experts at the intersections of technology and policy, as well as data and ethics, to help them navigate these issues and develop strategies and policies that result in good outcomes for the public.

The advent of so-called "smart cities" is requiring local governments to grapple with important public policy and privacy questions. For example, the impending rollout of 5G networks and the deployment of a new generation of IoT devices that will take advantage of 5G capabilities will result in opportunities for increasingly pervasive surveillance technologies to be enabled. More public interest technologists, lawyers, and policy experts serving in government as technology policy advisors and chief privacy officers could assist local government leaders in a number of important ways:

- Technology and legal experts who can deeply engage with software and hardware vendors and other partners, such as universities, around complex technical issues and technology policy questions
- Technologists who can help educate the both the executive and legislative branches of local government on complex technical issues
- Provide "thought leadership" on technology policy issues, in written and spoken forums.
- Effectively use their knowledge of technical platforms and solutions, both open-source and proprietary, to negotiate better deals for the government and taxpayers
- Assist with policy development in areas such as open data, privacy policies, data policies, policies related to smart cities, and so on

Based upon my own experiences in local government, the technology policy arena is a fascinating space within which to contribute and is one of the most effective ways to have real and lasting impact.

CULTURE CHANGE

"Culture eats strategy for breakfast"—or so the old saying goes. I'd often wondered if that statement was true or what it truly meant. A few years ago, I was fortunate to be an employee at Microsoft right about the time that this massive organization instigated a radical shift in its culture when Satya Nadella took over as CEO in early 2014. I had a front-row seat as huge cultural and strategic changes were rolled out, and I started to realize the true impact that culture has on the ability of an organization to reinvent itself and thrive. I finally began to understand the true meaning of that old saying about culture. Added to that, I learned to appreciate the huge supporting role that data can play in any cultural transformation. Fast-forward to my time serving in local government at the city of Seattle, where I began to think and write about whether there were lessons that government could take from that example when it came to how to change its own culture.[17]

In the final chapter, I will explain in more detail about why nothing will significantly change in how local government operates unless and until there is a real and sustained effort to change the culture in local government, specifically related to innovation, technology, and data. However, more technologists serving in local government can help build the pressure from the ground up to push the executive leadership to drive these organizational culture changes and to then help embed those culture changes into the fabric of the organization. Technologists can help develop that innovative culture by helping local governments move from being reactive to proactive through the effective use of data, reduce the backlog of IT projects while improving the experiences of the public availing themselves of digital services, and speed up the transition of local government infrastructure to the public government cloud. The point here isn't to transpose the tech sector's culture of innovation directly into local government; rather, it is to have more technologists from the private sector bring with them into government service the most positive aspects of that culture, such as a sense of urgency and beginning every technology conversation from the perspective of the customer.

EDUCATION

Often overlooked as a way to serve in the public sector, teaching in public universities and community colleges is a great way to have positive social impact and empower the next generation of technologists with the ideals and passion for public service. This can be accomplished as a full-time lecturer or by teaching part time in an adjunct or other capacity, which is a common way that experienced private- and public-sector technologists contribute. Having more technologists who are serving in government who can increase the awareness of the public sector as a viable career option is needed. While I was serving at the city of Seattle, I regularly did guest lectures at local universities and colleges and always relished the opportunity to engage with students and learn about how they were using the data that the city was making available. It was also a valuable way to learn about what software development tools and programming languages were trending in popularity and how the next generation felt about some of the most pressing technology policy issues. This created a useful feedback loop of data that I could then share internally within the data programs at the city.

This need for education isn't limited to our public colleges, however. There is also a real need for technologists within government who can educate government leaders on the value of data and how it can transform government. Technologists with solid communication skills are a hugely valuable asset to any organization, but especially in government, where there is still a reluctance to fully embrace open-source software, cloud computing, and other emerging trends in enterprise IT. Being able to create easily accessible, compelling, and convincing rationales for why government leaders should build a culture of innovation based around data and technology is a valuable way some technologists can contribute to their government.

A QUANTUM LEAP IN THE POWER OF TECHNOLOGY

While these lists are primarily focused on the technology and data challenges of the present time, new technologies and platforms continue to emerge that could lead to even greater technology policy issues that government will need to wrestle with. From blockchain and its ability to power a new class of applications to the advent of quantum computing and its exponential increase in the power of computer processing, these current and future technology questions will continue to require a continuous pipeline of talented technologists to enter into public service and help our state and local governments navigate these challenges.[18]

CHAPTER 5: KEY TAKEAWAYS

- Public statements from local government leaders can give useful insights into how they prioritize technology and data as part of their government service delivery obligations. Their priorities may at times seem at odds with the sentiment and desires of civic technologists who are attempting to change government from the outside.

- Based on the known top priorities of government IT leaders in the state and local government sectors, we examine at a high level some of the main areas where technologists can have impact:
  - *Building resilience*: Governments need to develop the capacity to prevent service delivery outages.
  - *Cybersecurity*: Election security concerns and ransomware attacks are just some of the major cybersecurity issues that

local governments are struggling to grapple with. More investment in talent is needed.

○ *Service delivery*: The need to accelerate the delivery of new and enhanced digital services.

○ *Operations*: Help develop the capacity of local government to improve their operational efficiency.

○ *Project management*: The need for more robust program and project management and what can go wrong if this critical aspect of management is neglected.

○ *Data analytics*: There is a huge need for local government to view data analytics as an investment, to have more experienced data scientists and technologists serve as CDOs, and to build overarching strategic data plans.

○ *Customer focus*: Helping local government to improve how it uses data and customer feedback to improve its service delivery, as well as improving customer feedback loops.

○ *Technology policy*: Local governments are grappling with complex public policy questions related to emerging technologies and the ethical collection and usage of data within our cities and communities. Technologists, especially those with expertise at the intersections of policy and law, can play a leading role in helping government leaders develop the policies, regulations, and laws needed to mitigate these important issues.

○ *Culture change*: "Culture eats strategy for breakfast"— how nothing will significantly change in how local government operates unless and until there is a real and sustained effort to change the culture in local government, specifically related to innovation, technology, and data.

○ *Education*: Often overlooked, teaching in public universities and community colleges is a great way for technologists to have positive social impact and help empower the next generation of technologists with the passion for public service.

• With the advent of quantum computing delivering an exponential growth in the power of computing, along with new platforms like blockchain, local government has an opportunity to be among the early adopters of these exciting technologies and to develop new services and experiences that will excite the public.

NOTES

1   "Technology—Technology Subtopics," National League of Cities, accessed September 13, 2019, https://www.nlc.org/topics/technology.

2   "State CIO Top 10 Priorities," National Association of State Chief Information Officers (NASCIO), accessed September 14, 2019, https://www.nascio.org/Portals/0/NASCIO_CIOTopTenPriorities.pdf.

3   "State of the Cities 2019," National League of Cities, accessed September 14, 2019, https://www.nlc.org/sites/default/files/2019-05/StateOfTheCities%20 2019.pdf.

4   "Results Washington—Home," State of Washington, accessed September 14, 2019, https://results.wa.gov.

5   "What's Wrong with the Washington State Data Center?," ZDNet, last updated December 11, 2014, https://www.zdnet.com/article/what-wrong-with-th e-washington-state-data-center.

6   "Accelerating Enterprise Cloud Adoption," U.S. Department of Defense, last updated February 15, 2018, https://www.defense.gov/Newsroom/Releases/Release/Article/1442705/accelerating-enterprise-cloud-adoption.

7   "Ransomware Attack Map," StateScoop, accessed December 15, 2019, https://statescoop.com/ransomware-map.

8   "Mobile Voting Project," Tusk Philanthropies, accessed December 15, 2019, https://mobilevoting.org.

9   "2019 Top 100 GovTech Companies," Government Technology, accessed January 6, 2020, https://www.govtech.com/100/2019/.

10 "AWS Works Hard to Keep Ahead of the Public Cloud Herd," TheNextPlatform, accessed December 15, 2019, https://www.nextplatform.com/2019/12/04/aw s-works-to-keep-ahead-of-the-public-cloud-herd.

11 Michael Lewis, *The Fifth Risk, Undoing Democracy* (New York: W. W. Norton, 2018).

12 "Seattle Begins Three-Year IT Consolidation," GovTech, last updated November 30, 2015, https://www.govtech.com/dc/articles/Seattle-Begins-Three-Year-IT-Consolidation.html.

13 "New Central IT Agency Positions the State of Washington for the Future," State of Washington, last updated July 1, 2015, https://watech.wa.gov/about/news-room/news/news-release/new-central-it-agency-positions-state-washington-future.

14 "About the Civic Analytics Network," Ash Center for Democratic Governance and Innovation at Harvard Kennedy School, accessed November 22, 2019, https://datasmart.ash.harvard.edu/news/article/about-the-civic-analytics-network-826.

15 "State Chief Data Officers Network," Beeck Center at Georgetown University, accessed November 22, 2019, https://beeckcenter.georgetown.edu/state-cdo-network.

16 "Tableau Blueprint Overview," Tableau, accessed November 22, 2019, https://help.tableau.com/current/blueprint/en-us/bp_overview.htm.

17 "What Government Can Learn from Microsoft's Cultural Transformation," David Doyle, accessed November 22, 2019, https://www.linkedin.com/pulse/what-government-can-learn-from-microsofts-cultural-david-doyle.

18 "A Quantum Leap for Open Data?," David Doyle, accessed November 22, 2019, https://www.linkedin.com/pulse/quantum-leap-open-data-david-doyle.

III

THE "HOW"

6

— CHAPTER —

KEY DIFFERENCES BETWEEN THE PUBLIC AND PRIVATE SECTORS

One of the most frequent questions I get about my own experience working in government is how I managed the transition into the public sector after such a long time in the private sector. While there are many differences between those two worlds, there are also a lot of similarities. After all, large private-sector companies are also large bureaucracies and often exhibit similar behaviors at times. Although at times I was bemused, bewildered, and frustrated with some of the things I encountered in government, I always tried to step back and see the bigger picture and think about the broader mission and to keep an open mind and have a sense of humor. This isn't to say that conditions in the private sector were always ideal—far from it. The one thing both of these sectors have in common is that they are inhabited by humans, where each person has their own unique point of view and way of doing things.

The level of complexity in the public sector is hard to describe to those who have never worked there—from the multilayered political considerations regarding most major decisions, to having your work and communications be open to public disclosure laws, to having union representation and bargaining agreements in sections of the workforce, and to being a public representative for the work that you do and dealing directly or indirectly with the public and press, and a lot more besides. It's one of the main reasons, in my view, that government sometimes doesn't move as fast as people on the outside would wish or expect; I came to respect and appreciate that need for extra time and space to deliberate before making decisions or implementing a new piece of technology or service. How to accelerate the innovation processes to improve the delivery of services within local government is challenging work, but work I found incredibly enjoyable when partnering with our city staff and other local governments.

In this chapter we outline some of the things you can expect when you work in local government, from the obvious to the not-so-obvious. I wish I had previously known or better understood some of these things before I began my public service, and while this is not an exhaustive list or may not mirror the experiences of others, I hope that these insights can help educate you on what to expect when entering this somewhat foreign and complex environment, help you ask more informed questions when going through the hiring process, and set yourself up for success from day one.

THE SOMEWHAT WELL-KNOWN THINGS

In this section, we examine some common questions and concerns that people have when considering a move into public service from the private sector. These topics can be considered somewhat well known, as most people appear to have at least some knowledge of or hold an opinion on these aspects of public service.

HIRING PROCESS

The hiring process in local government has several key differences from the tech sector that are worth understanding before you embark upon your own journey. These differences may or may not exist in the local government that you are applying to, but regardless, being aware of these anomalies will help you make better decisions.

Compared to the private sector, job classifications in local government can look very different. For a start, there are a bewildering number of titles in use within local government. One way to explore these is to look at any major job search site where government jobs are listed. You will likely find an amazing array of job titles there. Not all are related to technology roles, of course, but it is worth getting a sense for how diverse the work of local government truly is. With that in mind, getting a better understanding of how the work you're interested in gets classified in the public sector is important in helping you discover all of the opportunities that are out there. One important thing to watch for is whether the job will require membership in a labor union. A requirement to join a union as part of your local government employment is a possibility for some individual contributor technical roles, particularly in support roles with IT departments. For managerial positions, as well as director-level and executive-level positions, the is usually no requirement to join a union. These positions are known as "exempt" and typically will have a description in the job title and/or job description highlighting that designation. The key difference between these designations is related to tenure. Being hired as an "exempt" employee, you are subject to at-will employment law and as such can be fired much more easily than if you were a member of a union. There are some other differences also, such as having different arrangements for annual pay raises and extra vacation days being awarded for good performance in lieu of a cash bonus.

Title inflation can also be a problem. Based on some of the titles I've encountered over time, it can be hard to truly understand what a person does, what their span of control is (i.e., how many people they oversee in the organization), and what the scale is of the services that they are responsible for delivering, and so on. This is important information for technologists, as you will need to be able to accurately assess how your current job can be calibrated against the local government position you're interested in. Employees in the tech sector use a variety of websites to help solve this problem for their sector, such as www.levels.fyi or www. teamblind.com. Tech-sector employees will voluntarily share compensation and other information from the major companies, and a general alignment can be established—for example, what is the equivalent level at Amazon or Google to level X at Microsoft. At the time of writing, I'm unaware of such a service that includes government jobs. You'll have to establish other means for gathering this intelligence, typically through networking and informational meetings, which we will discuss in more detail later.

Jobs being advertised with the relevant hourly or salary range are the norm, where you will likely encounter some wide ranges. This can be especially confusing to those who are not familiar with this system. Typically, the hourly rate will depend on the person's previous experience, as well as the internal budget for that role. While there can be some room for maneuver outside of the published hourly rates, achieving an exception is fairly rare and requires sign-off from a senior leader like a Chief Technology Officer (CTO) or above. Although it will be tempting to go for the maximum hourly rate immediately, keep in mind that it will likely be a good idea to leave some room for salary growth, especially if you're considering staying for several years. This hourly rate will likely be one of the main areas of negotiation if you receive a job offer, so be prepared for some haggling, and make sure you have a clear idea of what you're willing to settle for ahead of time. Remember that in government your salary is likely going to be a more important consideration than in the tech sector, as it will constitute almost the entirety of your total compensation for the year. We will discuss the intricacies of local government compensation in more details in a later section of this chapter.

APPLYING AND INTERVIEWING FOR GOVERNMENT JOBS

Applying, and later interviewing, for government positions can feel quite different from the typical hiring process in the private sector, especially in the tech sector. First off, the process can often appear to be more formal and longer than what you might be used to. However, some governments have been taking steps to make the experience better, and from my observations, the job application process at the local government level appears to be less onerous than at the federal government level. Many applications will list the closing date for receipt of applications, which is useful information. Most applications will require a cover letter along with a resume, so if you've never written a cover letter before, this is a skill that is well worth developing. Writing a cover letter adds valuable context to your resume and LinkedIn profile for the person reviewing your application. It has the added benefit of forcing you to write down your rationale for why you want the job and why you're the best person for it—not as easy as it sounds. This rationale is something you will repeat in the interview process, so this is a really valuable exercise, and I highly encourage you to spend time crafting your letter. If required, answer any additional supplemental questions. These are general and agency supplemental questions. Depending on the hiring agency, this section may be blank.

It is also worth noting that having an initial informational meeting with the hiring manager may not be possible. This is sometimes possible within the tech sector, even if you're an external candidate. However, this is very much the exception and not the rule within government for external candidates. To get around this limitation, in your information gathering process, it should be possible to speak with people who work in that department. Reaching out via LinkedIn is a common tactic, as well as getting a referral from someone in your network, if that's possible. I would recommend you ideally try to speak with someone in the organization prior to applying or interviewing, and even before you accept an offer if you make it to that point. As is the case in any sector, the gap between the idealistic job description and the cold, hard reality within the organization can be quite wide. Always do your homework and check your assumptions before making any big decisions.

For technical roles in local government, you'll likely have an initial screening process should you make it through the initial scrub of job applications. And yes, just like the private sector, there will likely be an initial scrub, usually by humans and not via an AI seeking certain keywords and phrases. In larger local governments, it is quite common to have at least several dozen candidates for individual contributor and frontline management technical roles, and over one hundred candidates for senior leadership roles such as chief data officer, chief technology officer, and chief information officer. Another aspect of the job search process that surprised me was how many people from across the country would apply for positions in local government, with a view to relocating if successful. I had been hardwired to think that relocating was something that was only done in the tech sector, and I myself had been relocated by Microsoft from the European Product Development Center in Dublin, Ireland, to their headquarters in Redmond, Washington, in 2003. The lesson here appears to be that interesting and challenging technology jobs within local government don't become available very often and that there will likely be fierce competition for those jobs. The scale of demand for those jobs is also a signal that if more of those available, local governments might not struggle to fill them. In other words, many technologists appear to be interested in working in local government, and we have an opportunity to develop that extra capacity.

Aside from the initial screening process, you may also be required to complete an exercise prior to your in-person interviews, which is also a common practice in the private sector. The formal interviews are often in panel formats with the hiring manager and several other staffers with whom you would directly or indirectly work with if hired. From my experience, this is a big difference from the tech sector, where the norm for technical roles is to have a grueling series of one-on-one interviews over the course of a day. You will likely have only one panel interview, usually one hour long, followed at a later date by a second interview, which is possibly the runoff interview where the top two or three candidates meet with a senior leader. The goal of those runoff interviews is to allow senior leaders to assess the panel's decision on who they chose as their top candidates and to check for culture fit and other cross-group concerns that may not have surfaced in the initial panel interviews. Another major difference

I experienced with my panel interview process was that I was given the interview questions thirty minutes prior to the actual interview so I could review them and sketch out my answers before bringing them with me into the interview itself. You may or may not encounter something similar in your interview process, but I found this to be an interesting approach—it certainly helped with reducing nerves before the actual meeting and I think led to a better conversation in the room. I later discovered that this extra step is primarily designed to help candidates who speak English as a second language. I think the tech sector could find a similar approach when interviewing for certain positions to be beneficial.

COMPENSATION AND BENEFITS

The topic of overall compensation in local government is probably one of the most frequently asked questions I have received over time, and also one of the most frequently misunderstood considerations when deciding whether to serve in government. First let's walk through the various elements of the overall compensation package in local government, before comparing the overall packages between the public and private sectors.

As mentioned earlier, government jobs are typically advertised with an hourly salary range, and sometimes with an annual salary range listed. While all jobs have salary ranges, the big difference in the public sector is that you have that information up-front, which can help with negotiations if you succeed in getting an offer. One important thing to watch for— as mentioned earlier—is whether the job will require membership in a labor union, and this will be listed somewhere in the job description. A requirement to join a union as part of your employment will mean, among other things, the payment of monthly dues to the particular union. Depending on the union in question, these dues can be significant enough to warrant some discussion and negotiation with the recruiter. It may be possible to negotiate a slightly higher hourly rate to negate the effect of these monthly dues, so don't be shy about that. If you're a talented technologist and they really want you to join the team, they will find some wiggle room in the budget to accommodate requests like this. For the most part, the more senior technical jobs do not require joining a union, but if you encounter this requirement, it is something to consider.

There may be a requirement for new hires to be under probation for the first six months of their tenure. This was the situation I found myself in, and as someone with considerable professional experience prior to joining my local government, I found this requirement to be quite odd. I was new to government, so I expected to have to learn a lot in those first few months, but I felt an official probation period was overkill for someone who was in a union-exempt position. I didn't make a fuss about it—but I did pass along this feedback to my manager and human resources (HR) representative. Another tactic that can be employed when negotiating for a slightly higher salary than what's being offered is to use the six-month probationary period as a way agree to a salary bump once you've proved yourself. For example, start at a certain hourly rate and after six months have passed satisfactorily, the salary is increased to the new level. I would suggest a range of 1 to 5 percent is likely feasible. One negative side effect of this probationary period was that I was severely limited in how much vacation I could take in those first six months, and another restriction being that the government's matching pension funds didn't begin until after the first six months. I do think this is one area where local governments can be more flexible and creative in creating compensation packages that are more in tune with what professionals are used to in the private sector.

Another interesting difference from the private sector is that your salary information will be public. It is very rare for an exemption to be made, so expect to have your salary information be fully transparent to the public, whose taxes are paying for your salary. The data is usually shared via the government's own websites, usually in the form of a searchable database or via an open dataset that can be downloaded. Sometimes the data will be made available on a yearly basis, or in some cases the local government will update the salary information on a more regular schedule. It is also possible that a local news organization will request the data via public records requests and then create a searchable database on their website. Having your salary information be completely open can feel a little weird at first, but over time I found this not to be a major issue. My own feeling is that local governments should be as transparent as possible and be proactive about sharing the data. This is yet another way that local government can build trust with the public, and the transparency can lead to healthy discussions around compensation equity for existing staff as well as new hires.

While it varies from local government to local government, annual salary increases are possible and likely when economic conditions are right. In my own case, there was a modest cost of living increase each year, about 2 percent. These raises are kept quite close to current inflation. If you are among the represented (union) staff, then there will likely be a multiyear deal in place with raises scheduled per those contracts and agreements. Unlike the private sector, there is not an expectation that you will receive performance-related salary increases. The usual way to grow your salary by a more significant amount is to seek a promotion or make a lateral move into another internal team at a higher level.

The largest difference in terms of overall compensation is the area of bonuses and stock awards. In short, there are none in government at any level. At all. This is usually the biggest pain point for experienced technologists and other professionals moving into the public sector. Having had a long career at Microsoft, I understand this pain. While salaries for technology positions in larger local governments are reasonably close to those in the private sector, expect to take a significant cut when working in government in terms of overall cash compensation due to the lack of bonuses and other cash compensation. In addition to the absence of equity opportunities, moving into government will require some level of personal monetary sacrifice. I believe this is an important part of the overall mission of service, insofar as the sacrifice isn't excessively onerous. This is a major reason why many technologists will return to the private sector once their "tour of duty" has been completed.

Rounding off the other elements of the overall compensation package, benefits such as vacation time and health insurance are generally comparable with the private sector. Note that as a government employee you will likely have a few extra government holidays per year that are typically not observed in the private sector, such as Presidents Day. When it comes to retirement savings accounts, there are no 401(k) programs like in the private sector. Instead, you have the opportunity to enter the public-sector pension plan system. These systems vary by location, but for most long-term government employees, their guaranteed pension is the ultimate reward for a distinguished career in public service. For those of us who wish to serve in government for a shorter span of time, these programs are less appealing, and this is something to review when fielding offers to serve in local government. Note that it can be possible to use the time served in one local government in another local government's pension system—for example, if you move from a city government to a county government in the same region. It may even be possible to consolidate the funds into a single pension pot, similar to how a 401(k) could be rolled over to a Roth IRA. If you are planning to spend more than five years working in government, I would highly encourage you to work with your benefits representative to ensure you're getting the maximum benefit from the available plans and regional system. As always, be sure to do your research well ahead of time. Fortunately, most of this information is made publicly available on local government websites.

How Career Paths Differ from the Private Sector

These days it is fashionable for firms in the tech sector to have flat reporting structures, where the number of levels between a frontline employee and senior leadership has been greatly reduced, resulting in mid-level and senior managers typically having a large span of control. It is basically the opposite in local government, depending on the size of your organization. Governments at all levels tend to be very hierarchical, not just within the departments themselves but also within the overall government itself. While most local governments make their organizational charts available on their websites, it's not unusual for these to be out-of-date. Regardless, these charts will provide some great insights into the structure and nature of the organization, and if an org chart isn't readily available, your recruiter should be able to provide one upon request. Always remember that any documentation created by government is a public record, and you have a right to request it.

For technologists entering local government at the senior executive level, some roles may require mayoral (or equivalent) approval as part of the interview process, followed by approval by the relevant council or legislative body. Technology roles at the executive level such as chief technology officers, chief information officers, and chief data officers will typically need to follow this kind of approvals process, followed by a swearing-in ceremony.

Another important distinction between the private and public sectors is around promotions, or the lack thereof. Of course, promotions do happen in public service, but in my experience, it is something that happens less frequently than in the tech sector. The idea of moving up several levels within an existing job classification (like with engineering levels in the tech sector) doesn't really exist within local government. It is also difficult to compare levels of expected competence, responsibility, and span of control across similar jobs within other local governments. This is partially due to the vast array of job titles and classifications across local governments. Most people seek to advance their careers within public service by making lateral and/or upward moves in the bureaucracy or, for example, by moving from a municipal to a county government. Understanding the path for growth within the area of government within which you will operate should be a key piece of knowledge a new technologist gains prior to joining a particular government organization, as it is easy to assume that being really good at your job will lead to rapid promotion. Often, it will not. There can be an element of waiting your turn with respect to gaining a promotion within public service, especially with roles that are represented by a union, and understanding these often-unwritten rules is something I highly advise all new public-sector technologists to do.

OLDER TECHNOLOGY

On day one of my own government service, I was given a laptop that doubled as my desktop when docked. Upon booting it up, I was expecting to see the latest and greatest version of Windows running on the device. Instead, I saw an operating system that I hadn't seen in quite some time, Windows 7, which at that time was seven years old. Not quite end of life for an operating system (O/S), but rapidly approaching that point. As I had been working in the Operating Systems division at Microsoft prior to my government career, I hadn't used Windows 7 since it shipped in 2009—we all immediately moved over to the initial builds of what would become Windows 8, and later Windows 10. Seeing that familiar Windows 7 logo appear when I pressed the power button on my new government-issued laptop made me realize that I wasn't "in Kansas anymore." That little jolt helped me understand that I was truly in a new domain where I shouldn't expect to have the latest and greatest version of whatever software I was used to having in the past. Later that first week, I discovered that I needed to submit timesheets into a rather antiquated system. I hadn't had to submit timesheets in about fifteen years, as salaried employees in the tech sector generally don't do this. There were times that first week when I wondered if instead of getting the bus to work, I had instead hopped into Marty McFly's DeLorean and been transported back to the early 2000s.

These and subsequent episodes where I encountered what I considered to be legacy technology reminded me of the famous book *Crossing the Chasm*, published in 1991.[1] In his book, Geoffrey A. Moore described how a chasm existed between early adopters of technology and the more conservative groups in the "Technology Adoption Life Cycle." Most governments fit squarely into the Late Majority or Laggards cohorts, and this can make sense when we realize that government is essentially a large enterprise, with complex mission-critical IT systems and as such tend to be quite risk averse.

However, with the advent of cloud computing, O/S as a Service, widespread adoption of open-source software, and Software as a Service (SaaS), there is room to speed up this technology adoption lifecycle within local government. One of your main challenges as a public-sector technologist will be to partner with key stakeholders within your organization to push the organization forward in this regard. Begin with the IT strategic plan, if one exists, and understand the long-term vision, timelines, and budget requests required to achieve these new technology implementation goals. Then look for ways where you may be able to influence the direction that your organization plans to take. Waiting three to five years for a major software implementation to happen is not going to work for most technologists, who are eager to drive progress, so seek out intermediate steps that will unblock progress while waiting for those longer-term capital investments to occur. Open-source solutions can be a great short- to medium-term solution in most cases, and could lead to great conversations about the problems that could be solved without having to always default to large IT deployments with multiyear contracts and an army of consultants required to complete the implementation.

SOME NOT-SO-OBVIOUS THINGS

One of the most interesting, sometimes frustrating, and hopefully rewarding, aspects of any new job is running into those situations that appear completely obvious to everyone else around you, whereas you may be wondering what the hell just happened. One of the most common soft skills that is required in the tech sector is "dealing with ambiguity," and if that is a skill you have in abundance, then public service may be just the place for you! Some of the experiences and insights I outline here may or may not be scenarios that you will encounter in your own public service, but hopefully they will provide you, the reader, with some idea what to expect as you navigate your own career in public service. I would encourage you to pay particular attention to these kinds of scenarios as you encounter them over time, as apart from providing the most useful organizational learning you'll take away, these scenarios often lead to some of the most interesting opportunities to have real impact. Understanding the various quirks and inconsistencies of your organization can provide you with a gap to push through an initiative or save you some time from chasing dead ends.

LEVELS OF COMPLEXITY IN DECISION-MAKING

One of the biggest learnings I had while in government, which I have referred to several times in this book and in other writings, is how complex the decision-making processes are there. By this I mean that the decisions themselves can require an enormous level of thinking, internal discussion, public consultation, and forecasting before committing to a particular course of action. Why is this the case in the public sector?

One major reason is due to risk tolerance—government simply doesn't have the same level of risk tolerance as the tech sector does. For example, online services frequently release updated features to sections of their user base, with some of those customers seeing one version of the feature and another group of customers seeing a different version of the same feature or experience. These so-called "A/B tests" allow companies like Facebook, Twitter, and Amazon to figure out which version of that feature their customers prefer and then ship that version to the entire customer base. Trying to replicate A/B testing scenarios with government services is not trivial, as any disruption to vital public services can have devastating consequences for the more vulnerable sections of our society. Tweaking a feature on Instagram or LinkedIn doesn't carry nearly the same level of risk. Thankfully, this is beginning to change as government gets better at experimenting with new technologies and policies in short time horizons and using their findings and data to influence their longer-term policy decisions—for example, some cities have been experimenting with different approaches regarding new mobility solutions, such as electric scooters and bikes, running localized trials with strict conditions and reviewing the outcomes before deciding on their longer-term approaches.

Another explanation lies in the fact that the decisions government needs to make are often multidimensional problems, requiring multifactor solutions. A good example of such a problem is the issue of people experiencing homelessness in many of our cities. Local governments are beginning to realize that they cannot solve these incredibly complex issues independently. Regional efforts to address homelessness are now starting to take shape, such as the establishment of a new Regional Homelessness Authority in the Seattle metro area.[2] Understanding every dimension of the problem and clearly understanding the impact to every stakeholder in that scenario is a must in government. Taking shortcuts is not an option. This is especially the case in local government, where the impacts of decisions made at the local level are often visible much more quickly than at other levels of government. Believe you me, you will hear about those decisions quickly and loudly if they are resulting in negative outcomes for one or more sections of the community. Even problems that on the face of it seem fairly straightforward can become fiendishly difficult to solve when all of the organizational dimensions and political and socioeconomic factors are added to the mix. How to meet these challenges head on will often require taking some of the following steps:

- *Constituent feedback* – Depending on the service you will be responsible for providing, where possible, seek feedback and comment from the public *before* you deploy a service into the public domain. This is not as easy as it sounds and will often require in-person meetings at the community level that can often lead to robust debates and tough feedback being shared. Engage with your fellow government staffers who have experience in running these kinds of events to avoid potential problems and ensure these meetings run smoothly. Online feedback and comment is becoming more common and may be sufficient depending on the kind of initiative being undertaken.

- *Politics, politics, politics* – View everything through this lens. We will discuss politics in more detail in Chapter 9, but understanding the politics surrounding your area of expertise will help prevent you from getting into some hot water with some vocal sections of the community that you may have overlooked, or your political masters in your government, or both.

- *Oversight requirements* – Some initiatives will have direct or indirect council/legislative oversight. Ensure you understand which committees and elected representatives have oversight authority over the programs/funding you are responsible for, what level of oversight is required, and whether building relationships with their staff could help with ensuring a smooth review process when it is required. It is important to understand if and when to engage regarding oversight requirements and factor that into your overall project planning schedules.

As technologists, mastering these kinds of complexities will require time and patience. You will encounter many situations where an obvious engineering solution will only play one small part in the overall solution, whereas in the tech sector the opposite is often the case. Practicing humility and listening closely to all stakeholders, internal and external, will more often than not result in tremendous learning opportunities for you and better outcomes for the government and the public.

BARRIERS TO INNOVATION

Having discussed the challenges of creating a new culture of innovation in local government in some detail in Chapter 5, it is worth calling out one key element of that equation that may not be immediately obvious upon entering public service and how that element can affect the ability of technologists to be successful in local government—and that is the barriers to innovation that exist within the organization. The ideal of innovation within government is probably one of the most discussed subjects on government blogs, news sites, conferences, and podcasts, and yet at times it can seem as though we have barely moved the needle. As public-sector technologists, you have a wonderful opportunity to help more governments move beyond the words and aspirations and make the development of a culture of innovation a real and lasting achievement.

Some of these barriers assume subtle forms that can be initially hard to detect, but could slow down your momentum if you're not careful. For technologists coming from organizations that pride themselves on their disruptive and innovative cultures, hitting up against a culture that in some ways is the exact opposite can be quite jarring and may require some time to adjust to. Here are some of the ways that these barriers may manifest themselves, along with some suggestions for how to approach going over, under, around, or through these barriers and create some initial successes that push the organization forward.

Manage up. As we discussed earlier in the book, a true innovative culture flows from the top down. If possible, try to gain an understanding of the views of the executive leadership team when it comes to technological innovation. Look at their actions and not just their words. If you're involved in highly visible projects, ensure you have the support of your executives and get them to do more than simply speak words of support in public. Having them drive expectations around how the entire organization thinks about innovation is a good place to start. For example, think of ways where executive orders could be a useful tool to enforce new innovative policies, without adding undue burdens onto existing staff. Having senior leaders lead by example is a powerful motivator.

A lack of talented technologists serving within government is a barrier to innovation in itself. Have capacity building as one of your key objectives.

Related to those key objectives, strategic plans play a key role in articulating the vision for innovation efforts. Creating a set of principles that act as the "North Star" for others to follow can make pushing your innovation agenda easier with your team, key stakeholders, executives, and the public. One of the first deliverables in my time as open data manager was to create the first strategic plan for the program, and I was able to reference key elements of it on an ongoing basis with internal and external audiences, as well as establish metrics that we wished to be held accountable to.[3]

Most local governments work under the biennial budget cycle system. Long budget cycles can affect innovation, and two-year budget cycles can seem like an eon in terms of technological progress. Ensure your longer-term strategic aims are protected within those long-term budget projections, while also having enough buffer in the budget to take advantage of those short-term innovation opportunities that are sure to arise on a regular basis.

Government services are typically not set up for feedback loops, such as the Net Promoter Score (NPS), and therefore it can be hard to get feedback on how things are working. Moving more government services to digital/mobile scenarios would help with creating initial baselines of data, which can then inform the innovations that may be required to improve those experiences.

In-house innovation teams do exist within local government. The Bloomberg Philanthropies' What Works Cities programs fund many of the innovation teams within municipal governments, with the aim of having these teams get funded through the regular budget cycles once they have been established. Chief innovation officers are also an emerging class of technologist within local government, and while innovation should be a part of everyone's job, it is true that in organizations where there is a real cultural deficit, it makes sense to create a critical mass of expertise that can inspire and lead the rest of the organization to develop a broader innovative capacity.

If your role requires working across multiple departments, it is important to remember that each department can have a unique culture, including when it comes to thinking about things like innovation. A one-size-fits-all approach may not work in all cases. And remember, don't become your own barrier to innovation! By this I mean, don't overpromise and then underdeliver. If you overestimate the capacity of the organization to be innovative or to absorb change, then you run the risk of having some initiatives fail, causing lasting damage. Developing a culture of innovation where one didn't really exist is not something that can be achieved quickly. It will require patience, planning, and constant effort to reinforce those new values. But it can be done.

BUILDING A TEAM OF YOUR OWN

If your new role in government will involve hiring new staff and building a new team or retrofitting an existing team, there are a number of important things to be aware of when hiring staff into the public sector. When seeking to hire software engineers or data scientists or technologists who possess highly valuable and sought-after skills in the private sector, the reality is that you face an uphill battle. During my own public service, I needed to backfill a couple of positions in the Open Data team, one being a software engineer and one being a data warehousing role. In a city like Seattle, where there is a shortage of technical talent and hundreds of open technology roles at any moment in time, writing a job description and creating a hiring package that included *none* of the following was an interesting experience:

- No sign-on bonus.
- No annual cash bonus.
- No equity opportunities.
- A salary that is likely to be lower than what the tech sector would offer, with limited scope for increases.
- No 401(k) matching program (government has a defined pension scheme instead).
- Rigid office hours and conditions regarding working remotely.
- None of the perks that workers in the tech sector have become accustomed to.

- Oh, and you might need to join a union! And pay them monthly dues.

I used to joke that the only extra I could offer on top of salary and benefits was "the thanks of a grateful mayor." Of course, it's not all negative. Governments offer good benefits and the opportunity to avail oneself of a pension scheme that in the long term can be quite attractive to people who wish to serve for many years in the public sector. In municipal government, salaries tend to be fairly competitive for most technical roles. Limitations such as the ones I've outlined here are known issues within government, and I would expect to see more experimentation and movement to address some of these impediments to hiring, but this will take time.

In the end, I did manage to hire one engineer for the data warehousing role who had previous public-sector experience and was highly motivated by the mission of public service. The software engineering role was filled by someone already employed at the city of Seattle and who had been helping out our team. Both people were great additions to the team and had immediate impact. This was an important lesson for me—not to overlook the talent that already exists within your organization and to actively seek it out. It is easy to forget that there are already talented technologists working within local government, and many may be seeking the kind of growth opportunity that a role on your team might offer.

There are some other considerations when it comes to building a team of technologists within local government; some will be similar to hiring best practices in the private sector, but in any case it is useful to call them out:

- Be sure to include staff in your interview panels who can assess for diversity and culture fit.
- Before commencing a hiring process, ensure you understand all of the legal and policy requirements. These can vary quite widely from the private sector. Review the documentation, then sit down with the HR manager and have them walk you through

the process and what requirements are "must have" versus "nice to have." This will save you a lot of time and result in a smoother hiring process and a more positive experience for the candidates.

- Related to that, be sure to clearly understand the differentiation between "exempt" positions versus "represented" positions (i.e., those that require the employee to join a labor union).

- If you find yourself in the unfortunate position of having to terminate someone's employment within local government, then the earlier advice is doubly important and particularly when it comes to "represented" staff.

Finally, there is the issue of coaching staff in the public sector and how that might differ from the tech sector. The evidence presented here is anecdotal, sourced from my own experience and from speaking with other managers in other local governments regionally and nationally, and it is not encouraging. I was surprised and disappointed at the lack of a culture of management coaching within local government. A number of factors have led to this situation, some of which are related to how government in general thinks about management and leadership, which I discuss in the next section.

MANAGERS VERSUS SUPERVISORS

Before I joined the city of Seattle in 2016, I had been a people manager in some shape or form for over fifteen years. During that time, I had directly or indirectly been responsible for teams of people on three different continents (Europe, Asia, and North America), usually a mixture of full time employees (often referred to as 'FTE') and contract staff, with the occasional intern, and both in-house and offshore teams. I had managed teams as small as four people and as large as thirty-five. One of my last teams at Microsoft consisted of seven FTE, whose members originally hailed from France, South Korea, China, Thailand, Bulgaria, and the

United States, with myself being from Ireland. This was pretty typical of the teams within my division at that time, and I loved that kind of diversity. I had the privilege of managing amazing teams of people with fascinating background stories and a wide range of skillsets. Each required a unique managerial approach when figuring out how to motivate, coach, and inspire them. They, in turn, taught me a huge amount about how to be a better manager, and their hard work helped contribute to my own success. I remain in contact with many of those I managed, and I treasure those memories and their friendship. Because of these experiences, I can claim to know a little about people management and how to build a highly functioning team.

Upon entering local government, one major difference I immediately noticed was the lack of a comprehensive organizational framework that focuses on employee development. While there was a rudimentary annual review process within the IT department where I worked, its application was quite informal and seemed to be devoid of any cross-managerial review process—basically an employee's review rating was based solely on the input of their supervisor. Readers familiar with "review calibration meetings" in the tech sector will understand exactly what I am referring to. Another observation was that there appeared to be almost zero consequences for poor performance, and on the flip side, little incentive to go above and beyond. In Seattle, there was an award of extra vacation days for good performance, which was very welcome, but other local governments may not have similar rewards. I will admit I did find myself yearning for those big bonuses and stock awards at annual review time, but such is the life of a public servant. Thinking about this further, I began to realize that this lack of an organizational culture around performance was likely one of the main factors behind the perceived differences in output between government and the private/tech sector.

To be fair to the government in Seattle where I worked, they had been attempting to instigate some new processes to address these gaps, and I did have the opportunity to participate in one "360 review," which provided me with some helpful feedback. A pilot annual review process had been established in my department, but alas, these efforts were sporadic and lacked the consistency that I was used to in the tech sector. As someone who greatly values coaching and employee development, this lack of an employee development mentality puzzled me, and so I began to think about how this type of culture could initially be established and later endure. One difference that I had immediately spotted was that frontline managers of people were typically called "supervisors." I thought this choice of title was not fitting in an environment where people were supposed to be encouraged to do their best and to push for personal and professional development. Changing that one title to better reflect the expectations on both sides of the manager/direct report relationship could lead to an initial step in rethinking innovation in the local government workplace. I like to think of it as a government culture hack.

Government culture hack: One easy change governments can make to create a more innovative culture is to stop using the term "supervisor" when referring to people in management roles.

- *Why*: A supervisor is typically responsible for making sure a task gets completed, a process still functions, or that no harm comes to the subject (think babysitter or chaperone). That's it. There's no expectation of making improvements or unlocking innovation, including developing the people they manage.
- *How*: Instead, titles such as "lead" or "manager" suggest a more proactive managerial approach is expected. Based on my own experiences in local government, I believe that using titles other than "supervisor" allied with accountability measures (people management outcomes, staff development goals, promotion velocity, etc.) would lead to positive organizational culture change.
- *What*: Aside from managers/leads knowing they need to manage their people as well as their tasks, their staff would know that a key part of their manager's role is to help them grow their skills and careers, creating space for career-oriented conversations. And best of all, it's a relatively low-cost change to make.

Simple changes like these can have both immediate and lasting impact on how the organization thinks about itself, the roles we all play in building an innovative culture and how those various roles intersect, and create the space for valuable conversations to happen that help inculcate that culture into the organization.

COMMUNICATION

Privacy is a topic that we hear about on an almost daily basis these days, from issues related to how social media companies are sharing and selling our data in ways that make many of us uncomfortable, or how easy it is for communications we thought private to be easily shared with others. Similarly, in the private sector many corporate communications have ended up in the public record as a result of investigations or court cases. Our expectations of privacy when using online services and our various devices have diminished greatly in recent years. New government regulations to help address some of the most serious concerns are likely. Yet most people working in the private sector have a certain expectation of privacy when it comes to communications such as emails, text messages, and so on. Not so in the public sector.

In fact, as a public servant, you have no reasonable expectation of privacy when it comes to the work that you do. If you only understand one thing prior to beginning your career in the public sector, understand this concept. If you will have a public-facing role, this is even more important to grasp. I share this not to alarm you, but rather to ensure that you fully understand that everything you will do in your career in public service is essentially a public record, and as such could be requested by a member of the public or the press or other interested parties. There are some exceptions for sensitive issues, but these are few and far between, and in some cases these exceptions can end up being litigated. Better to assume that you're on the public record all the time. So, what does this mean in practice? Here are some key ways you can be effective in your job while adhering to the letter and spirit of the public records laws:

- It means that you need to be prudent about what you write about and share over email or other forms of official communication. The rule of thumb that I used was "how would I feel if what I am writing was made public?" If I had reservations or was simply unsure, I would seek clarification or, better yet, I would scrub the text and attempt to write a more measured version.

- You'll do a lot of business over the phone and in coffee meetings. Sometimes I would send an email to a colleague, only for them to call me back because they didn't want to share their information over email. Over time you will get a good sense for when to commit something to a memo or an email and when an initial in-person conversation makes more sense before sending that written communication.

- Anything you touch is basically a public record. For example, if you have a notebook where you take notes in a meeting, those notes could be requested in a public records request.

- Make sure you understand the data and documentation retention rules and schedules. Often these can be quite rigid, but depending on the scenario, there may be ways to archive critical information for easy access beyond any initial limits. For example, it is common to set a ninety-day retention policy for regular email you send and receive as a government employee. After ninety days, your email would automatically be archived, making it quite difficult to quickly access it after that time. There may be an option to mark some emails as exempt from this policy.

- Similarly, do not expect your local government to use Slack or Microsoft Teams or other such collaborative tools. This is partially due to communication retention policies, many of which require adjusting due to these new technologies. While some governments are beginning to experiment, typically they can only be used for engagements that don't require an official decision to be made. If you are using one of these tools and an "issue of substance" arises, one way to handle that is to move the conversation to an email thread.

- It is likely that you will have an official government smart phone to be used for official government business. This is because in the event of a public records request that ends up in litigation or as part of an official investigation, it might be required that the actual device containing certain communications also be handed over. While I was confident that I would never find myself entangled in any such scenario, I made sure to create that firewall between my personal communications and my official government communications. Trust me, it's worth the pain to carry two phones around.

Don't let these considerations put you off entering into government. Like most processes in government, it sounds more onerous than it actually is. Once you establish some basic personal rules and adhere to the policies, you'll soon get used to these extra requirements and considerations, and upon reentering the private sector, these will be good rules and practices to bring with you. In the unlikely event that you do become part of a public records request, don't panic. Local governments have well-established practices for handling these requests, and my advice is to work with your public records coordinator and discuss the request, as perhaps there are other ways for the request to be satisfied without having to share vast tranches of emails or documents.

Similarly, my insights on the kinds of communication styles you will likely encounter are not meant to discourage the sharing of information that may be of interest to the public. In fact, the opposite is true. The tech sector is notorious for the vast amounts of email and messaging communications that are generated daily—I would typically have to field several hundred emails a day in my tech-sector career. This is partially due to the culture and partially due to the fact that often remote teams are collaborating on the same project. In local government, communication is localized often to the building you're physically located in, or perhaps another building across the street. The preference for short, in-person chats or quick phone calls within government can actually be more efficient and prevent long email threads from escalating and unnecessarily dragging many more, increasingly senior, people into the bureaucratic quagmire. Over time, you'll develop a sense for when to write and when to talk. If you have an opinion on an issue that you feel others need to hear, then don't let the public records element of the equation dissuade you from sharing those—even if something were to be made public, if you are doing the right thing, you will have no issues with defending your stance in public. And always remember, the public has a right to know what we as public servants are doing on their behalf using their money. Public records laws are vital to a transparent and open government operating on behalf of its citizens. Remember, it's "government of the people, by the people, for the people."

LEARN FROM OTHERS

The examples of key differences I have shared are based upon my own experiences and observations. Fortunately, other resources are available online that delve into these comparisons, and many stories are shared by people who have made similar journeys, albeit along different career paths.

OTHER LOCAL GOVERNMENT STORIES

To hear the stories of others who made the move into local government, for example, a series of interviews called "Finding Local Government" is available on the Engaging Local Government Leaders (ELGL) website.[4] Although a few years old, some of these personal stories may resonate with readers. Their podcast, which is referenced in Chapter 8, is also highly recommended as a source of interviews and insights into how people made their way into local government and the myriad differences they encountered between the private and public sectors.

FROM THE PRIVATE SECTOR TO THE NONPROFIT SECTOR

As it happens, these differences between the private and public sectors are also largely applicable to the nonprofit sector. This is a useful realization, as the private sector often combines local government and nonprofits when developing "social impact" initiatives. Many technologists volunteer within the nonprofit sector, and some go on to work there or found their own nonprofit organization at some point in their career. If you find yourself being one such technologist in the future, then many of the same key insights in this chapter will also be appliable in the nonprofit sector. There are, however, some subtle differences. In a fantastic three-part series of blog posts on this very topic titled "From IT to Public Health," Jenny Richards outlines the key lessons she learned in her career transitions from the private sector into the public health (nonprofit) sector.[5] Part 1 deals with the transition process, part 2 with the lessons learned, and part 3 with her recommendations. Jenny was an amazing collaborator while I served in local government and someone who has played a huge role in the publication of this book and whose advice I would urge readers to take on board if you are indeed interested in serving as a technologist in the nonprofit sector.

OPPORTUNITY COSTS

Whereas people in the private sector tend to focus on the possibly negative financial implications of making such a move into the public sector, it is important to point out that there are other positive considerations to bear in mind. Some of these are financial; others are more experiential, such as the exposure to public speaking and personal development opportunities that can be less accessible via the private sector. For example, part of my role involved public speaking, such as at national conferences or giving guest lectures in local colleges and universities. I also got to partner with nonprofits and universities on specific projects and/or developing research and regularly communicate and share knowledge with other governments at the local, state, and federal levels. As a result, my professional network grew considerably. The new skills and experiences developed in the public sector can be invaluable should one decide to move back into the private sector at a later stage.

A good way to think about these differences between the sectors is in terms of opportunity costs. By having a long career in public service, you will gain the benefit of a middle-class salary that remains pretty constant over time, more job security, and a generous pension upon retirement, whereas the opportunity cost is that you forego the opportunity to work in a more risk-adverse environment with the potential for more financial upside via stocks and equity deals. Similarly, you can view work–life balance, other quality-of-life decisions, and organizational missions through this prism. Simply boiling down government service into binary choices such "government = less money" can prevent potential public-interest technologists from including public service as a realistic option in their career decision-making process. Be sure to step back and look at the bigger picture when considering public service, and don't let the naysayers drown out the many positives.

THE LANGUAGE OF PUBLIC SERVICE

Finally, another key difference you'll encounter in the public sector is the language and mind-set of public service. The difference can be profound. The first such occasion where I realized that I was dealing with an entirely new paradigm was during my very first meeting with my new boss. It was my first day, and he had just given me a tour of the useful places to know about and how to get there, and especially where the best coffee was (this is vital in Seattle). Immediately afterwards, we had a quick meeting in his office where he began to set out some expectations for the first few weeks and months of my tenure as open data manager. Toward the end of our conversation, it became clear to me that we were speaking two different dialects of the same language, much like how I speak two different dialects of the English language—what I like to refer to as "Americaneze" and "the Queen's English." In this particular meeting, I was speaking the "organization focused on the bottom line and shareholder value" dialect, whereas he was speaking the "organization focused solely on providing services to the public" dialect. As I left his office, I felt as if my head had been turned 180 degrees. It was at that moment that I knew I had much learning to do, that I needed to talk to as many people as possible, and to be patient while I adjusted to this new world.

I also realized that while my previous career experiences to that point provided me with some credibility, I needed to be humble and not be the person who continually brought up how great it was in the private sector—and for the most part I was successful with that (although I am sure some of my former colleagues would disagree!). There were times when those experiences were called upon or were useful as a reference point, but for the most part I forced myself to listen and learn from those other public service professionals who had been doing the work far longer than I had. Watching and listening allowed me to realize the sheer scale and complexity of the work that local government does, often invisibly and most certainly underappreciated. In some ways, that very first meeting I had laid some of the groundwork for what would eventually become the book that you are now reading. In time I hope you will also learn to understand and speak this dialect, as it will allow you to ask what you can do for your government in new and exciting ways.

CHAPTER 6: KEY TAKEAWAYS

- In this chapter, we explore some of the main differences that technologists may encounter between the private and public sectors and some suggestions for how to navigate those situations in local government.

- The somewhat well-known things—such as hiring processes, applying and interviewing for government jobs, compensation and benefits, how career paths differ from the private sector, and encountering older technology.

- And some not-so-obvious things—like the levels of complexity in decision-making, potential barriers to innovation, how to build a technical team, managers versus supervisors, and important differences in communication.

- Learn from others—listen to the stories of other technologists who have made the transition to local government and from the private sector into the nonprofit sector.

- Opportunity costs: Don't just factor in the possible negative differences in compensation when thinking about serving in local government. There are positive opportunity costs that you should also consider, such as career growth opportunities.

- The language of public service—how understanding the subtle differences in the language used in the public sector can help technologists integrate more quickly and have a more immediate impact with their work.

NOTES

1 Geoffrey A. Moore, *Crossing the Chasm*, 3rd ed. (New York: Harper Collins, 2014).

2 "Regional Homelessness Authority—Home," King County Regional Homelessness Authority, accessed January 6, 2020, https://regionalhomelesssystem.org.

3   "2018 Open Data Plan," City of Seattle, accessed November 22, 2019, http://www.seattle.gov/Documents/Departments/Tech/OpenData/City_of_Seattle_2018_Open_Data_Plan.pdf.

4   "Finding Local Government," ELGL, accessed January 16, 2020, https://elgl.org/?s=finding+local+government.

5   "From IT to Public Health: Part 1 (Transition)," Jenny Richards, last updated October 1, 2015, http://www.jnnyrchrds.com/journal/2015/9/23/public-health-transition-part-1.

7

HOW TO GET STARTED

So far in this book we have discussed *why* government needs more technologists and *what* challenges and opportunities await there. Hopefully you are now inspired to strongly consider working in local government. If so, then the next obvious question is, *how*?

The *how* question, in all its forms, is actually one of the most frequent questions I get about my own journey into local government. How did I know this was something that I wanted to do? What resources did I use to learn more about local government? Whom did I talk with? How did I find out about volunteering opportunities? And so on. The truth is, it all happened organically and over a period of several years. It is also true that I was somewhat deliberate in my approach, especially when I had a clearer idea of which aspect of local government I was specifically interested in. After I had begun my local government career, I became aware of yet more resources and programs and literature that would have been beneficial to me while I was in the evaluation phase. In this chapter, I will attempt to stitch together the knowledge I gained from my own journey into local government into a cohesive and practical guide for aspiring public-sector technologists.

BUT FIRST, UNDERSTAND YOUR "WHY"

Before getting into the *how* discussion, it's important to make sure you fully understand your own reasons for wanting to serve in state and local government. In other words, are you truly clear about your own *why*? I get the *why* question far less often than the *how* question. I have outlined earlier in the book lots of reasons why state and local government is so important, but understanding your own reasons for why you would want to serve in local government can be driven by very different motivations. Being able to clearly articulate your *why* will allow you to make better decisions as you navigate your own journey into public service, using my own journey as how this can be the case.

MY JOURNEY

It was on a cold January night in 2014, sitting in the library at the University of Washington Bothell, that I read a paper commissioned by the Ford Foundation that would alter the course of my life. It was titled "A Future of Failure? The Flow of Technology Talent into Government and Society,"[1] and it was the first time that I had read a description of the journey I was attempting to make and to have a framework and language to describe what I was trying to accomplish. That paper led me down many more paths of research, and ultimately led me to the world of open government and open data, which I have been researching and working in ever since. How I came to be sitting in the library that night is a key part of my journey. In my late thirties, and at that time about fifteen or so years into my Microsoft career, I began to realize I was no longer satisfied in my job and began to seriously think about my "Career 2.0," what that might look like, and how to move into a new role that would feel more fulfilling. Changes in my personal circumstances in 2013 meant that I had more free time, and I began to seriously think about getting a second master's degree to cross-train for a new discipline. But in what?

After a lot of reading, thinking, and talking with some close advisors, I thought that policy might be a good fit, and specifically technology policy. Why? I had been thinking a lot about the pace of change being driven by rapid advances in technology (some of which I was privy to as part of my work at Microsoft) and my sense that our laws and policies were struggling badly to keep up. I sensed there was a niche for people who could help bridge the worlds of technology and policy and that those needs would only grow in time. Added to that was my love of reading widely on many topics, researching, writing, and thinking about long-term strategic issues, and so I felt I was on a good path. Once I had settled on technology policy as a possible viable future career path, I found a program that allowed me to pursue this goal while at the same time balancing working full time and being a parent.

I decided to visit Washington, DC, for the first time that spring of 2013, and I spent three days wandering around the monuments, museums, and other historic sights seeking inspiration and affirmation of my career change goal. I fell in love with DC, and that visit made me realize that I craved a career that would allow me to do work more closely associated with technology policy issues in DC and perhaps even work there someday. I was hooked.

Starting out in this new program in the fall of 2013, while I had a vague sense of wanting to focus on technology policy, I really had no idea where it would ultimately take me, and that was part of the attraction. "Serendipity" quickly became my favorite word and my favorite tactic, and four months into the program I had my epiphany on that January night. I focused on open data for the remainder of my studies, and upon graduation began the process of getting involved in the local open data community and researching open data and policy job opportunities. In the meantime, I was very fortunate to be allowed to switch my focus at Microsoft to run a data insights team that taught me vast amounts about big data, how to have a lot of impact within an organization by helping inculcate a more data-driven culture, and have a lot of fun along the way. All the while I was seeking out opportunities to move into a new role that was more policy focused, and eventually I was fortunate to be selected as the new open data manager at the city of Seattle, leaving Microsoft after eighteen years of service in early September 2016.

THEN, UNDERSTAND YOUR "WHAT"

Typically, people will have a basic understanding of the *why* when wanting to make a major career transition, but it is figuring out the *what* that is perhaps a much tougher step. Long before I read that Ford Foundation article that would transform my own journey and help myself in answering this *what* question, I began writing in a journal on a regular basis to help with framing my thoughts. This allowed me to identify patterns and drill into certain ideas over time. I used mind-mapping techniques to help me visualize my current working environment and possible future working environments and how they might intersect. I identified what activities I enjoyed doing in my spare time and whether I could integrate those into my future work—for me, those were things like reading, researching, and writing. I identified the activities I liked in my current job that I hoped to integrate and expand within a new role, which helped me narrow my focus onto specific roles. Once I had found a role or area that was intriguing to me, I went to talk with people who operated in that space—what I discovered is that people are often very happy to be approached for advice, and this can be invaluable from a networking perspective. These things and more helped me identify my *what*.

WHETHER TO CHANGE YOUR DISCIPLINE OR DOMAIN

An important part of the *what* decision-making process is the decision whether to change the type of job you do or the environment within which you do your current job. This is a really important question to answer, and especially when it comes to moving from the private to the public sector. Early on in my career transition process, I got fantastic advice around changing either my "domain" or my "discipline" but not both at the same time. In my case, "domain" = private sector and "discipline" = running an engineering team (focused on data). By changing domains (from private sector to public sector) but not moving to a new discipline, I was able to mostly focus on adapting to the change in domain. Once I had time to figure out my new operating environment, I was then able to focus on the discipline change (i.e., for me, that would mean moving further into the technology and data policy space and away from managing software engineering teams). This is something I would urge everyone to think about when making any kind of career transition, but especially when moving from the private to the public, or vice versa.

LASTLY, THE "HOW"

Once you have your *why* and *what* figured out, we can properly begin to think about those *how* questions. While I share some of the main insights I gained during my own journey from the private to the public sector, not everyone who reads this book will be looking to transition into a public-sector role after a career similar to my own. Perhaps some readers will seek to join the public service straight out of college, some will be in the early stages of their career in the private sector, and some readers may have already served in government. Regardless of your own journey into government, and perhaps back into the private sector afterwards, your journey will be unique. Aside from the author's insights and personal anecdotes, there are a number of practical steps that anyone who is seriously considering a career in local government can take as part of their own decision-making process. While we examine some of these topics in detail here, readers can also keep up to date with useful local government online resources at the website accompanying this book: https://askwhatyoucando.com.

EDUCATION

One common way that people approach building a career in public service is to obtain new qualifications in areas typically related to government work. Attending college or taking online courses are usually the first things that spring to mind; however, there are many other options and useful resources that readers can avail themselves of (often for free!) that can be hugely beneficial.

FORMAL COLLEGE EDUCATION

When we think about formal college qualifications related to government, often full-time undergraduate degrees that are dedicated to political work, such as political science, or postgraduate degrees such as a master's in public administration (MPA) immediately spring to mind. In my own case, I obtained a master of arts in policy studies degree via a part-time program while working full time. At the time that I started this program, I had a general direction in mind, which was to explore the technology policy, and it was during my studies that I was able to narrow my focus upon issues related to open data. If this is an option that would be appealing to you and you have the time and resources to take this on, then looking for programs available for working professionals is a good place to start—usually at your local university or community college. These programs are designed for working adults and generally not able to attend class during regular office hours. Sometimes classes are held on the weekend; other times they may require attendance a couple of evenings a week. If you are looking at a graduate degree option, then the time commitment will range from one to two years, depending on the program. And remember, regardless of the full-time or part-time status of the program, the class time is just one aspect of the time and energy commitment. There will be considerable amounts of reading required for class, as well as completing assignments, so be sure to factor that into your planning.

PROFESSIONAL CERTIFICATIONS

If you don't want to commit to a full degree or graduate degree program and instead want to supplement your existing technical qualifications with an extra public-sector-oriented qualification, then you will likely have several options. One common method is to obtain a certificate in your area of interest, such as privacy or ethics. These courses can range in length from several weeks to several months, and are also usually offered at times suitable for working professionals, and usually in the same institutions where the full degree options are available. These intermediate courses can be a great way to test out your interest in and aptitude for the kind of work you may be interested in pursuing in local government. They can also provide excellent opportunities to meet with government officials who may be part of the teaching staff for those courses and become aware of interesting opportunities in that space.

One of the most common ways that technology professionals, and indeed non-technologists, gain the credentials and know-how for specific areas of policy are through professional certifications. One of the most common qualifications that I noticed during my time in government was the "Certified Information Privacy Professional" qualification. Other common certifications included those related to data governance, IT project management, and procurement. These qualifications are typically offered via nonprofit organizations that specialize in these areas, with a great example being the Internet Association of Privacy Professionals (IAPP),[2] or via professional associations within government itself.[3] Depending on what stage you are at, there are many options for you to consider if you think that having an extra qualification would prove useful in a current or future public-sector career.

Of course, there is no requirement to seek an extra qualification in order to work within government. For most technologists, their existing professional experiences and qualifications should prove more than sufficient in order to secure a role within government. Where an extra qualification may prove useful, however, is when your work as a technologist intersects with an area of policy or regulation that you may not be already familiar with. As an added bonus, these extra qualifications often prove to be highly valued in the private sector also.

BOOKS

Before we delve into the more interactive elements of learning that readers can avail themselves of, it would be remiss of the author not to strongly encourage those of you interested in learning more about government to read yet more books on the subject. Many interesting books about government are available, some of which I use as sources for this book and have referenced within some chapters, and these are books that I highly recommend readers also check out. In the case of my own journey into the public sector, I read quite a few books related to government, both academic and more general, and found them to be very helpful in learning about the frameworks with which to view how government operates, as well as providing valuable context on how government functions as a massive system. If you are interested in understanding government at a macro level, I highly encourage readers to seek out relevant books, either online or at a local public or college library (where there are often some hidden gems in stock). A general search query on Amazon should be sufficient to get your search started, and some of the online resources listed later will also contain pointers to recent books that could be of interest.

Here are some book genres, with examples, that I found useful both during my own career transition research process while working in government and at the time of writing as I think about my future career progression both inside and outside of government. It is worth noting that I didn't choose books where I knew I would agree with the arguments or conclusions being made by the authors; rather, I wanted to get as many viewpoints as possible on subjects and ideas that I was interested in and to challenge my own thinking. Reading these books as part of a book club or having the ability to debate their findings with friends and colleagues can also be a great way to develop your knowledge of these complex subjects and prepare yourself for the kinds of debates that can happen as part of government service.

Social science:

- *Winners Take All: The Elite Charade of Changing the World* (Anand Giridharadas)
- *Weapons of Math Destruction* (Cathy O'Neil)
- *Hillbilly Elegy: A Memoir of a Family and Culture in Crisis* (J. D. Vance)

Technology policy:

- *The Fixer: My Adventures Saving Startups from Death by Politics* (Bradley Tusk)
- *Tools and Weapons: The Promise and the Peril of the Digital Age* (Brad Smith, Carol Ann Brown)
- *Habeas Data: Privacy vs. the Rise of Surveillance Tech* (Cyrus Farivar)

Data science:

- *The Case for the Chief Data Officer* (Peter Aiken, Michael Gorman)
- *Factfulness: Ten Reasons We're Wrong About the World—and Why Things Are Better Than You Think* (Hans Rosling)
- *Small Data: The Tiny Clues That Uncover Huge Trends* (Martin Lindstrom)

Computing:

- *Technology-as-a-Service Playbook* (Thomas Lah and J. B. Wood)
- *How the Internet Happened: From Netscape to the iPhone* (Brian McCullough)

- *A Shortcut Through Time: The Path to the Quantum Computer* (George Johnson)

Biographies of government leaders:

- *The Power Broker* (Robert Caro)
- *The Education of an Idealist: A Memoir* (Samantha Power)
- *A Thousand Days: John F. Kennedy in the White House* (Arthur M. Schlesinger Jr.)

Books on government:

- *A New City O/S* (Stephen Goldsmith and Neil Kleiman)
- *The Fifth Risk* (Michael Lewis)
- *Innovative State: How New Technologies Can Transform Government* (Aneesh Chopra)

One of the most useful, and often overlooked, aspects of reading books related to government is that they will usually contain a large number of citations to other books, research papers, and useful resources related to the topic of government. In fact, some of the sources referenced and cited in this book were sources I originally discovered from reading some of the books listed here.

ONLINE LEARNING RESOURCES

As with any industry vertical, a huge number of online resources are available for those who wish to learn more about that sector and the types of opportunities that may be available. As with all online research efforts, there are many wonderful rabbit holes to go down, and the worlds of state and local government are no exception. This section of the book attempts to help curate some of that vast array of resources, and while it isn't meant to be an exhaustive list, it should provide the reader with a great jumping-off point for their own research. Readers will find an updated list of resources at www.askwhatyoucando.com.

ONLINE TRAINING WEBSITES

Online training services such as those provided by LinkedIn provide excellent online training opportunities. While at first glance it can seem that these services are not really tailored specifically for the public sector, there are many instances where relevant courseware can be located if you use the right search queries. For example, searching for generic terms like "smart cities" or "governance and society" will lead to some talks and classes that should provide a good grounding in those topics, as well as pointers to related resources. As government needs more technologists at all levels and in all areas of expertise, course related to software development, IT services, cloud computing, data science, DevOps, etc., will be just as relevant for the work you will need to do in government as in the private sector.

MASSIVE OPEN ONLINE COURSES

Another incredible source of online learning comes from massive open online courses (sometimes referred to MOOCs, pronounced "moouks"). These are university-level programs developed by some of the top universities in the world that are made available to anyone who wishes to enroll online. These courses can provide an easy way to explore topics of interest before committing to a longer-term program either online (via a MOOC or directly with another online college) or by attending a traditional college campus. Aside from the ability to take full online degree programs from prestigious universities, these services are increasingly providing opportunities to get other types of certifications in certain topics, often for a very reasonable fee, and their qualifications are increasingly being recognized within the private sector. Some of the most popular MOOCs include Coursera (coursera.org) and edX (edx.org).

PODCASTS

There is a tremendous wealth of knowledge about government available for free via podcasts. This medium is an incredibly effective way to learn about government at all levels and the many private-sector, research, and philanthropic efforts that intersect with government. Podcasts are available about federal, state, and local government levels. Personally speaking, I have discovered some of the most interesting and insightful things about government through the many government-related podcasts I subscribe to, as well as getting context on many government initiatives that I learned about elsewhere online from listening to interviews with the people driving those initiatives. While there are several excellent podcasts solely dedicated to local government, many other podcasts are available that provide great insights into the intersection of government and technology, data, ethics, and so on. Following is a list of some of the podcasts about U.S. government that I have personally found to be incredibly valuable. Note that some of these podcasts may not remain active over time, but their archives still provide tremendous value.

State and local government:

- GovLove
- Go Public
- GovConnect
- StateScoop Radio

Federal government:

- Fedheads
- Gov Actually

- Government Digital Service podcast
- The Business of Government Radio Hour (IBM)

Technology policy:

- Firewall
- Recode Decode
- Intersections (Brookings Institute)
- HBR PolicyCast
- Code & Conduit (Bloomberg Law)

Data science in government:

- GovEx
- Follow the Data (Bloomberg Philanthropies)
- Numbers Geek (Geekwire with Steve Ballmer)
- The PolicyViz Podcast
- AWS Public Sector podcast (Amazon)
- Gov Pod (Microsoft)

As the world of podcasting is constantly in flux, an updated list of useful podcasts can be found on the accompanying website for this book: www.askwhatyoucando.com.

SOCIAL MEDIA

Another great way to learn about government programs, resources, initiatives, conferences, podcasts, articles, research, etc., is via Twitter. When I first joined government, I was surprised by just how much traffic was generated by governments and affiliated organizations on Twitter. It is far and away the most powerful platform for driving awareness of government-related activities. As a result, it is also a fabulous way for you to curate your own knowledge of all things government and keeping up-to-date on a daily basis. I like to think of Twitter as a supercharged RSS feed. It is also a great place to start developing your own personal branding as a public-interest technologist—for example if you decide to start writing your own blog posts, posting about your articles on Twitter can help amplify their reach and impact. If you are looking to follow some useful Twitter accounts that are related to government, my advice is to begin with a few organizations or interests (i.e., a local government, a state government agency, a think tank, a philanthropic organization, school of government, etc.) and then see who they follow and who follows them. Before long, your Twitter feed will have organically grown into a valuable source of real-time data and insights right at your fingertips.

WEBSITES AND BLOGS

Several quality news organizations are dedicated to providing insights to the public about the work that government is doing on their behalf. These news organizations do their own reporting, as well as curate news and articles from other online sources. In addition, there are websites from universities and philanthropic organizations engaged in work to improve government that also provide curated news and original content. These websites review what is happening across all levels of government throughout the United States, as well as providing awareness of interesting government-improvement programs elsewhere in the world. Some blogs also play a role in providing useful original content, often taking a contrarian view, which can be useful when we think through our ideas about how to improve government. While some of these websites also have accompanying Twitter feeds, for those readers who prefer to consume their news on a larger screen, I would suggest using an RSS reader app to provide a quick and easy way to scan through the daily news updates, or for most websites there is an option to sign up for a daily email summary, which I also found to be useful. Following are some examples of websites

I believe readers will find useful and provide further reading on specific topics of interest.

Useful websites:

- fedscoop.com
- statescoop.com
- govloop.com
- datasmart.ash.harvard.edu (Data-smart City Solutions, Harvard Kennedy School)
- governing.com
- citylab.com
- nextgov.com
- sunlightfoundation.com

Another useful news source about government can come from within government itself. It is not uncommon for a federal or state government agency or city government department to run their own blog that provides updates and news to the public, which can later be picked up by the national government news websites. For example, the city of Seattle runs a blog out of their IT department called "TechTalk" (techtalk.seattle.gov), which provides weekly updates about how the city is pushing forward its government improvement agenda through technology. Similarly, local governments with innovation teams are also likely to have accompanying blogs highlighting major achievements in improving how local government uses data to improve operations and increase their evidence-based decision-making. Again, my alma mater at the city of Seattle provides us with a good example of such a resource via their blog (innovation-performance. seattle.gov). These hyper-local news resources can provide aspiring public-interest technologists with valuable insights into the work currently being undertaken by their local government and ideas for opportunities to get involved. Be sure to check out what resources your local government provides that you may not previously have been aware of.

University Programs Focused on Improving Government

Leading universities in the United States with schools of government often have programs dedicated to improving government at all levels. These organizations and initiatives are usually connected to coordinated efforts between government and philanthropic organizations. These programs provide cutting-edge research and guidance for government, and their websites contain a wealth of information and ideas for future research. Some also provide curated news updates on happenings within their spheres of influence and provide newsletters that anyone can sign up for. These organizations sometimes hold conferences related to their work, which can be invaluable to government staffers, as well as academics and advocates for good government. Some of my most valuable learning as a public servant, and useful connections, came as a result of engaging with some of these organizations. Some great examples include:

- GovEx (Johns Hopkins University)
- Ash Center for Democratic Governance and Innovation (Harvard Kennedy School)
- Tech Policy Lab (University of Washington)
- Cascadia Urban Analytics Cooperative (University of Washington and University of British Columbia)
- Center for Technology in Government (University at Albany)

Philanthropic Organizations

The funding behind many of the programs I reference in the previous section comes from some major philanthropic organizations. The largest example of this type of engagement is the work being driven by the Bloomberg Philanthropies' Government Innovation team, via two programs known as What Works Cities and Results for America. These programs fund and oversee the impact of initiatives that help government build their technical and data science capacities, typically through the establishment and funding of innovation teams in municipal governments throughout the United States. Bloomberg Philanthropies have pumped hundreds of millions of dollars into these efforts and share the outcomes and progress via their website. To my knowledge, this is the largest such effort by far in the United States, and most major municipal governments have had some involvement with these programs to date. Similarly, The Volcker Alliance is a philanthropic effort whose mission is to "advance effective management of government to achieve results that matter to citizens." Founded in 2013 by former Federal Reserve Board Chairman Paul A. Volcker, this group advances their work through a series of partnerships with academic, business, governmental, and public-interest organizations. These two philanthropic organizations were established by leaders with significant experience at the highest levels of government and who have firsthand knowledge of the scale of the problems facing government, as well as insights into the size of the opportunities that exist to improve how it functions.

Some major technology companies also contribute toward these efforts to improvement government or the public sector in general. It is important to remember that the public sector doesn't just include government; it also includes other sectors, such as nonprofit organizations, and public education organizations such as schools, colleges, and libraries. Several large technology companies have established programs via their own philanthropy efforts that typically focus on providing software, training, staff volunteer time, and grants to these kinds of public-sector organizations. Good examples of this type of philanthropic outreach are the nonprofit programs funded by Microsoft Philanthropies[4] and the Tableau Foundation, which aims to donate $100 million in software, training, and financial support by 2025.[5]

These and similar programs provide good insights into the types of issues that external organizations have identified as being necessary to address within government itself and are worthy of their support. As such, they can provide the reader with a good sense for how their own skillsets in technology, data science, software engineering, design, operations, and customer experience can be brought to bear within government itself.

"SINGLE-ISSUE" ONLINE RESOURCES

If the idea of thinking about government in its entirety and how you might play a role in helping shape its future seems a little daunting, and perhaps overwhelming, then an approach that might be more beneficial would be to think about government service through the lens of an issue that you are passionate about. For example, if you are someone who is passionate about issues related to race and social justice, researching what programs your local government has in place to develop that agenda and what organizations they partner with can be an excellent place to start educating yourself about what that work looks like in practice. Similarly, identifying organizations that seek to effect change or produce positive social impact on a regional or national scale can be a great first step in educating yourself about the types of issues where technology and data can play a leading role in driving significant policy change. Some examples include Measures for Justice (measuresforjustice.org), which is an organization founded to "develop a data-driven set of performance measures to assess and compare the criminal justice process from arrest to post-conviction on a county-by-county basis. The data set comprises measures that address three broad categories: Fiscal Responsibility, Fair Process, and Public Safety." Similarly, Code for America (codeforamerica.org) focuses its work on three main areas: Criminal Justice, Social Safety Net, and Workforce Development. The focus on solving issues related to these areas, which are common to all governments across the United States, means that the solutions developed will be generally applicable across most governments. If having impact at the larger local government scale appeals to you, this can be an incredibly valuable way to serve as a public-interest technologist, and could lead to future opportunities to serve within government itself at a later date.

STATE AND LOCAL GOVERNMENT WEBSITES

Often the best place to start, and often overlooked, are the websites of state and local governments themselves. If there is a particular issue you care about, this can be the best place to start your research. This is what I did when researching open data government programs in Washington State, and it led to me to connect directly with the government staff working in those programs—and with whom I continue to stay in close contact with to this day. These online resources usually contain a wealth of information about those programs, including plans, reports, and insights into current areas of work. The civil servants running these programs are often happy to engage directly, and these can be incredibly valuable networking connections to make.

PROFESSIONAL ORGANIZATIONS

One of the challenges of researching opportunities in a new domain or sector can be finding out about all of the amazing work being done and by whom. While searching on social media, websites, and the other resources I have pointed readers to here is helpful in the initial phase of your journey, it overlooks the power of good old-fashioned professional networks. Although these are organizations one would typically join upon entering government, these can provide a lot of useful information about the people and government organizations who are most active in your field of interest and may provide a useful list of people to contact or organizations to target as part of your job search. One of the most useful, and fun, organizations for local government is the Engaging Local Government Leaders organization (elgl.org). If you're a fan of the *Parks and Recreation* TV show, this is the organization for you. They also produce the excellent podcast "GovLove." To find other professional organizations that may be of interest either during your search process or after you have become a public servant, there are some useful lists of professional organizations online.[6]

VOLUNTEERING

Joining a local civic technology group can be a great way to dip your toes into the world of public service. Most major metropolitan areas have these groups, and they are usually in the form of a local Code for America brigade or an organization focused on data science for social good. It is common for these groups to partner together when hosting events, such as hackathons, and to also partner with local technology firms and universities. For example, in Seattle the local Code for America brigade (known as "Open Seattle") would host its monthly meetings at the headquarters of Socrata, which was a leading GovTech company based in Seattle. These partnerships and monthly interactions led to many serendipitous engagements and ideas for new projects. These groups also interact regularly with local government officials. For example, as open data manager for the city of Seattle I would regularly attend and/or speak at these monthly meetings. It was a useful way for me to gather feedback about the initiatives we were pursuing regarding open data, as these civic technologists were one of our biggest customers! It also allowed me to get a sense of where the energy was in terms of platforms, development practices and tools, and what the needs of the civic technology community were in terms of the datasets and other resources we could provide. If you live in an area where no such civic technology infrastructure exists, think about getting involved in setting up an organization.

NONPROFITS

Not-for-profit organizations can also provide an excellent way to get insights into how governments, especially local governments, provide services to the public and by extension get some real-world insights into the process and problems governments are tackling. The fact that some nonprofits help provide vital services on behalf of local government can often fly under the public's radar. Take homelessness, for example; although local government agencies are primarily responsible for tackling this crisis, many of the direct outreach and service provision elements of those programs are provided directly by nonprofit organizations, whose work is funded by the government. Nonprofit organizations, both large and small, also have many technical needs, and acting in a volunteer capacity is a typical way that public-interest technologists can assist. Websites such as idealist.org are an excellent place to search for nonprofit opportunities. Aside from the social impact opportunities provided by these organizations, the professional experiences gained through volunteer or paid work at nonprofits are highly valued within local government and could be a useful differentiator when seeking employment within government.

COMMITTEES, BOARDS, AND COMMISSIONS

Local government committees and commissions are another valuable way to get insights into how government operates. These are officially sanctioned groups that act as intermediaries between the public and the government and provide a way for the government to interact with and get feedback from committee members, as well as members of the public. For example, before I left the private sector to go into local government and while I was researching opportunities related to open data, I came across a board at the city of Seattle called the Community Technology Advisory Board (CTAB), which had a subcommittee that focused on issues related to open data.[7] I attended one of their monthly meetings, which are open to the public, and in addition to hearing directly from city officials about mayoral priorities and their work in areas related to technology, data, and related policies, I was also recruited for the subcommittee focused on open data and e-Government. Aside from being a great networking opportunity, I began to get a much better sense of how some of the issues I was interested in were being handled by the government and what the challenges around technology and data science were. My experiences within this city of Seattle committee and board proved to be quite helpful in my application process for the open data manager position, as some of the hiring panel (including the Chief Technology Officer) were already familiar with me and I with them. After I had been hired into the open data manager role, I moved from being a member of that subcommittee to becoming the city official who liaised with that subcommittee and would give presentations on our open data work to the board and subcommittees in their monthly meetings. Understanding how those committees functioned allowed me to be a more effective official liaison and champion for their work within the government.

Almost all local governments have committees, boards, or commissions and are usually crying out for volunteers. If you attend one of these meetings, it is likely that you will be approached about joining that group. The time commitment is usually quite manageable and can be a fantastic way to start learning the ropes of local government. The organizations will typically be listed on your local government's website under "volunteer opportunities."

ATTEND PUBLIC MEETINGS

If volunteering your time and talents with local government committees or commissions isn't a viable option, another way to gain some insights into the challenges facing local governments is to attend some of their public meetings. These could be their regular council meetings, either for the full council or their related subcommittees. The agendas for such meetings are usually published in advance on their website, so you can choose to go to a meeting that is covering a topic of interest. If you're just curious about how your local government's legislative branch and its elected officials are providing oversight over the executive functions of that government, then these meetings can be very revealing and will give you a good sense of the types of challenges that they are most interested in addressing. If attending these meetings in person isn't possible, many local government both stream and record these meetings, and you can watch them later on-demand. Some governments may also publish transcripts of the meetings on their website. These resources can help us track how government is dealing with the issues that we care about and provide insights into how our elected officials and civil servants view issues related to technology and data and the progress they are making in developing their internal technological capabilities and associated polices.

NETWORKING

All of the activities outlined earlier will enable a common scenario, which is to provide opportunities to network. Networking is something that can be difficult for most people to do. In fact, based on my own experiences of mentoring other professionals and students, it is frequently raised as one of the things that makes people the most nervous, and they will actively shy away from it. As an introverted person myself, I fully understand these feelings and often find myself having to literally force myself to go to some events. It is always the case that I am glad when I do, and I will have made at least one connection that is meaningful, which in turn may lead to other connections being made.

What is the secret to successful networking? How do you know if you're doing it well? In my experience, there is no secret sauce to successful networking. It is a unique experience for everyone, and like all skills you develop, it requires practice to get better at it. In order to find the career opportunities that will enable you to do the most impactful work possible, it is almost certain you will need to go and speak with humans that you don't already know. Lots of them.

If you abhor the idea of large networking events, then simply start by meeting one on one with people of interest. Personally, I find these types of meetings to be much more beneficial than the rapid-fire introductions that happen at larger networking events or conferences, as you have time to have a proper conversation where both parties can focus without constant interruptions. If you're looking to meet with people from a domain (e.g., government) where you don't have existing connections and are not sure where to start, tap into your existing network for suggestions on who may be useful for you to connect with. This is one of the most common next steps I take when I mentor students and young professionals—to connect them with people within my own network who may be in a better position to help advise and guide them in the longer term. Most highly experienced professionals are incredibly generous with their time and knowledge, and frequently will connect you with others in their network if they see real potential. Paying it forward is a very important aspect of professional development—after all, every single person in a position of authority was at one point the beneficiary of someone's guidance and faith. Don't be shy about asking for ideas about who else you could talk to.

Networking events are also incredibly useful for making those serendipitous connections that can later turn into valuable professional relationships. These events can come in all shapes and sizes; some are officially designated as "networking events," whereas any conference, panel discussion, hackathon, meetup, or kickoff event is often a place where the best networking opportunities lie. When attending such events, always be ready to grab any opportunity to introduce yourself to as many people as possible—some of the best connections I have made over the years have come from randomly chatting with people at such events, and it is pretty rare for me to leave without at least one or two business cards or opportunities to connect with someone at a later date. Professional networking organizations may also exist in your area that could be loosely aligned with your interests and that may intersect with local government. For example, I became a member of the Irish Network Seattle organization, whose members (not all of whom are Irish!) hail from both the public and private sectors and host fun and interesting events that generate great networking opportunities. These organizations can provide more relaxing environments for networking. Basically, any scenario where people are gathering to connect around an issue or topic of interest should be considered a networking event.

STARTING YOUR JOB SEARCH

If you are now at the point where you wish to pursue opportunities in the public sector, the next step is understanding where to find relevant opportunities and how to assess those organizations that may be of interest.

ORGANIZATIONAL ETHNOGRAPHY

One relatively quick and easy way to gain a sense of an organization you may be interested in is to develop an ethnography of that organization. Ethnography is the scientific description of the customs of individual peoples and cultures. In this case, it means performing some basic qualitative research on the organization and its people, its structures, and how it views itself by using the information made available on their website. This is a technique that I was introduced to during my public policy master's degree program, and one that I continually use to this day when assessing both public- and private-sector organizations.

Start at the organization's home page on the Internet and ask yourself a series of questions. What are your first impressions? Is an org chart readily available? How would you describe this organization based on what you see in their org chart? Do they have a mission statement? If so, does it reflect your values as an individual? What symbols are used throughout the site? Are metaphors employed in the site content? How does the organization see itself? By asking questions such as these, you'll be able to develop a sense for how good a fit this organization may be for you. You could, and probably should, extend this into their social media presence and other public outlets.

INTERNSHIPS

For newly minted technologists, either close to graduation or having recently graduated, taking advantage of internship opportunities in government can be a great way to dip your toes into the public sector. Getting real-world professional work experience and exposure to the opportunities to have a real impact within government can be a great first step toward encouraging more graduates to commit to working there in the longer term. These opportunities can be made available to both undergrad and postgrad students in all areas of government and usually will provide a stipend. For those readers still in college or pursuing an advanced degree, be sure to look for state and local government internship opportunities facilitated within your schools. For example, in my role as open data manager, I partnered with my counterpart in state government on some open data literacy projects in conjunction with the University of Washington and their funding partners. We hosted some students during the summer and put them to work on helping us solve some real-world problems we wished to tackle. These programs provided a real win-win for all parties, giving government useful existence proofs and case studies with which to advocate for more resources to continue the data science work within government itself and gave the students some valuable professional experience and networking opportunities. In some cases, the students could continue to pursue the work as part of their capstone or thesis requirements for their degrees.

JOB SEARCH RESOURCES

Aside from the usual generic job search sites, such as Indeed and LinkedIn, there are several other resources that can help readers with their government job search process. For general public-sector roles, the first place most people start is the relevant government website and search their open positions there. Like almost all organizations, state and local governments will typically use a third-party service to manage their listings and application intake processes. In my experience, governmentjobs.com is the service most local governments use. If your search is broader than just your immediate local government, several jobs boards are available that curate all open positions locally, regionally, and nationally. Similarly, if you are looking for executive-level positions, some jobs boards do a good job of highlighting those positions separately from other positions. For roles specifically targeting the technology policy arena, some job boards specifically focus on both public and private opportunities. The most well-known examples of these jobs boards are listed next.

Public sector:

- https://www.sgrjobs.com (includes executive-level searches)
- https://governmentjobs.com
- https://elgl.org/jobs

Technology and policy positions:

- https://daybook.com
- https://jobs.thebridgework.com
- https://jobs.codeforamerica.org

Note that federal government jobs are usually handled in separate systems.

COMPENSATION INFORMATION

One advantage that job seekers in the public sector have is the ready access to wage data for those roles and similar roles elsewhere. This is because the amount of money a civil servant is paid while working in government is considered a public record. After all, it's taxpayer money that is funding their salaries, expenses, and benefits. Rather than having to request that data, it is typically made freely available to everyone either as an open dataset or via an online searchable database. Great examples of each include the city of Seattle Wage dataset[8] and the state of Washington salary database.[9] Similarly, almost all government job advertisements come with the expected salary ranges in annual, monthly, or hourly rates. As all government salary data is public knowledge, the government job boards also provide useful contextual information—for example, even if you're not looking to relocate, these job boards can provide useful information on salaries, benefits, and other conditions for similar positions in other jurisdictions. This can help you assess whether the government you may work at is providing a good offer. This salary transparency data provides candidates with the information they need to have the best job offer negotiation possible. This is especially important when we consider issues of pay equity related to women and people of color.

CIVIC LEAVE PROGRAMS

Towards the end of my tenure at Microsoft, I became aware of a very interesting approach toward expanding the pipeline of talent from the private to the public sector, which was the concept that had initially grabbed my attention when earning my master's degree in public policy and which I have written about elsewhere in this book. A senior Microsoft executive, Kurt DelBene, had recently returned to the company after spending some time working within the federal government to help fix the so-called Obamacare online service, healthcare.gov. The launch of the online health insurance marketplace had experienced a disastrous launch in 2013.[10] In 2014, President Obama tapped DelBene to help address the healthcare.gov issues. DelBene was one of the senior executives responsible for helping transition the hugely successful Microsoft Office suite of desktop products into online services and was seen as someone who could quickly help address the architectural issues with the giant government online service. During his service in federal government,

DelBene had also come to the realization that government needed to build its internal technical capacity, and upon his return to Microsoft in April 2015, he set about creating a new program, known as "civic leave," that would allow Microsoft engineers to take a leave of absence and temporarily serve in the U.S. Digital Service arm of the federal government. Rotations were typically six months to one year. In 2018, the Microsoft CEO, Satya Nadella, met with the U.S. Digital Service staff for a discussion on the impact of this program and its future direction.[11] Efforts to expand these programs continue, with ongoing interactions between a group of major tech companies (led by BSA | The Software Alliance industry group) and the White House.[12]

While much of the focus of these civic leave programs to date has been at the federal level, there are efforts to replicate this model into state and local government. In October 2019, the state of Colorado launched its own version of the U.S. Digital Service, where it hopes to attract engineers, data scientists, designers, and program managers to complete civic tours of duty with the state government.[13] As more state and local governments begin to create similar digital service programs and more civic leave programs get established within the private sector, the number of opportunities for technologists to engage in tours of duty within government itself will increase and perhaps lead to more technologists choosing to join government in a more permanent capacity once their initial service has been completed.

For readers who work at technology companies that offer these type of civic leave programs or other forms of leave that could be used for government service, these programs can provide an excellent opportunity to complete a tour of duty in government, gain some incredible professional experience, and test out whether a future career in government could be a good fit without having to leave your current role. If this is not an option currently being made available in the workplace, perhaps this could be an opportunity to speak with management about the possibility of implementing such a program.

INTERVIEWING

Finally, you reach the stage where you find a role that you're interested in and wish to apply for. Applying, and later interviewing, for government positions can feel quite different from the typical hiring process in the private sector, especially in the tech sector. First off, the process can often appear to be more formal than what you might be used to. However, some governments have been taking steps to make the experience better, and from my observations, the job application process at the local government level appears to be less onerous than at the federal government level. Many applications will list the closing date for receipt of applications, which is useful information. Most applications will require a cover letter along with a resume, so if you've never written a cover letter before, this is a skill that is well worth developing. Writing a cover letter adds valuable context to your resume and LinkedIn profile for the person reviewing your application. It has the added benefit of forcing you to write down your rationale for why you want the job and why you're the best person for it—not as easy as it sounds. This rationale is something you will repeat in the interview process, so this is a really valuable exercise and I highly encourage you to spend time on crafting your letter. If required, answer any additional supplemental questions. These are general and agency supplemental questions. Depending on the hiring agency, this section may be blank.

It is also worth noting that having an initial informational meeting with the hiring manager may not be possible. This is sometimes possible within the tech sector, even if you're an external candidate. However, this is very much the exception and not the rule within government for external candidates. To get around this limitation in your information gathering process, it should be possible to speak with people who work in that department. Reaching out via LinkedIn is a common tactic, as well as getting a referral from someone in your network if that's possible. I would recommend you ideally try to speak with someone in the organization prior to applying or interviewing, and even before you accept an offer if you make it to that point. As is the case in any sector, the gap between the idealistic job description and the cold hard reality within the organization can be quite wide. Always do your homework and check your assumptions before making any big decisions.

For technical roles in local government, you'll likely have an initial screening process should you make it through the initial scrub of job applications. And yes, just like the private sector there will likely be an initial scrub, usually by humans and not via AI seeking certain keywords and phrases. In larger local governments, it is quite common to have at least several dozen candidates for individual contributor and frontline management technical roles, and over 100 candidates for senior leadership roles such as Chief Data Officer, Chief Technology Officer, and Chief Information Officer. Another aspect of the job search process that surprised me was how many people from across the country would apply for positions in local government, with a view to relocating if successful. I had been hardwired to think that relocating was something that was only done in the tech sector. The lesson here appears to be that interesting and challenging technology jobs within local government don't become available very often, and that there will likely be fierce competition for those jobs. The scale of the demand for those jobs is also a signal that if there were more of those available, then it doesn't appear that local governments would struggle to fill them. In other words, many technologists appear to be interested in working in local government and we have an opportunity to develop that extra capacity.

Aside from the initial screening process, you may also be required to complete an exercise prior to your in-person interviews, which is also a common practice in the private sector. The formal interviews are often in panel formats with the hiring manager and several other staffers with whom you would directly or indirectly work with if hired. From my experience, this is a big difference from the tech sector where the norm for technical roles is to have a grueling series of 1:1 interviews over the course of a day. You will likely have only one panel interview, usually one hour long, followed at a later date by a second interview which is possibly the runoff interview where the top two or three candidates would meet with a senior leader. The goal of those runoff interviews is to allow senior leaders to assess the panel's decision on who they chose as their top candidates, and to check for culture fit and other cross-group concerns that may not have surfaced in the initial panel interviews. Another major difference I experienced with my panel interview process was that I was given the interview questions 30 minutes prior to the actual interview so I could review them and sketch out my answers, before bringing them with me into the interview itself. You may or may not encounter similar in your interview process, but I found this to be an interesting approach, it certainly helped with reducing nerves before the actual meeting and I think led to a better conversation in the room. I later discovered that this extra step is primarily designed to help candidates who speak English as a second language. I think the tech sector could find a similar approach to be beneficial in certain cases.

CHAPTER 7: KEY TAKEAWAYS

- One of the most frequently asked questions I get about my own journey into government is how I went about making it happen. In this chapter, I share insights from my own transition from the private to the public sector, as well as suggestions for readers to try out as part of their own decision-making process.
- First, understand your "why."
- Next, understand your "what"—and keep in mind that it is usual to change the discipline or domain, but not both at the same time.
- Finally, we explore the "how":
    - We start with education and all of the amazing resources that are available to help you research working in local government.
    - Volunteering opportunities and how these can help you discover exciting opportunities within local government.

○ Networking and how it can help you meet with current government staff who can provide you with amazing insights into working within local government and what the best opportunities are.

○ How to start your job search should you decide to serve in local government.

○ Insights and tips about interviewing for (technical) positions with local government.

NOTES

1 "A Future of Failure? The Flow of Technology Talent into Government and Society," Ford Foundation, accessed September 16, 2019, https://www.fordfoundation.org/library/reports-and-studies/a-future-of-failure-the-flow-of-technology-talent-into-government-and-society.

2 "International Association of Privacy Professionals—Home," IAPP, accessed September 16, 2019, https://iapp.org.

3 "31 Government Associations You Should Join," GovLoop, last updated September 27, 2016, https://www.govloop.com/31-government-associations-you-should-join.

4 "Nonprofits," Microsoft, accessed September 16, 2019, https://www.microsoft.com/en-us/nonprofits.

5 "About Tableau Foundation," Tableau, accessed September 16, 2019, https://www.tableau.com/foundation/about-tableau-foundation.

6 "31 Government Associations You Should Join," GovLoop, last updated September 27, 2016, https://www.govloop.com/31-government-associations-you-should-join.

7 "Community Technology Advisory Board," City of Seattle, accessed September 16, 2019, https://seattle.gov/community-technology-advisory-board.

8 "City of Seattle Wage Data," City of Seattle, accessed September 16, 2019, https://data.seattle.gov/City-Business/City-of-Seattle-Wage-Data/2khk-5ukd.

9 "State Employee Salaries by Year," State of Washington, accessed September 16, 2019, http://fiscal.wa.gov/Salaries.aspx.

10 "The Failed Launch of www.HealthCare.gov," Harvard Business School, accessed September 17, 2019, https://digital.hbs.edu/platform-rctom/submission/the-failed-launch-of-www-healthcare-gov.

11 "A Fireside Chat with Matt Cutts, USDS Administrator, and Satya Nadella, Microsoft CEO: Civic Service Leave," U.S. Digital Service, accessed September 17, 2019, https://medium.com/the-u-s-digital-service/a-fireside-chat-with-matt-cutts-usds-administrator-and-satya-nadella-microsoft-ceo-civic-3bcaad68680e.

12 "The White House Wants to Make Civic Leave for Technologists Normal and Accessible. Will It Take Off?," FedScoop, accessed September 17, 2019, https://www.fedscoop.com/civic-leave-white-house-technology-company-employees.employees

13 "Introducing Colorado Digital Service," FedScoop, accessed September 17, 2019, http://www.colorado.gov/digitalservice.

8

YOU GOT THE JOB, NOW GET STARTED

Congratulations! You have joined the cohort of very special people that call themselves "public servants." Probably the first questions you'll ask yourself as you embark on this exciting phase of your career is "How do I have impact?" or even "How do I get things done?" If you have moved from one domain (the private and/or tech sector) into this new domain (the public sector), trying to answer those questions right off the bat can be quite difficult, if not impossible. Instead, focusing on learning as much about your new environment as possible and learning from others in similar positions is a good way to begin.

It is common for people embarking on a new role in any sector to have a thirty-, sixty-, and ninety-day plan of action, complete with some metrics, to assess if they are hitting the ground running or perhaps think about what success looks like after six months or a year. In federal government, the "first hundred days" nomenclature is often invoked when describing the desired early progress in a new role or administration. On March 4, 1933, the administration of President Franklin D. Roosevelt began its first term of office with an intense period of action that became known as The First Hundred Days. Over the course of 105 days, fifteen major pieces of legislation were passed by the U.S. Congress with the aim of getting the U.S. economy back onto its feet after the devastation of the Great

Depression. Unless the local government you're entering is in similar dire straits, the need to have an impact equivalent to FDR in the first hundred days of your new role is unlikely. Instead, my advice is to use that time to build a new network and develop an understanding of the organization that will help you make the right decisions on what issues to tackle first and in which order. I personally like the "first hundred days" metric, as it roughly equates to three months and is enough time to get a true sense of your new environment.

MOVING FROM "NEW HIRE" TO "OPERATIONAL"

With this in mind, technologists entering public service will first need to think about how to get from being seen as a new hire to being fully operational and productive. Academic frameworks, such as the technology enactment framework, can provide technologists in executive-level government roles (such as chief information officer, chief technology officer, or IT department director) with useful tools that may help preempt some difficulties downstream.[1] For the vast majority of technologists entering local government, something more immediate and practical is required to speed up this transition process.

As with any job in any sector, there will be a huge body of knowledge that one develops over the course of one's tenure that would have been very helpful to have known ahead of time. Following is a selection of some of the main insights I developed over the course of my public service and that will likely be relevant in any local government environment. These do not subscribe to any framework or claim to be scientific or quantitative in any way. These are my personal reflections and some of the things I wished I had known in advance. These are also the anecdotes I most frequently share when I'm asked about my experiences. They are not listed in any particular order of importance, and hopefully will prove useful to most readers who make the leap into public service.

BUDGET

In government more than in other organizations, the budget is the real source of power. Think "appropriations" and "the power of the purse," and you'll quickly understand why Congress is so powerful and how membership in committees like Appropriations and Ways and Means are highly sought after by representatives. This is one of the main ways that the legislative branch acts as a "check and balance" on the executive branch. Regardless of the size and scale of the projects and initiatives you'll be working on, it's vital that you factor your budget into the equation right from the beginning. Proceeding with an initiative only to later discover a budget issue that derails your project is one sure way to destroy your credibility.

Therefore, you should understand the budget and how it works. Budgets within government can be labyrinthine, so take the time to understand it for your own department and internal teams first before looking across the entire government budget. There will likely be a budget analyst who will have direct oversight of your area of the government, so meet with them early and often. I would have quarterly meetings with my relevant budget analysts, and these meetings were invaluable. In addition to knowing where my program's actual spending versus projected spending (i.e., my budget) was, I discovered several pockets of funding I was previously unaware of. These meetings would enable me to query the analysts on where the hard lines were in terms of spending and where there was more flexibility within the overall department budget should I need to overspend in some areas. These meetings also enabled us to alert each other to potential spending or budget issues well ahead of time and to help mitigate any other issues that subsequently arose. This communication also helped establish trust that I could tap into when a problem arose.

Related to this last point, become best friends with your department's budget director, or at least get into their good books (working well with their analysts is a great start). Sooner or later you'll hit a budget issue or will have a major budget request that will require a supplemental budget request, and you will need their support in order to help get it through the appropriations process, especially if this extra budget will require legislative approval. The budget director will understand the higher-level politics when it comes to your department or area of government and will be able to advise on the feasibility of your budget request. These suggestions do not mean to keep your management chain out of the loop—rather, it means that you can work with your management to roll up your budget requests within a larger department budget request or have your manager act as a supporter of your specific request. The best advocate for your budget request is you, but your manager will be able to help you shape the proposal and avoid any pitfalls, and their proactive endorsement will be instrumental in getting overall approval. It is likely they will also have a good sense of the politics surrounding such a request.

It is common in local government to have a biennial (i.e., two-year) budget cycle. As a new public-sector technologist eager to start making some changes, this can make getting new requests approved tricky. Two years can seem like an eon to technologists used to the aggressive timelines in the product development cycles in the private sector. Responses from your budget director such as "Come back to me in two years" are not what you will want to hear early in your tenure. Depending on when you join, you may be at the beginning, middle, or end of a biennial budget cycle, so it will be possible to figure that out once you're in place and begin working with your budget team. As mentioned earlier, methods are built into the budgeting processes to help with issues that arise during those biennial cycles, usually in the form of a supplemental budget request. As with the overall budget process, ensure you understand the supplemental budget request process and the relevant timelines, and factor those into your planning. These requests should be used sparingly, so building up a good relationship with your budget analysts and budget director will help you assess their tolerance and that of the relevant legislative or executive branch approvers for such requests.

Finally, in the early stages of your tenure you should spend your budget allocated to the most critical projects of your area of ownership. If you don't, there is a risk that you will be appropriated less money in the next budget cycle. It is vital to do this early in your tenure, while you are still learning how the system works and where the gotchas are. One trap that is easy to fall into as a technologist is that you have confidence in your ability to innovate your way into generating significant efficiencies before realizing there are a host of other nontechnical considerations that you failed to appreciate. Avoiding this overconfidence can be a difficult skill for technologists in government to develop. I struggled to contain this urge until I better understood the culture within government regarding driving efficiencies. Take the time to understand the budget and the various systems within which you'll be operating before you consider giving up any budget, as it is very difficult to get it back later and especially with reduced credibility.

UNDERSTAND THE POLITICS

All organizations have internal politics, and some also have external politics to contend with. The larger the organization, the more complex the politics invariably is. It is a fact of life and something everyone needs to deal with at some stage of their career. One of the key differentiators between working in the public sector versus the private sector is the level of external politics that you may have to contend with when pursuing initiatives involving public-facing technology and/or data systems and the policies related to them. A great example of this is the emergence of privacy policies and their importance when providing external digital services or implementing new methods for data collection within the jurisdiction of the government. Politics is defined as "the art of the possible," and while at times it feels the letters "im" should be added to the beginning of the word "possible," it is possible to navigate a highly political environment such as a local government and have impact as a technologist.

The first step is to understand the politics surrounding the issues and projects you are working on. No government leader wants to be on the front page of their local newspaper for the wrong reasons, and especially in an election year. Once you have a better sense for the politics surrounding a project or policy, you'll be in a better position to navigate the politics and have fewer meetings where you might leave the room wondering what just happened. I experienced a few of these meetings during my public service, where it was clear that no matter how much supporting data I had, the decision-making process was operating under other opaque considerations. Those meetings reminded me of a scene from *The West Wing* TV show (Season 5, Episode 15, "Full Disclosure") where the character Toby Ziegler is about to enter a contentious meeting with trade union bosses. Here is the dialogue[2] from that scene:

[Toby walks up to the meeting room that has been allocated for the meeting with the union reps. Ed and Larry are standing there.]

ED: *Here are the latest numbers on our trade deficit with China.*
TOBY: *Don't need them.*
LARRY: *You want us to stay for the meeting?*
TOBY: *No. This meeting is about politics, facts won't help.*

[He walks into the room.]

This is not to say that the politics surrounding a certain issue or project means it's doomed never to move forward. The key is to quickly recognize that you are in such a situation and step back to see if there is an underlying issue that you're not aware of or whether there are other political considerations at play. This is a soft skill that may take some time to develop, but it is invaluable. The key to solving some of these impasses is through the development of those personal relationships that will help unblock you. Should you hit a roadblock with a particular leader, manager, or stakeholder, seek ways to learn more about what the root cause might be. Remember, it is highly unlikely you'll get the full story within the context of a meeting with others in the room, and you will definitely not get an explanation in writing. Reach out and have a quiet informal chat over a coffee, or if that's not possible then see if your manager or someone else within your organization has developed a relationship with that person. It is likely they will have a longer history than you within the organization, and they may be able to act as a mediator. My boss was able to perform this role for me on more than one occasion, allowing us to reassess our approaches when attempting to partner with some other departments.

RISK TOLERANCE

The next important step is to develop an understanding of the risk tolerance of your stakeholders before embarking on certain initiatives. Politics and risk tolerance may seem like they mean the same thing, but the difference is subtle. A stakeholder may not have any political concerns about your project or idea but can have concerns about other risks. These can include issues like previous failed attempts to do something similar, cost overruns, procurement delays, overly aggressive schedules, or other "gotchas" that you may not be aware of. Technologists tend to be really good at getting excited about the possibilities of what is possible and perhaps overestimating the capacity to achieve the outcome in a realistic time frame. I know I am certainly guilty of this, and it was something I had to work on during my government service. The best ways to temper your enthusiasm into a robust proposal that has a high chance of success is to do a lot of (you've guessed it!) meeting with people individually and developing the new relationships required to get the support needed. Ideally, you will do this in advance of any group meeting to announce the idea. By building a "coalition of the willing" and, if needed, finding an executive sponsor, you'll ensure that your initial kickoff meeting is more of a formality to announce the work will proceed, rather than hitting everyone in the room with new information and seeking their support on the spot. These people will help you identify and address any glaring omissions or invalid conclusions in the early stages of ideation, rather than after you have publicly committed to achieving an outcome that you suddenly realize may no longer be achievable as first conceived. If you are building a proposal based on the assumption that you can leverage resources in other teams or departments, these initial background meetings are especially critical. Local governments are far less flexible than a technology firm when it comes to the rapid reallocation of their resources and talent for new project ideas, especially if the project work is funded by grants, which have strict stipulations on how that money can be spent.

NO SURPRISES

This "no surprises" rule is especially important in government—and at all levels. Ensuring everyone is briefed in advance of any major initiative rollout is absolutely a must-do, and this includes the relevant executives within the organization—for example, the relevant policy advisor in the mayor's office. Even if it seems like overkill, sharing in advance with key policy staff is usually greatly appreciated and may prevent some last-minute "no-go" decisions coming down from on high. This is also true of reports or strategic plans. Before I published the city's first Open Data Strategic Plan, one of my final ports of call was to the mayor's technology policy advisor, who gave their blessing after we reviewed the central goals of the plan. If nothing else, the proactive sharing of information, reports, and initiative proposals can be seen as being respectful of the various offices and their roles in the oversight process and can lead to future goodwill being developed. If you're not sure who to consult with, and when, your managers will likely have great insights here based on the rollout of previous projects.

LOCAL ELECTION CYCLES

Another useful thing to do is to figure out where you are in the local election cycles. The window of time for certain projects or initiatives to get approved can often be surprisingly short. Hearing responses that begin with phrases such as "as this is an election year" is generally not a positive indicator of success. If there is a chance that the administration will be replaced within the following twelve to eighteen months, you might start to encounter this issue. Some of this can be related to budgeting concerns and the lack of desire to seek supplemental budget, or it could be that the current administration doesn't want to prioritize a particular issue until after they hope to be reelected. This may seem a little counterintuitive to technologists, as we are trained to get as much done within a certain time frame as possible. This is one of the ways where the differences in time horizons between the public and private sectors becomes apparent. This is how it is possible to delay the provision of a new service even when the need becomes increasingly urgent.

DON'T OVERREACT

Lastly, try to avoid the "Streisand effect," which is defined as "a phenomenon whereby an attempt to hide, remove, or censor a piece of information has the unintended consequence of publicizing the information more widely, usually facilitated by the Internet." Named after the famous entertainer and actress Barbara Streisand, it refers to how her attempts to suppress the publication of photos of her Malibu residence backfired spectacularly.[3] In local government, when things invariably do go wrong and there may be some negative public reaction, or if an article or podcast where you are quoted out of context is published, it is natural to want to immediately correct such inaccuracies (as you see them), and in some cases it will absolutely be necessary to do so if the error is egregious. However, there may be cases where doing so will attract more attention to the initial quote or statement than if had you simply ignored it. These can be tricky situations to handle, and usually it is best to loop in your communications staff (if they were not already involved in the initial public relations (PR) process) and work through the issue with them. Government communications staff often have working relationships with local reporters and may be able to engineer a correction should one be required. Avoid the temptation to go it alone when it comes to government PR, and especially when it comes to using social media to do so.

ALIGNING WITH THE COMMON MISSION

One of the best things about working in local government is that every single person working there is aligned around a common mission—serving the public. There are many thousands of local government entities, yet all of them have the same basic mission. Therefore, describing yourself as a "public servant" and your work as "public service" is important. This framing will help you remain focused on the overall mission when you invariably need to deal with the realities of government bureaucracy and the longer time horizons that local government operates within. It will take some time to get used to these descriptors and to truly understand what they mean. It will require viewing the work you will do through a different lens, adjusting your metrics for success, and thinking more deeply about the outcomes that you wish to achieve.

This is very different from the "bottom-line" approach of the private sector. The goal of serving within government isn't to maximize value for the shareholders or to build disruptive technologies. It is to provide the services that are necessary to the public, within budget, for as long as is required, which is essentially indefinitely. It is a completely different mindset and will take some time to adjust to. In a highly political environment such as local government where issues can arise thick and fast and require faster responses when compared to state or federal government, it is important to keep this overall mission of providing services with a long life span at the back of your mind when dealing with the pressures for rapid responses to gaps in service provision.

Build Relationships

As in any large organization, there will be a critical cohort of people that it will be highly beneficial to build relationships with. This was something I spent an enormous amount of time doing both at the beginning of my tenure and later throughout my two years in local government. When starting out, these initial conversations are vital to help avoid making rookie mistakes and therefore building your credibility. Later, building lasting relationships and continually developing new ones will allow you to develop an internal network that can help you achieve your desired outcomes. Note that this internal network could be within a single department or across every department in that government.

In my own case, I ran a program that required me to implement a policy across twenty-seven departments at the city of Seattle. Each department varied hugely in size and areas of responsibility. Some had more than a thousand staff, others fewer than twenty. Yet all were expected to contribute data to the city's open data portal. I was fortunate that a network of data stewards had been established prior to my arrival, with most departments having at least one steward already in place. As these data stewards were going to be critical to the success of the program I was about to manage and provide the amazing datasets that would provide real value for the public, I immediately set about building relationships with them. This involved one of my favorite activities, drinking coffee. Lots of coffee. Again, I was fortunate to be working in a building that had its own Starbucks in the lobby, as well as three more Starbucks and a fabulous coffee kiosk in the adjoining buildings (it is Seattle, after all). In a period of about three weeks, I met with at least thirty of these staffers from across the city government. Aside from the meet-and-greet aspect of the meetings, it gave me a fabulous opportunity to develop an organizational ethnography. I was able to uncover what was unique about each department, what their culture was like regarding data, how supportive their department leadership was of the program I would run, and what barriers they faced in complying with the policy. These meetings allowed me to develop a rapport with everyone I would need to work with, while understanding what their most basic needs were and how my team and I might be able to quickly address some of the most common process issues raised. I firmly believe that these fifteen or twenty hours of informal coffee meetings likely saved us from months of wasted effort on things that truly didn't matter. Maintaining those relationships is just as important, and in my case we were able to do so primarily through a regular monthly meeting where all data stewards were required to attend, which often led to follow-up conversations and offers of new staff who were eager to join the effort.

Aside from the hard work required at the beginning, building and maintaining an effective network requires constant effort. As a rule of thumb, I would have at least two or three "networking" meetings on my calendar each week. These could be coffee meetings, chats after work during happy hour, or talking over lunch. Sometimes these were meeting other city staffers not directly associated with my program but who could lead to potential partnerships in the future. Other times, due to the nature of the program I was managing, I would meet with people in other regional governments or representatives from the community who were using the data we were providing. There were many benefits to these meetings, from becoming aware of interesting initiatives that we were able to avail ourselves of to creating opportunities to showcase our data platform and help establish public trust.

One thing I made sure to do was to constantly share the high-level outcomes and knowledge gained from these meetings with my team and management. Doing so helped my team develop an understanding of how I was helping them to achieve the outcomes that we had all agreed to in the strategic plan and to better understand my role as manager. Sharing information about the networks being developed meant that my team and others were able to tap into those connections at a later point if needed. I also received valuable feedback and new ideas that I could then go back to those partners with, often leading to a virtuous cycle.

Outside of your immediate team and management structure, there are a number of other teams within your greater organization that are very important to your overall success in your role. I outline some of those roles for you next, based on my own experiences in local government, but each organization and government has its own unique structure and culture, and there may be other individuals within your organization who play a key role in your ability to get things done. Identifying and befriending them should be a priority.

WORKING CLOSELY WITH YOUR HUMAN RESOURCES TEAM

If you are in a role where you will manage a team and may need to hire staff, building a good relationship with your human resources (HR) partners is critically important. While this is true of any organization in any sector, managing and hiring staff in local government has some unique situations that you will need to navigate with the assistance of your HR staff. Some of these situations will include managing staff who are members of labor unions. You may also need to hire staff who will need to join a union upon accepting their offer. There are many rules and regulations to be aware of, and leveraging their years of experience in dealing with unionized staff and their representatives will prevent you from unwittingly finding yourself in some very tricky situations that could lead you to expending vast amounts of time and energy to unwind. Related to that, in general there are salary ranges for government positions, and so your HR partner can advise you on how to negotiate with prospective new hires once an offer has been made. For exceptional candidates, it is possible to exceed the top end of the range, and HR will be able to guide you on that. Finally, they will provide a lot of assistance when it comes to the hiring process itself, from crafting the job descriptions to where those job advertisements can be placed, the length of the hiring process, process related to reviewing resumes, holding the interviews, and finally choosing your preferred candidates and making an offer. There will likely be rules and requirements that you don't need to adhere to in the private sector for all of these steps in the process, so ensure you work closely with HR at each stage.

COMMUNICATIONS TEAM

If your work as a technologist within local government has a public-facing component to it, then it is critical to establish a great working relationship with the communications team. Think of your communications staff as your marketing team or public relations (PR) team. These components can include any outreach activities, such as speaking at conferences and being on panel discussions, managing social media activities for your program, being interviewed by local news media, providing quotes for government-related articles or press releases, being interviewed on a podcast, and so on. Your communications partner can guide you on the content, tone, and messaging of these outreach activities. Another critical function they can play is in providing a detailed history of the politics related to certain issues that you may be speaking to. They are often some of the more connected people within your government and will have a good pulse on where the focus of the leadership is at any moment in time, which is valuable information when you are considering whether the timing is right to pursue some of your major initiatives.

ADMINISTRATIVE TEAMS

I'm a firm believer that administrative staff are often some of the most critically important people you will ever work with in any organization. A great administrative professional is worth their weight in gold, and then some. By leveraging their skills in creative ways, they'll be able to help you and your team scale your impact. There are myriad ways in which your administrative staff can help you on large and small projects, freeing up valuable time for you and your team. Often these staff are able to help in ways that you may not have previously realized was possible. It is highly recommended that you get to know your administrative staff early into your time in government and learn about the many ways that they may be able to assist you and your team. Depending on your role, you may have an administrative assistant assigned to your team—but there may be other administrative professionals in your government organization who will prove invaluable, such as the executive assistants of the Chief Technology Officer / Chief Information Officer or administrative staff in other departments. Aside from helping you ensure that you make the best use of an executive leader's time, they can often provide useful insights and advice about the issue you may be working on. Building constructive and respectful relationships with key administrative staff (including chiefs of staff in some areas) will help you be more effective in achieving your goals.

FIND "THE KEYMAKER"

"The Keymaker" is a fictional character in the 2003 film *The Matrix Reloaded*. As a computer program manifested in human form, he possesses an enormous number of physical keys wrapped around his body. These keys act as backdoors into various areas of the Matrix—essentially, they are shortcuts that only he knows about. This knowledge makes him incredibly valuable to heroes and bad guys alike. Navigating government IT systems can sometimes give you the impression that you are trapped in an environment as complex as the Matrix. As a new technologist attempting to navigate within this labyrinthine world, finding that person who fits the bill as "The Keymaker" can prove invaluable. Trust me, there is always one person within the local government IT department who literally has the keys to the kingdom. They will save you countless hours of frustration and lost effort. This person is usually one of the longest-serving members of staff, and it's quite likely they will seek you out if they hear about your new ideas. The goal here isn't to use their knowledge to circumvent existing IT policies and take risky shortcuts; rather, it is to partner with them so that they can point out all of the technological "gotchas" and alert you to possible alternative methods and systems that can help you achieve your aims. They will supercharge your learning and connect you to other "Keymakers" in the organization. More often than not, they will relish a new challenge and volunteer to help with some work items. If you are a seasoned technologist who has fond memories of legacy technologies, it's a lot of fun to reminisce with these folks. Most importantly of all, they will help you see the Matrix. Find them.

BRANCH AND DEPARTMENT INSIDERS

If your work spans several departments, or indeed the entire government, then building a network of "champions" is a common method within local government to help you achieve your goals. This can be a formal or informal network of advocates, depending on the role and the nature of the work. Often there is little or no funding for some policy initiatives related to technology and data. For example, the open data policy that I was responsible for implementing was known as an "unfunded mandate," which meant that the work was to be accomplished without any additional budget to pay for staff to do that work. Hence, the only possible way to achieve the program goals was to establish a network of data stewards, or "champions." Each department had to nominate at least one data steward, and this was often extra work that this person did on top of their regular job. While not ideal, one of the benefits of this system is you will have staff advocating for your work inside of their respective departments. Depending on the nature of the projects you undertake, having this network of advocates can provide a powerful voice for systemic change. Related to that, each department within a large government will likely have its own "micro-culture" with specific political and policy viewpoints, and your network of advocates will provide you with valuable insights that you can use to assess the levels of support for your technological initiatives.

If your work will fall into the technology policy side of the equation, then having good connections within the upper reaches of the executive branch (for example, the public policy team within city hall) are very helpful in understanding the tolerance for change for larger initiatives. Communication between the executive and legislative branches tends to be channeled through a key set of staffers, so ensure you understand those protocols before initiating any contacts regarding your technology initiatives.

OWNERSHIP

One of the most effective ways to have impact within local government is to be willing to show up and to be willing to own things. It really is that simple. This is especially true if you're working across departments. I was surprised at how often other staff were reluctant to step up and take ownership of some deliverables or initiatives. While there was a reluctance on their part to step up, sometimes for reasons I never quite fully understood, once there was someone who was willing to take the lead and drive the project forward, then they were happy to contribute to the effort. I believe this is a part of local government culture that having more technologists can help improve, where it is more in our nature to want to take on new technical challenges and drive improvements where we see obvious gaps. Instilling the desire to take action when obvious opportunities present themselves can lead to others feeling empowered to follow suit.

Even before taking on the ownership of a deliverable, simply showing up is another great way to start having impact. This doesn't mean simply attending meetings that others have called. Look for other opportunities to just "show up." These can be committee meetings, council meetings, local conferences where your government is involved, or random invites to exploratory meetings with other technology-focused teams in other parts of your government. Some of the most meaningful and interesting conversations and learning I experienced while in government came from those kinds of organic interactions, both inside and outside of my immediate organization. Projects, initiatives, and great ideas looking for someone to help bring them to fruition are everywhere in local government. Always be on the lookout for opportunities to take some sort of ownership role in the wide range of interesting projects happening all around your local government ecosystem. Partnership opportunities with nonprofits, universities, and regional agencies can be especially interesting and rewarding. Make sure to clear this with your management in advance, ensuring that they fully support your desire to look for opportunities beyond the immediate scope of your job description.

Finally, if you own it, deliver. This is a highly sought-after quality in government and will get you noticed. Unfortunately, it is often easier to push out deadlines in government than it would be in, say, a private-sector product development environment. The level of accountability isn't as strict, and this can lead to schedule and feature creep. I would argue that this is one of the behaviors within local government that I would love to see changed, and this is certainly an area where experienced technology leaders can help. Beware of falling into that trap yourself! It is quite natural to want to take your foot off the gas if the organization around you isn't reacting as nimbly as you'd like. One way to counteract this is to constantly share updates on your progress, both with the short-term deliverables and, more importantly, how these are contributing to the overall success of the larger mission or strategic plan. Some project timelines in government can be quite long, so keeping focused on the delivery of various stages of the project can be a great way to build momentum. I like to think about this in the context of huge government projects like the effort to get to the moon in the 1960s. There were three main stages to that immense project—Mercury, Gemini, and Apollo. The first two stages (Mercury from 1958 to 1963 and Gemini from 1961 to 1966) had distinct yet overlapping goals, and each stage was critical to the success of the final stage (Apollo from 1961 to 1972), which was to land a man on the Moon and return him safely to the Earth. If it wasn't possible to successfully exit either of those first two stages, the overall project would have failed. Throughout those stages of the overall mission, NASA constantly gave updates on their progress and provided great transparency even when disaster occurred. While no local government project will ever reach the levels of complexity of a Moon shot, those basic project management and communication principles can help ensure that complex technology enablement projects within your government can be broken down into digestible chunks that help others understand the outcomes and how they relate to things that they care about, as well as keeping you and your team focused and energized.

CREATE REAL THINGS AND SHARE THEM

One of the best things about working in local government is that there is a real willingness across the entire community to share ideas and new ways of thinking about addressing problems. As referenced elsewhere in this book, there are many resources and channels of communication where local government employees seek to empower each other in the pursuit of that common mission of public service.

However, based on my own experiences within local government and from attending conferences and events across the United States, there does appear to be a bias toward speaking to what is needed to be done rather than showing what actually has been done, at least in terms of the work related to technology and data. The ratio of words spoken versus software bits demonstrated seemed skewed in the wrong direction, to my mind at least. This was why I made a conscious effort to avoid speaking about "vaporware" (i.e. software or services that will never actually materialize) when I had a chance to speak to students or other local government staff in any capacity, and always attempted to demonstrate some of the real solutions that my team had developed. I would say that my most meaningful successes came from sharing these tools and processes that others could build upon, and the reaction of those in the audience afterwards helped confirm that there was a real need for more local government technologists to do likewise. Counter to the prevailing culture, I elected to share early and often! This included code via GitHub or demonstrating prototypes and beta-stage releases. More than once I had other staff query my decision to do so. Regardless, I learned that this early sharing of ideas and prototypes can help develop support and acceptance of new ideas where the pace of technological change had been traditionally slow and where exposure to open-source tools and languages was minimal to nonexistent.

Similarly, I was not shy about learning from other local governments and reusing their tools and processes for our work. I built some great relationships with my peers in other U.S. local governments, and they were only too happy to assist my team if needed. There is a huge opportunity for technologists to develop the network effects that can empower a large number of local governments across the United States at minimal cost through the sharing of code, tools, know-how, and encouragement.

CAPACITY BUILDING

One of the most striking things to a new technologist starting out in local government will be the realization of the extent of the reliance that government has on consultants and outsourcing. When it comes to the rollout of major IT projects, I can't think of a single instance in my time in local government where a seemingly small army of consultants performed a lot of the heavy lifting. As all government contracts are public record, you can research your own local government's reliance on consultants for yourself. Of course, all companies and organizations rely on consultants for services that are outside of their core competencies, but the scale of the reliance that exists within government at all levels is on a different plane. I am not proposing that we need a huge wave of technologists to enter government to completely eliminate this need—of course, there will always be a need for outside help when that makes sense. Rather, I am suggesting that one way you as a public-sector technologist can have impact is to look for those opportunities to build the internal technical capacity of your organization so that a healthier balance is established and that more taxpayer dollars can be allocated toward deriving more value from the internal technology staff. By helping to build the internal capacity for innovation, your government will be in a better position to maintain existing services and continue to deploy new or updated services in times when budgets are tight. Another benefit is that the internal technology staff will have more challenging work to focus on, growth opportunities will be more plentiful, and it will lead to the development of more highly technical roles that will be more attractive to private-sector technologists.

Before all of those positive outcomes can become reality, however, one useful way to build some short-term capacity is to use interns for suitable limited-term projects. Interns are often funded through partnerships with philanthropic organizations and local universities, so the only real costs to the local government are associated with hosting them for a summer (desk space, etc.), plus the extra management and coaching time you'll need to allocate to them. The project funders will typically cover a stipend for the student intern. If you have existing projects where you're looking to quickly scale, hiring some interns can be a great way to accelerate progress. I had the privilege of hosting some amazing interns within my team, with skillsets including software engineering, data science, program development, and policy analysis and evaluation. Aside from the fantastic work they produced, their enthusiasm and energy were infectious, and they demonstrated to existing staff new ways of thinking and working. Probably most importantly of all, they showed what could be accomplished in a short amount of time with the right amount of focus and determination. They are typically motivated by the desire to work in the public service, and so interns can be a fantastic pipeline of potential new full-time hires.

PROVIDE THOUGHT LEADERSHIP

A truly rewarding way to contribute to the public service mission is to provide thought leadership in your areas of expertise. Luckily, one of the many benefits of working within local government is that you will have no shortage of opportunities to do so. One strategy for building longer-term thought leadership opportunities is to look for opportunities to help your government differentiate itself from other localities. This is especially true when it comes to policy innovation. For example, the city of Seattle is known as a leader in data privacy, and you will find many examples online where city staff (such as the chief privacy officer) have contributed to articles, talks, panel events, conference presentations, podcasts, and so on. As privacy is such a topical issue at the time of writing, it means that Seattle is often at the forefront of these public conversations. Other cities are known for their own areas of expertise or focus, either in terms of policy or in terms of applications they have developed that other cities can leverage. As a technologist in local government, you will have opportunities to develop a nationwide profile as a leading thinker and doer in your areas of expertise that will be hard to replicate from within the private sector. Take advantage of them.

As mentioned earlier, governments are great about sharing ideas and know-how. The most effective online channels for doing so are Twitter, LinkedIn, articles in the state and local government press, and podcasts focused on (local) government. Focusing on these four channels alone should provide you with a broad audience. When it comes to providing content via these channels, I found that a hybrid approach of short-form content (e.g., tweets, LinkedIn updates) and long-form content (e.g., blog posts, published articles) works well. The great thing about social media is that it can greatly amplify the impact of the longer-form content. For example, if your local government has a blog, then be sure to add high-value content to it and then use Twitter to share its availability. By reviewing the analytics of your content postings, you can quickly discern what topics are resonating with the public and/or other government staff. For example, I noticed that posts about machine learning (ML) were hugely popular and that helped me think about future content that I could provide.

In terms of in-person channels, public speaking is an obvious must-do. This can be in the form of speaking at conferences, taking part in panel discussions at smaller events, or giving guest lectures at local universities and colleges. In addition to sharing your expertise, another great benefit in taking part in these events is that you'll often get great feedback and be exposed to new thinking. Similarly, developing partnerships with universities and other local governments can lead to opportunities to co-create content that will be beneficial to the broader community—such as generating research papers or even writing a book on your area of expertise.

SPEAK UP! OTHERS MAY SECRETLY WANT YOU TO

There will come a time in your public service where you encounter something so broken that you have no choice but to speak up, even if it's in an area totally outside of your span of control. Picking up things and helping fix them isn't really a part of the local government culture as it would be in the private-sector technology world, and so this can be one of the tough things to adapt to initially. My advice is to not to shy away from those situations, but in speaking up be thoughtful about how you might help unblock others from being able to act. Let me give you an example.

Part of my role at the city of Seattle involved traveling to conferences several times a year, and I was fortunate to be able to do so and very much enjoyed this aspect of my work. I had seen many tools and processes that hurt my head, but I was willing to accept dealing with these as part of the experience of working within the government, and I would frequently crack jokes about them. However, the travel reimbursement process was on another level. It was a mind-bogglingly complicated set of forms that required extensive documentation. The many rules and regulations that had to be precisely adhered to ultimately led to many follow-up emails and phone calls and, in my specific case, being hunted down by the finance staff. We had to use a spreadsheet to calculate certain values for hotel rates by city, per diem rates, and so on—it had so many macros embedded within that I seriously considered sending it to my old colleagues at Microsoft so they could use it in their memory leak testing for the Excel application. It was truly a masterpiece, a Jenga-like structure of paperwork worthy of inclusion in a future Government Bureaucracy Hall of Fame.

On a particularly wet and miserable Seattle morning, after months of laughing off bad processes like this one, I finally broke. I began to rage against the machine. At first I began stalling on submitting my exports—a form of silent protest. This resulted in visits from the unfortunate finance staffers, who also had deadlines to meet. They would appear at my desk with a look on their faces similar to how I would glare at my young daughter when she failed to precisely follow my instructions for the umpteenth time. My boss eventually had to get involved in the cajoling, crucially pointing out that our expenses reimbursement system was a bureaucratic hydra, with other departments being the source of many of the arcane requirements. Researching the varied sets of documentation helped me realize that these lasagna layers of processes was a great example of how a system is designed to suit existing processes and ways of doing things, rather than starting with the customer experience.

I decided to change course. I became a model of compliance with the travel approval and reimbursement processes and pivoted from protesting to attempting to help address the root causes. I mapped out the experience from my perspective and developed a detailed memo, complete with workflows, that outlined the less-than-optimal user experience. Most importantly, I suggested several steps where changes could be made reasonably quickly, from my perspective at least, to improve the process by removing unnecessary or duplicative steps. In my previous job, I also traveled for work and so understood what an efficient and relatively painless approvals and reimbursement process looked like. I pointed out that making the process better would result in better quality data, less time spent following up with laggards and more time spent on higher-value activities, and approval and reimbursement deadlines being met ahead of schedule. In short, it would be better for literally everyone involved. I volunteered to take part in any pilot programs for new processes. I sent the memo to the key staffers and their managers.

A week or more went by before I received a reply. I had been expecting a somewhat defensive reply, as feedback can be difficult to absorb initially, and as an experienced manager I had received plenty of similar feedback in the past. To my surprise and delight, the response was quite positive. In the time since I had submitted the memo they had reviewed my feedback and suggestions carefully and, most encouragingly, had had an initial meeting with the central finance department to see if there were ways to streamline their processes.

What this episode taught me was that by speaking up in the way that I did and providing possible solutions to the problems outlined, I had empowered these staffers to advocate for some changes. As mentioned earlier, government is somewhat more territorial than the private sector, and unlike in technology firms, it is not common to proactively step into other areas of control without advanced delicate diplomacy. The other major difference is that government doesn't seek feedback from its customers at nearly the same level as the private sector—internally or externally. When you don't have customer data to suggest there is a real problem, there is far less of an impetus to proactively solve those problems. By using me as the customer and my memo as the data, the finance staff had an excuse to instigate these meetings and create the space needed to explore changes that those same staff had privately told me were badly needed. In other words, sometimes your colleagues in local government will secretly want you to be a squeaky wheel.

BE A RESPONSIBLE TECHNOLOGIST

One of the hardest things about working in technology is that when new ideas occur to you, it's really hard not to jump in two feet first, make all kinds of wild assumptions, start building prototypes immediately, and excitedly share the news with anyone who will listen. Much less exciting is dealing with the realization that in order to actually get from that initial cool idea to making it a reality requires a lot of painstaking work, building relationships, validating assumptions early and often, and leaving behind high-quality documentation. This is especially true when first encountering an environment such as local government, where many seemingly tantalizing opportunities to improve things exist. Yet acting in a responsible way as a technologist is one of the best ways you can have impact when working in local government. Here are some ways you can demonstrate these qualities.

To begin with, it is important to respect the experience of those who are already working in government. It is quite likely that there will be others you will work with who may have had the same idea as you but couldn't make it happen—for example, they didn't have the budget or the buy-in from senior leaders. This is where having as many initial conversations as possible in your first one hundred days will prove valuable, as it is likely those previous attempts may surface in those conversations. Don't be shy about asking your new peers to talk about what projects were previously attempted and ran into problems. This will be a great way to gather data on what kinds of projects typically succeed and the reasons why they typically fail, as well as getting a sense of what projects may be good candidates for a reboot. If you do have an idea that is truly new, you'll be in a better position to know that in advance or who to ask to validate the idea.

Related to the last point, assume that these projects began with the best of intentions. Making assumptions about the intent or competency of staff who previously attempted to solve these problems can be an easy trap to fall into, especially at the beginning of your service. Just because your new peers and teammates don't use the latest open-source tools or still employ older software development methodologies (e.g., "waterfall" program management processes are still fairly common) does not mean they lack the skills needed to be good engineers or project managers. The rules concerning IT environments tend to be quite rigid within local government, and most staff will not have had the same opportunities as those in the private sector to explore new methods and tools and development environments. While this is slowly changing, this is yet another great way to have impact in your role and is a great way to reenergize staff who are looking to learn and grow and expand their skills. You can be a great advocate for this type of change, so look for support from your leadership to create safe spaces for innovation. You'll be amazed at the creativity that will be unleashed.

In addition to creating the space for innovation to occur, it is important to build open, interoperable systems. As one of your goals should be to share as much of your work as possible with others both inside and outside your organization, using open-source tools and generating open-source code is a must. There is a concerted movement within local government to use more open-source tools and languages, so be sure to make that a pillar of your strategy. Choosing the right tools is thus critical to the longer-term success of your technology initiative. Choosing industry-standard tools that are more likely to be maintained is key. For example, don't propose a new startup Content Management System (CMS) system just because it is cool and the new in-thing. Think about the longer-term interoperability requirements, training requirements, product updates, privacy, and other data-related policies, as well as the need to have the system serviced for many years. Remember that typical enterprise support agreements last for at least ten years, and these can sometimes be extended by paying extra. In government, always remember to expand your time horizons. This is why it is vital to leave behind high-quality documentation. People come and go, but major technology deployments have a habit of sticking around for quite a while. Assume that anything you help build or deploy as a government technologist will long outlive you, and ensure that you put in the effort to document everything as you go.

Aside from the technical aspects of your work, it is always important to ensure that you consider the many people who will be using your creations. One of the biggest differentiators between local government versus state and federal government is that the impact of your work can be quickly observed at the local level, especially in municipal governments. This is why it is important to research and collaborate on best practices for rolling out new digital services to the public, including communications. Before you get to that point, it is also vital to put residents first in your decision-making. This will include creating personas to help with service design goals and understanding your customers. Later it will include elements such as using human-centered design techniques and gathering as much early feedback as possible from the public to ensure that their experience in using the digital service surpasses their initial expectations. It is also vital to view your work through an ethical lens. Having a set of ethical principles to abide by is a good start, but being willing to listen to and act upon critical feedback will ensure you develop services that help lead to more equitable outcomes.

SELF-AWARENESS

Finally, having a good sense of self-awareness will be invaluable in your time working within government. Yes, this is true of any organization, but it is especially true of government. The key insight I gained during my time in government, however, is that no matter how prepared you think you are to deal with this unique environment, you will encounter situations that will test your patience and willpower to the limit. You will likely become highly agitated and frustrated at the seemingly slow pace of decision-making or the unwillingness of some people to do what on the face of it appears to be completely logical and the right thing to do. There will be days when you will seriously question your decision to join the public service. I am speaking from experience.

In order to deal with these emotions, here are a few things that I suggest may well help you also. If you already have a great sense of humor, then you have a head start. Being able to reduce the tension with a well-timed joke or anecdote can really turn your day around and that of your colleagues. My boss was especially gifted at this, and his frequent injections of clever wordplay and hilarious memes into contentious situations helped reduce tensions a great deal. "Have a good sense of humor" was one of the criteria, or "preferred qualifications," in our job descriptions. Being able to step outside of tricky situations to gain perspective is critical, so take lots of breathers, walks outside, coffee breaks, whatever works. Not responding to emails when agitated is good advice in any work environment, but especially true in government. After all, do you really want your email rants to be exposed via a public records request? Take advantage of every opportunity to network and socialize with your government work colleagues, both in your own government and when you get a chance to go to conferences. The camaraderie is fantastic and can feel like group therapy when you're dealing with challenging issues. You will also gain useful insights into how to approach tricky situations, or perhaps a colleague who is willing to partner with you in solving an issue. The old saying "a problem shared is a problem halved" is especially true in government. Oh, and watch the *Parks and Recreation* show if you haven't already; otherwise, you'll miss out on a lot of insider jokes.

ASK WHAT YOUR GOVERNMENT CAN DO FOR YOU

I won't lie: being a technologist brimming with ideas, passion, and energy can be a challenging role at times within local government. As this book is primarily arguing that we need more technologists to serve within local government itself, it is natural to ask what local government itself is doing to make it easier to attract and retain talented technologists and how it is empowering them once there. In the final section of this book, we'll explore some ideas that our state and local government leaders could explore, and some proposals they could enact, to speed up the digital transformation of local government.

CHAPTER 8: KEY TAKEAWAYS

- In this chapter, we explore how to move from being a "new hire" to being mostly "operational" within this new world of public service.
- Specially, you'll learn about important things in the world of local government in no particular order of importance, such as:
  - Understanding the budget cycles and how they may affect your work.

- Understand the politics surrounding the projects you'll be involved in.
- Know what the organization's tolerance for risk is.
- The "no surprises" rule and why ensuring that you overcommunicate is critical.
- Local election cycles and why they may affect your ability to move big projects forward.
- Don't overreact! Things will invariably go astray, and in a public role like local government, it is important to be very deliberate when responding (or not) to public feedback or criticism.
- Aligning with the common mission of government is very important, so make sure you truly understand what that common mission really is.
- Building relationships is especially vital in local government, as many decisions get made in person and not using electronic communications (think public records!).
- If you will be managing a team of people, work closely with your human resources team at all times. Many rules and regulations don't apply in the private sector, and many staff are members of unions.
- When communicating externally in any way, especially early in your tenure, work with your communications team to avoid any obvious gotchas. Over time, you will learn how to navigate the complexities of speaking on behalf of your agency to the public.
- The administrative staff in your division, and across the entire government, can be of immense help and value to you. They are literally worth their weight in gold. Leverage their knowledge and insights, as well as their ability to help with operational issues.
- Find "The Keymaker" in the technology department, the person who has the keys to the IT kingdom. They

can save you days and weeks of time and frustration and help you navigate the labyrinthine local government IT environments.

○ Figure out who the right "insiders" are in each section of government that you will need to interface with—those with the most useful knowledge about their department or branch of government and who are willing to share those insights.

○ Taking ownership of projects and deliverables is a great way to have quick impact and to establish credibility. Due to the rigid structures within local government, stepping up to own extra deliverables is not something that is as common, or expected, in the tech sector. Lead by example.

○ Government loves to talk about what they plan to do. In fact, it could be said that the metric of success in local government is being able to speak about future initiatives and less about actually making them happen. Create real things and share them with the local government ecosystem across the country. This is a very effective way to gain credibility and to have impact outside of your specific government.

○ Use your skills to help build the internal capacity of your local government so that programs and initiatives can continue to function well after your eventual departure.

○ Providing thought leadership in the form of blog posts, teaching, and public speaking is a fantastic way to develop your profile within the local government world and to expand your impact.

○ Speak up! Others may secretly want you to, which is especially true in a more formal environment like local government.

○ Be a responsible technologist while also pushing some boundaries and creating the space for innovation to happen. Also, don't assume that your ideas haven't already been attempted. Be respectful of the current and former staff who may have tried and failed, for reasons outside of their control, to innovate within local government.

o Finally, having good self-awareness is critical in an environment like local government. There will be lots of opportunities for social engagements with your new colleagues—use that time to develop great working relationships and learn from their experiences.

NOTES

1 Jane E. Fountain, "Enacting Technology in Networked Governance: Developmental Processes of Cross-Agency Arrangements," National Center for Digital Government Working Paper No. 06-003, (November 2006), http://scholarworks.umass.edu/cgi/viewcontent.cgi?article=1018&context=ncdg

2 "The West Wing 5x15 – 'Full Disclosure,'" westwingtranscripts.com, accessed October 16, 2019, http://www.westwingtranscripts.com/wwscripts/5-15.txt.

3 "Streisand Effect," Wikipedia, accessed January 16, 2020, https://en.wikipedia.org/wiki/Streisand_effect.

IV

OK, WHAT'S NEXT

9

ASK WHAT GOVERNMENT CAN DO

The primary argument this book is making is that there is a real need for more technologists to serve in government at all levels, but especially at local government levels. By building the capacity of technical talent within local government itself, we can accelerate the digital transformation of local government. The book also challenges technologists to more seriously consider public service as a viable option at some point in their career and to perform "tours of duty" in addition to any civic technology volunteering that they already perform. The focus of the book is then on the role of the technologist within government and how they can have positive social impact.

Another important question arises, however, and that is for existing government leaders to ask themselves what they can do to make local government a more attractive proposition for talented technologists. In Chapter 8, I discuss some of the issues I faced when trying to attract talented engineers into my team, but before we get into the nitty-gritty of those specific questions, I think it is important to first outline some ideas that can help existing government staff think about new approaches they can take when developing a new culture of innovation within their own local government, as well as helping attract and retain a new wave of technologists entering local government. Some of these ideas are my own, and some you may have seen elsewhere, but combined I believe that these suggestions also provide new technologists joining local government with interesting ideas for how they can add future technical capacity building into their own job descriptions and amplify their longer-term impact.

THINK BIGGER

Earlier in this book, we outlined the sheer size of the state and local government ecosystem in this country and the scale of the economic and social impact within its span of control. If some of our largest metropolitan areas have economies greater than many developed countries, then bold planning and a truly exciting vision for the future will be required to maintain and grow these local economies. Each local government should be asking itself questions like "What is the scale of our ambition?" Many cities and regions have future-facing plans with time horizons of twenty years or more, which is encouraging to see. These plans tend to focus on the externalities of government, however, and for the most part have not factored in the incredible changes in technology and data science being wrought as part of the Fourth Industrial Revolution and how they could be harnessed to help address some of the challenges that are identified in these visionary plans. Vision plans aside, how else can local governments think bigger?

VIEW DATA ANALYTICS AS AN INVESTMENT

One of my biggest critiques of the efforts to modernize local governments is their lack of ambition when it comes to investing in their digital transformation and how to leverage data as a strategic asset. Compared to the amount of time and energy that is expended in talking about the need to do these things, the actual monetary capital and political will that is deployed to make these aspirations a reality generally fall far short, as evidenced by the need for philanthropic funding to support many local government data and innovation programs. There is a real need for local government to view data analytics as an investment and not as a traditional information technology (IT) project or expense.

Let's use examples from my own recent experiences in the tech sector and local government to illustrate the differences in thinking. Toward the end of my tenure at Microsoft, I was a part of the Operating Systems Group (OSG), which was responsible for developing and releasing the Windows O/S in all its forms (Client, Server, etc.) worldwide, as well as a host of related activities, such as sustaining the O/S through the release of security updates. In total, there were about 12,000 full-time employees (FTE) in OSG. When the pivot was made to become almost entirely data-driven, a number of investments happened very quickly. One was the establishment of a data science team at the core of the division. Their numbers fluctuated over time, but roughly 90 to 120 FTE were dedicated to this group, with most being experienced researchers, data scientists, or software engineers with strong math and statistics backgrounds. Their core functions were to perform applied research, as well as having some capacity to perform "Research as a Service" for individual teams when they wished to uncover insights from the data Microsoft collected from its customers, and also providing training and support for the entire 12,000 OSG members and help them upskill. Essentially, a "train the trainer" model. This group of roughly 1 percent of the overall organization quickly transformed how the other 99 percent did their work, and over time more and more engineers had data science or analytics functions become a core part of their job description. Taking part in these trainings, and changing engineering workflows to avail ourselves of data, became a core priority. Funding was not an issue.

Fast-forward to my time at the city of Seattle, ironically an organization that also had roughly 12,000 FTE. The core innovation (data analytics) team numbered six people, with a smattering of data scientists and analysts across all departments. We estimated at the time that the total number of people who could be classified as working full-time with data were fewer than twenty. Some of those positions were funded using philanthropic grants. This comparison got me thinking about why local government struggled with seeing data as an investment and something that required bold action to remedy. There are many reasons why this is the case, but one issue I repeatedly encountered when advancing the use of data within local government was the need to educate the leadership on the positive benefits of doing this work. It took an enormous amount of time and energy, often with limited results. Another issue was convincing leaders that these investments need not be huge in order to really move the needle. The local government leaders I encountered had been conditioned to think of these requests in terms of multiyear IT projects costing millions of dollars, whereas our proposals were essentially to use open-source tooling and existing resources (including interns) to do more with the data that we already had. This is a common issue across local government. We need to come up with an easy way to explain and ultimately convince local government leaders to invest in data, using a reasonably sized request for new investment that wouldn't scare them away.

THE 1 PERCENT RULE

This led to the formulation of what I like to call "The 1 Percent Rule." It is essentially a rule of thumb that local governments of any size can employ to begin the process of transforming their ability to effectively use data. The rule is this: **At least 1 percent of total headcount should be specifically dedicated to data science and/or data analytics work.**

One of the reasons I chose this value was that it was an order of magnitude larger than current investments in data analytics, yet seems like a goal that should be easily achievable by any organization. If we take existing IT department sizes into account, this 1 percent goal becomes even more reasonable. For example, the IT department at the city of Seattle has a little over 700 staff at the time of writing, which roughly equates to 5.8 percent of the total number of employees. It is likely that this ratio is repeated in many local governments across the country. As IT departments continue to consolidate and migrate more services and infrastructure to the public cloud, opportunities to reassign existing IT headcount into data analytics headcount become available. This means that in some cases local governments may be able to reach the 1 percent threshold without having to create new headcount, or certainly without having to fund many new positions.

Rationale:

- One percent is a straightforward way for both government leaders and the public to think about data as an investment.
- One percent is not a large number, especially when the potential return on investment (ROI) can be significant.
- Even as the number of staff in government fluctuates over time, it will be easy to adjust data analytics operations and staffing using this rule.
- For smaller governments, these staff could form a central analytics unit.
- For larger governments, these staff could form a central analytics unit, plus have dedicated data staff in every department that act as a hub-and-spoke model. For example, many state and local government departments already have data officers or data stewards in place. This rule could help formalize these structures and their funding models.
- Ideally, a chief data officer (CDO) would lead the central analytics unit and oversee the development of a strategic plan for how the government will collect, store, analyze, and share data. They would also partner with chief information officers / chief technology officers (CIOs/CTOs) on developing a holistic approach to service delivery and data analytics needs within specific departments.

In the example I used earlier, following this rule would mean that the city of Seattle would move from having fewer than 20 staff dedicated to data analytics to about 120 staff. While this would mean roughly a six times increase in the number of dedicated data analytics staff, it is still a relatively small number when compared to the overall size of the organization, and the potential of this 1 percent to have a positive impact on how the remaining 99 percent of the organization performs their duties is significant. How significant? Well thanks to some great research by the team at the Harvard Kennedy School for Government, we have some insights into the scale of the impact that is possible through investing in data analytics.[1] Their report includes data from McKinsey, which states that in terms of monetary ROI, "research shows that efforts to apply data analytics to eliminating waste, fraud, and abuse in government can have returns as high as 10 to 15 times their cost." Additionally, when factoring in nonfinancial benefits, "as governments improve efficiency and decrease waste, fraud, and abuse, their esteem among the public grows and faith in government improves." This report outlines several examples from state and local governments that highlight the efficiencies, operational improvements, and elimination of waste and fraud made possible by their investments in data analytics.

There are other examples besides data analytics that could be listed here to highlight this need for local government to think bigger. I focus on data analytics specifically, as I believe it presents the largest opportunity for local government to transform itself in the coming decade and provides one of the best and most exciting ways for it to attract and retain a new generation of talented technologists.

CHANGE THE NARRATIVE

In the introduction to this book, I lamented the fact that the story of government, from state and local to federal and everything in between, is not being told. There is no "West Wing" for local government. Instead, the vast majority of the public only see, read, and hear stories that reinforce the negative stereotypes about local government. Stereotypes are enormously difficult to change, but not impossible. How? Change the narrative.

Technology, and technologists, can play a leading role in making that happen.

One way to start this process is to change how local government thinks of itself. It's a safe bet to assume that if any government at any level was to describe itself, the words "technology" or "data" or "innovation" wouldn't appear in that description. Instead, the language would include references to services, people, community, diversity, inclusion, and so on. This is not unlike how major private companies also publicly describe themselves. Let's look at one example that everyone reading this book will be familiar with, including the author: Starbucks. Their mission statement is "to inspire and nurture the human spirit—one person, one cup and one neighborhood at a time." As mission statements go, it does a great job of giving us a warm feeling about the place where many of us spend a lot of time. However, if you pull back the curtain and really examine what Starbucks is, you'll discover that in fact it is a technology company that sells coffee. This is not just my analysis; senior leaders at that company regularly make this inference when speaking to the media or at conferences. Starbucks has an enormous technical capability, from software engineering to advanced data science. Think about how many innovations have been added to their app during recent years, how these extra conveniences have improved our experience as Starbucks consumers, and have in small but subtle ways made it more likely that we'll return as customers. Before the app even existed, there were Starbucks cards, which acted as physical payment cards, through which we could collect points toward "rewards" that allow us to get free drinks and food. Once their app was launched, it initially replaced that physical card, while allowing for location services to prompt the app once you entered a Starbucks to have your "card" automatically available on your lock screen for even faster access to their app. Later, mobile ordering was added, which was a huge innovation and has saved me and countless other customers many minutes of time where normally we would be standing in line. That innovation also meant that customers' names would be spelled correctly and that they would get the correct drink—thereby reducing wastage. Integration with a music service, Spotify, allows customers to easily check out and purchase the music that is playing in their stores, with Starbucks getting a cut of each transaction initiated via their app. There is also the merchandise, such as Starbucks mugs, which are another brilliant way to create attachment. I am a prime example; instead of buying a fridge magnet when I travel, I now prefer to buy a Starbucks mug from that city. I have over forty mugs at home as of this writing. Everything I have described here is just one aspect of how Starbucks is using technology and data to enhance their brand and customer experiences, in addition to some good old-fashioned analog merchandising.

Let's examine another side effect of their technology, one that the public is less aware of. Millions of Starbucks customers also preload their Starbucks virtual "cards" with money, often in an automated fashion when balances reach a certain threshold. By doing this, Starbuck's customers are essentially giving them an interest-free loan multiple times a year. In addition to having millions of customers whose coffee spending habits are known to them, Starbucks can accurately predict how much those customers will spend in the future—which makes future financial modeling easier. In fact, Starbucks has more money on deposit as a result of their app than many major U.S. banks. In any given quarter, Starbucks may have somewhere between $1.5 and $2 billion on hand as a result of customers preloading their card balances.[2] In effect, Starbucks is one of the largest banks in the United States as a result of having more customer money on hand than many banks have in deposits.[3] Next time you're in a Starbucks, take a moment to think about all of the ways that technology is playing a role in your experience there, as well as before and after you enter the store. Think also about the other possibilities that technology can enable in such environments, such as using machine learning to create more personalized experiences for their customers.[4]

Now, what if local governments were to attempt to reimagine the role technology could play in helping to completely change the experience that their customers had? What would that look like? What if local government was to think about itself as a technology enterprise that provides services to the public as one of its personas? What if we had the chance to go back to the drawing board and reimagine and redesign government from scratch. What if…

INVERT

In order for something like what I am proposing to be even remotely possible, we need to completely change how we think about government and how it functions today, and we need to be willing to work toward building a system that may not exist for some time. We need to be willing to make some big bets and to invest for the long term. Or to put it another way, we need to invert our thinking.

Blue Origin is a space company based in Kent, Washington. It is about twenty miles south of Seattle, and it is owned and privately funded by Jeff Bezos, the founder and CEO of Amazon. Its primary focus is on providing regular, repeatable space travel into low-earth orbit, whereas SpaceX (owned by Elon Musk) is primarily focused on deep space missions, such as the goal to transport humans to Mars. An extract from their mission statement states: "Blue's part in this journey is building a road to space with our reusable launch vehicles, so our children can build the future."[5] For several years, I couldn't quite figure out exactly what Blue Origin was attempting to do, until I happened to hear a rare interview that Bezos gave about their work at Blue Origin. At the 2016 Vox Recode Conference, he spoke about the need to invert heavy industry—in other words, move heavy industry off the surface of the Earth and into outer space and, by extension, use Blue Origin spaceships to transport heavy materials to and from Earth.[6] A new kind of Amazon Prime business, if you will. All of a sudden, everything clicked into place in my mind. Aside from the audacity of the long-term plan, which I loved, the idea that really grabbed my attention was the use of the term "invert." The more I thought about it, the more I realized that inverting systems was a common strategy that Bezos employed. Take Amazon Web Services (AWS) as another example. AWS originated from the brilliant insight that some of the internal infrastructure Amazon had developed to help them scale their online business and solve some of their most pressing computer storage and processing needs would also be useful to many other companies who would likely be facing similar challenges. Instead of assuming that every company would want to host their own servers and build their own datacenters, which is incredibly expensive and time consuming (and which was Microsoft's business model), Amazon realized that other companies might just want to lease that capacity on an on-demand basis. In other words, they inverted the enterprise model and helped create an entirely new way of building businesses that could rapidly scale their computing infrastructure at a relatively low cost. Platform as a Service (PaaS), Infrastructure as a Service (IaaS), and Software as a Service (SaaS) companies were born, resulting in tens of billions of dollars of new revenue for Amazon and their competitors scrambling to catch up—while also initially powering the rapid growth of online giants like Facebook and Netflix. The question I always ask myself about this is how come it was Amazon who essentially invented the cloud as we know it today? How come everyone else missed it? I believe that it is Bezos's ability to think about inversion that helps set Amazon apart from the rest.

We are also experiencing a form of inversion in how people choose to live and work. In his 2013 book *The Great Inversion and the Future of the American City*, Alan Ehrenhalt "reveals how the roles of America's cities and suburbs are changing places—young adults and affluent retirees moving in, while immigrants and the less affluent are moving out—and addresses the implications of these shifts for the future of our society."[7] A key factor in this population movement has been the ongoing trend of big tech moving their main base of operations directly into cities, as opposed to the suburbs where large tech companies traditionally located their headquarters (HQ). These shifts are having profound effects on the physical makeup of our urban areas, with many cities, both large and small, experiencing almost unprecedented levels of redevelopment. Aside from the many new buildings appearing on our cities' horizons, how people travel to and from work and their places of recreation have also been changing. New forms of mobility are continually being tested and experimented with, from ride sharing to car sharing to electric scooters and a host of other innovations in between, as well as increased investments in, and usage of, public transit. The pace of change being driven by the rapid deployment of new mobility technologies has led to public policy standoffs in many of our major cities, with local governments trying to cope with these hugely popular innovations without a clear policy or legal framework to guide them, as well as a lack of data on the consequences of these services operating as they would wish to.

If you're still not convinced about the powers of inversion that are at play in our cities and how our local governments are struggling to deal with them, consider the recent effort by Amazon to run a competition to identify its new "HQ2." In September 2017, Amazon announced that it wished to build a second HQ in North America and would seek proposals from cities in North America. At stake was an investment of $5 billion to develop a campus with up to 50,000 jobs and a promise that this new HQ would be a "full equal" to the existing Seattle HQ.[8] The outcome of this process is now well known, but that is not what is of interest here. Rather, it is how Amazon inverted the "request for proposals" (RFP) process. Typically, state and local governments issue RFPs. They do so when seeking bids from vendors and consultants who could fulfill the requirements for new systems and infrastructure to be deployed on the government's behalf. Amazon inverted that process with their HQ2 competition. They issued an RFP where the local governments were the vendors, offering their cities and counties as the best solution for what Amazon sought, complete with generous tax breaks and other incentives. 238 local governments submitted bids for this RFP, with some going to extraordinary lengths to entice Amazon to favor their bids.

How could local government apply these principles of inversion? At the very least, we can start formulating some of the big questions that might unlock some fantastic opportunities to invert current systems and change the way we all think about government. For example, why do all local governments try to solve the same problems basically independently of each other? Yes, they share a lot of information and sometimes some pieces of code, but basically they are trapped in the software vendor and consultant ecosystem. Government procurement is a massive multibillion-dollar enterprise, with state and local governments projected to spend an incredible $107.6 billion in 2019 on IT alone.[9] Procurement practices have been flagged as one of the major barriers to innovation within government, and civic technologists such as Code for America are trying to tackle these issues with some innovative approaches.[10] But what would it look like to truly invert that system? There are many, many other examples that we could explore.

Who will lead the drive to help us think through these inversion questions? Unlike the federal government, there is no central agency or power structure that oversees policies and appropriations that could help drive this work, no one JFK-type figure to declare that "we choose to go to the Moon." The major philanthropic efforts, such as Bloomberg Philanthropies, are one such, albeit limited, effort. Some of the larger tech companies have also been stepping up to challenge the status quo. In Toronto, a project is currently underway to design a "smart city" from the ground up. Led by Sidewalk Labs, a Google company, they are "designing a district in Toronto's Eastern Waterfront to tackle the challenges of urban growth" in conjunction with local government and the community.[11] This project is a good example of how pushing against some of the existing boundaries and norms of urban development can create controversy and pushback. The largest issue stems from concerns about how data collected from residents, visitors, and workers who will populate this new district will be controlled, used, and possibly resold. Due to the huge number of sensors being deployed, privacy activists have highlighted concerns about improper data collection and heightened surveillance. These are important conversations, and it is good that these issues are being openly discussed and worked through. Any effort to invert an existing system as large and complicated as a city will require tough conversations and a huge amount of effort to work through the technical, policy, legal, ethical, and equity challenges. We should not lose sight of the fact that without these kinds of projects such as the Sidewalk Labs Toronto project, no one will be able to create the "existence proofs" that demonstrate that *there can be another way*, that is it possible, and that others now have a new direction to follow. With the right level of investment and the political will to experiment and to drive these projects forward, perhaps it might be possible to invert our local government systems after all.

TALENT ACQUISITION

In the introduction to this book, I make the point that local government is generally quite passive when it comes to seeking out the technical talent it needs. Being so passive in a labor market that already has a huge demand for technical talent is not a viable long-term strategy—not if we want to really move the needle on what local government can do. The question of how to attract and retain talented technologists is one that now should be addressed with increased urgency.

Where to start in addressing this question? Having gone through the process of leaving the private/technology sector to enter local government myself, I believe that attracting a new generation of technologists into local government is possible, even in the current labor market. In order to do so, several changes should be enacted by local governments so that they can move closer to where they can meet technologists where they are at and not expect technologists to move into the space (physical, cultural, etc.) that local governments currently occupy. Meeting somewhere in the middle would be a great start, but I would argue that local government should go further, should be more risk adverse, and really experiment in some areas. These areas include articulating the mission of the organization, identifying clear problems that additional technologists can help solve, and creating more jobs that directly translate into the language of the tech sector.

Of course, local government will have many technical roles that don't really exist in the private sector. The job that I performed, open data manager, doesn't really exist in the private sector, but it is relatively common in the public sector. It was attractive to me because I had already identified open data as an area of technology policy that I was especially interested in as I pursued my master's degree in public policy, and when an exciting position opened up within my own region, I was ready to jump at it. This is true for other technologists serving in local government. Appealing to a new generation of technologists, however, will require some adjustments to this approach. Translating the needs of local government into modern language that appeals to technologists is crucial. In addition to the job titles and descriptions being structured to be more appealing to technologists, the language used within those job advertisements can play a huge role in whom those jobs appeal to. Augmented writing services, such as tools provided by Textio, can allow you to create language that will appeal to the very people that local governments would ideally want to hire, as well as appealing to their values and aspirations for how to have impact.[12]

Making it easier for people to apply for these positions is another important step in this process. Even with the introduction of government-focused online job application hubs, some of the requirements for applicants can be onerous and therefore off-putting. Reducing unnecessary steps and requirements for documentation where possible can have a significant impact in how many potential candidates fully complete an application. Indeed, this is an area that civic technologists often focus on helping local governments with: how to reduce the number of steps in their hiring workflows.

The physical infrastructure where people work is a huge part of the talent acquisition equation. It is easy to scoff at some of the perceived excesses in the modern workplaces provided by tech companies in particular, but there is a very good reason why some of these larger companies spend billions of dollars leasing and building this kind of infrastructure. These work environments are very attractive to Millennials, and coming soon, the Gen Z workforce. As a Gen X'er myself, I struggle with open-concept office spaces and a lack of privacy, but I also appreciate that the future of work is leading us in some new directions, and so it is good to embrace these changes as best as we can and find the right balance of closed and open spaces. Some larger municipal governments have already begun experimenting with the physical design of the spaces where their innovation teams work from.

There is an extra step that local governments can take, however, that can help with recruiting the next generation of technologists. Instead of expecting everyone to work at existing government locations, local governments can instead experiment with using coworking spaces for innovation-type teams and get them out of city hall and into the place where those civic technologists are already working. This approach could have multiple benefits, apart from exposing the work of local government to other technologists currently not thinking about government work: it would lead to spontaneous interactions that could lead to serendipitous outcomes. Having teams of public-sector technologists working out of a local coworking space for part of their week would do much to increase the coolness factor of city hall. Local governments should do more to meet the next wave of technologists where they already are.

Similarly, look for opportunities to bring other local government staff into environments such as tech companies, startups, and so on. As previously mentioned, bringing staff from the public and private sectors together can lead to all kinds of serendipity, and the key here is not to expect those private-sector employees to come to government buildings; rather, it is also very beneficial for government workers to get out of their own environments and experience how technologists and other professionals do their work. This is exactly how we foster more mutual understanding and respect between the sectors. I speak from experience. In 2017, as part of our efforts to empower our city employees to use data more effectively, we held our annual Data Camp training event that year at two separate locations outside of our government buildings. Staff were hosted at the Tableau and Socrata headquarters in Seattle, where they were trained on data visualization and storytelling techniques, as well as gaining exposure to new data tools and methods. Our city staff were then able to take those new skills back to their respective teams and use them to develop new insights from their many sources of data. These Data Camp events created many opportunities for networking and discussion and helped build empathy and more understanding between the groups.[13]

Finally, local government could do more to leverage programs that enable technologists from the private sector to take a leave of absence and temporarily serve in local government. Many of the larger tech-sector companies have developed "civic leave programs," where staff are allowed to take a leave of absence to go serve in government. Currently, these programs are focused on the federal government level only, and the jobs are mostly based in Washington, DC.[14] The most advanced of these programs is one developed by Microsoft.[15] I believe that there is scope to expand these programs to state and local government and create the opportunity to allow experienced technologists to investigate possibly working in these branches of government. Working in a location much closer to home, and their company HQ, would be a much better fit for most people and allow them to focus on issues closer to their communities, where the impact of their work will be more immediate and visible, and may even tie into public policy issues that the company itself cares about. There will likely be some conflict of interest issues to work through, as many tech companies count government at all levels among their largest customers, but I believe the potential upside here would make those investments very worthwhile.

Aside from the movement of technologists into the actual government itself, another approach is to avail ourselves of volunteer programs within tech companies. One of my favorite examples is the Tableau Foundation. Tableau, a leading data visualization software company based in Seattle, issues generous grants to many public-sector and nonprofit organizations via their foundation. Recognizing that simply issuing grants isn't enough, the Tableau Foundation amplifies the impact of those grants by having highly skilled volunteer staff from Tableau help with upskilling staff within the organizations receiving the grants in how to make better use of the organization's data.[16] Both of these approaches can generate tremendous opportunities for real and lasting impact by developing the infrastructure and know-how that empower governments to do more. State and local government should avail themselves of these opportunities to build these pipelines of talent into government and help accelerate their digital transformations.

CREATE THE SPACE FOR
INNOVATION TO HAPPEN

It is one thing to think about lofty concepts such as inversion, narratives, and talent acquisition; it is quite another to put in place the conditions where such concepts and ideas could be made real. Without local government being able to create the space for such innovative thinking to take effect, the status quo will remain. When leaders in government talk about creating the space to innovate, they typically will speak about organizational culture and leadership and perhaps even the physical environments where people can do their best work. As we have discussed elsewhere in the book, these are all important things to discuss and implement. There is, however, one policy lever that all local governments can pull that can create the conditions required for these kinds of innovative advances to actually take effect, but rarely do. This lever is within their budget, and it is how they treat spending on technology within that budget.

Most state and local governments view their IT departments as "cost-recovery" units, that is, IT departments are expected to recover all of the costs associated with the delivery of their services to all of the other departments. In most cases, this is 100 percent of costs. This typically means that IT departments spend large amounts of time and energy ensuring that they operate within the budget constraints of the various departments they are servicing. These budget pressures are often the real reason why IT projects in many state and local governments struggle to be completed on time and on budget—and the IT department often gets the blame in such cases. One major side effect of this approach is that IT departments up and down the land struggle to procure any budget allocations for innovation-related activities.

275

How to address this? For starters, local governments need to stop thinking about technology and data simply as an "expense" and to think about them as an "investment" that will lead to real, tangible returns in the short, medium, and long term. In other words, local government should invert its thinking with regard to technology and data. There is a good reason why the private sector invests billions of dollars in the latest tools, technologies, infrastructure, and acquiring data—the productivity gains and economies of scale realized from these investments can be huge. A great first step to is reevaluate the budget structures surrounding technology and data within local government and seek ways to add funding for innovation-related activities completely separate from the day-to-day running of the IT departments. Some of this funding could be achieved with contributions from each department, where there is an expectation that the innovations produced would result in process improvements and efficiencies that would flow back into those departments in terms of productivity gains and reduced spending in some areas. Additionally, investments in data analytics at the governmental and departmental level would lead to insights that could result in similar outcomes.

This isn't just an idea—some municipal governments have already demonstrated that efforts like these do produce real results. These are exactly the kinds of challenges that talented technologists seek out and thrive on. If the political will exists to make bold changes to how local government thinks about technology and data and how it invests in those activities, then the technologists will come.

UNDERSTAND "THE FUTURE OF WORK" AND ITS IMPLICATIONS WITHIN LOCAL GOVERNMENT

Before some of these objectives can be accomplished, local government leaders need to develop a true sense of what their own future labor needs will be. Ironically, while government at all levels is spending a lot of time and energy on issues related to "the future of work" in the overall economy, there is little evidence that government is also thinking about how these issues pertain to government itself. Without a clear understanding of how government *itself* needs to adapt to these changes caused by automation and AI, it will be impossible to develop those bold, futuristic plans that will encourage the kind of lateral and inverted thinking that will be required regarding the role of technology in how our civil institutions will function in the years to come.

Many studies have been completed on the question of what the future of work will actually look like. While it is basically impossible to accurately predict the outcomes, much of the research completed to date can provide local government with some idea of how to quantify the potential impact.[17] Using these frameworks and data, local government can begin to create assessments for where their current labor pools are most vulnerable to these advances and to start planning and having discussions with unions and other stakeholders ahead of time. It is imperative that local government understand that changes as a result of automation and artificial intelligence (AI) are inevitable. State and local governments will not be immune.

Building the capacity of technical talent in local government is one of the key ways that local government can help with planning for and managing these transitions. It will not be enough to simply follow the old models and rely on armies of consultants to do the heavy lifting. This is not a transformation that will be easily outsourced. It will require teams of dedicated public-sector technologists who are passionate about government and the civil servants that work there to help shepherd these changes through in the most humane and equitable way possible. This is exactly the kind of challenge that will attract a new wave of mission-oriented technologists into local government.

THE CEO DRIVES THE CULTURE

As the title of this book and its ongoing references to President Kennedy suggest, I am a big fan of his approach to making big bets, being able to articulate them incredibly effectively, and inspiring generations of people to follow that call into public service. Likewise, the Obama administration proved to be another high point in how our young people viewed public service and led to renewed efforts to reshape or rebuild major parts of the federal government and attempt to really move the needle on its digital transformation. What was it about these two presidents and their administrations that so captured the imaginations of new college graduates and professionals alike and enticed them into public service? How did they, for want of a less controversial description, make government cool again? Was it the person in the form of the president, or the mission, or both?

One of the key ingredients, I believe, is that they had a plan and they were willing to make significant investments in order to achieve their goals, with the race to the Moon being the ultimate example of how to create an incredibly ambitious plan, to craft inspirational speeches that still capture the imagination to this day, and then to put in place the people and machinery to deliver upon those objectives. To quote President Kennedy from his famous "Moon Speech" at Rice University in 1961, "we do these things not because they are easy, but because they are hard."[18] More than the heady language and coolness factor, there was a plan and the willingness to make it happen. There was also one other critical, yet intangible, element at play in those examples of governments getting things done. It was the organizational culture of the time, and in both cases that culture was set from the very top, by the president.

Just how important the person at the top is, who I'll refer to as the "CEO," in setting the culture became abundantly clear to me over the course of my final three years at Microsoft. It was during this time that Satya Nadella took over as CEO, only the third CEO in the company's forty-year history. He replaced two iconic figures, Bill Gates and Steve Ballmer, who had led the company for decades and who had ingrained a certain way of doing things into the fabric of the organization. At that time, the company was struggling to rediscover its identity after more than a decade of miscues and missed opportunities. It needed to reboot, and quickly. This massive company, with 128,000 employees at that time,[19] somehow was able to completely transform its culture and within five years was once again the most valuable technology company in the world with a market capitalization exceeding $1 trillion.[20] Initially watching this cultural transformation from within, and later from afar, I was fascinated by this metamorphosis. Nadella wrote a book in 2017 outlining how he led this transformation, primarily by instilling the principles of a growth mind-set into how the company operated and by changing the company's major business models to pivot toward a "Cloud First, Mobile First" focus, later adding AI as a central plank of their strategy.[21]

How, then, can you transcribe these kinds of cultural transformations into the public sector, and state and local government specifically? Due to the complex makeup of government, with its multiple branches and council oversight and complex labor union agreements, is something like this even possible? I believe so, and here are several takeaways from those historic examples and from my own observations in local government and personal experiences in leading teams that governments of all shapes and sizes could apply.

1. *The CEO owns and drives the culture change.*
   This is the biggest learning I took from my Microsoft experience. Without this top-down sponsorship, real culture change will not occur. The person at the top of the organization needs to passionately believe in, own, and drive the culture change— and build a leadership team to help them push these changes throughout the entire organization. Through their actions and spoken and written words, they continually reinforce the desired changes, use their power to quickly effect changes that help create the space for innovation to thrive, and engender the trust of the overall organization. In local government, the "CEO" would be

the mayor, or county executive, or governor, or agency director, etc. While it is unlikely we will see many experienced technologists running for mayor, it is incumbent upon us technologists to be vocal advocates for the person at the top to living these new cultural values while driving these changes across the organization.

2. *Articulate a clear vision.*

   Create an open-ended mission statement that every government employee can align their work with, as well as having it resonate with every taxpayer and resident that they serve. Develop supporting ideals that everyone in the organization can easily understand (e.g.. "One Government"). These can help staff think differently about their role in breaking out of entrenched silos. Empower your staff to work across boundaries with minimal preapproval, and support new employee-devised initiatives. As an experienced technologist, you already will be familiar with efforts such as these and can play a leading role in developing clear vision statements and then aligning the work to those values and goals over time.

3. *Push the organization to do more.*

   Think of new ways to incentivize local government staff around a big unified goal that will resonate with everyone—something that is measurable, whose impact is potentially significant, easily understood, and appreciated by the government and public alike. Then, create the space for staff to unleash their creativity, and reward innovators. Again, as an experienced technologist, you already will be familiar with efforts like these and can lead by example.

4. *Obsess about your residents (customers).*

   Always start from the perspective of the resident you are serving and work backwards from there. Directly and indirectly engaging with your residents (customers) should be a key part of any organizational culture: for example, passively via feedback and service usage data or proactively via human-centered design for new or existing services. Reimagine what it means to "serve the public"—ideally, this can mean enabling the public to help themselves without any direct government staff interaction. I believe that this is one of the most effective ways for new technologists coming into local government to have clearly visible impact in the short to medium term.

5. *Your data is an asset, so leverage it.*

    You cannot improve what you cannot measure. Without the capability to define success metrics and then track progress, you lose a key pillar in your strategy to drive culture change across the organization. Having data be a key part of everyone's job is critical to empowering each employee to play their part in driving culture change from their position. The one asset all governments have in abundance is data, and it gets more valuable the more you use it. Think of investments in data infrastructure and upskilling in terms of unlocking significant return on investment (ROI), rather than as a sunk cost or line-item expense.

Without the CEOs of local government, the mayors and county executives and other leaders, effectively articulating what the culture of their organization is and leading by example each and every day, real change in local government simply will not happen. No amount of bottom-up or grassroots-driven efforts will succeed in changing the culture of the organization unless the CEO truly believes in that vision. There is an army of young technologists just waiting for the right opportunities to engage with and serve within their local governments, to help realize a new culture of innovation within local government and enable a new paradigm for public service delivery, if only the current leadership would let them. Just like President Kennedy did, when 400,000 of the best and brightest technologists heard his call and ultimately realized his vision.

CHAPTER 9: KEY TAKEAWAYS

- In this final chapter, we invert the focus of the book and instead ask what government leaders can do to better attract and retain talented technologists in the future. It challenges government leaders and other advocates for better local government to think more creatively about how government can attract and retain a new wave of talented technologists and how to empower them to use its existing assets (e.g., data) and new technologies to build the next generation of local government.

- Think bigger:
  - Government needs to view data analytics as an investment—and not as a cost. Current expenditures on data analytics are simply nowhere near what's required.
  - The 1 percent rule—this author advocates for state and local governments to consider dedicating at least 1 percent of their headcount for data science and data analytics functions.

- Change the narrative—how local government can begin to think differently about itself, using the example of how Starbucks, to everyone's mind a coffee company, is essentially a technology company, and how it leverages technology and data to radically change their customers' habits and in doing so effectively become one of the largest banks in the United States.

- Invert—following from the Starbucks example, we examine how Amazon and Blue Origin have used the process of inversion to either completely upend large systems and norms or begin the work to do so. Systems and arrangements that were taken for granted as being institutional in nature are not immune to the forces of change. Many of the systems and processes within state and local government are institutional in nature, but some could be good candidates to be inverted and in doing so create new opportunities for real innovation in local government.

- Ironically, while government at all levels is spending a lot of time and energy on issues related to "the future of work" in the overall economy, there is little evidence that government is also thinking about how these issues pertain to government itself. Government is not immune to the impacts of automation and AI; in fact, the rote nature of much of the administrative and bureaucratic work executed in government makes it a prime candidate for automation to disrupt it. Leaders in government need to also focus on this internally as well as externally.

- Local government is generally quite passive when it comes to seeking out the technical talent it needs. Being so passive in a labor market that already has a huge demand for technical talent is not a viable long-term strategy.

- In addition to improving how local government attracts and retains technical talent, leaders in government should be more aggressive about creating the space for real innovation to happen. This will require a fundamental change in culture.

- The CEO drives the culture in any organization. The governor, the mayor, or the county executive is the leader who must drive any real and lasting culture change around how technology and data will be used to build a next-generation local government that the public will be satisfied with. Bottom-up efforts to shape the culture are not enough—the leader needs to believe in this change and drive its implementation on a daily basis in words and deeds.

NOTES

1   "The Case for Government Investment in Analytics," Ash Center for Democratic Governance and Innovation at Harvard Kennedy School, last updated September 3, 2019, https://datasmart.ash.harvard.edu/news/article/case-government-investment-analytics.
2   "Starbucks, Monetary Superpower," Moneyness, last updated August 21, 2019, https://jpkoning.blogspot.com/2019/08/starbucks-monetary-superpower.html.

3   "Starbucks Has More Customer Money on Cards than Many Banks Have in Deposits," MarketWatch, last updated June 11, 2016, https://www.marketwatch.com/story/starbucks-has-more-customer-money-on-cards-than-many-banks-have-in-deposits-2016-06-09.

4   "Starbucks Turns to Technology to Brew Up a More Personal Connection with its Customers," Microsoft, last updated May 6, 2019, https://news.microsoft.com/transform/starbucks-turns-to-technology-to-brew-up-a-more-personal-connection-with-its-customers.

5   "Blue Origin—Our Mission," Blue Origin, accessed November 7, 2019, https://www.blueorigin.com/our-mission.

6   "Amazon CEO Jeff Bezos at Code 2016," Vox Media, last updated June 1, 2016, https://www.vox.com/2016/6/1/11826718/jeff-bezos-amazon-full-video-code.

7   Alan Ehrenhalt, *The Great Inversion and the Future of the American City* (New York: Penguin Random House, 2013).

8   "Amazon to Build Second HQ in North America, Seeks Proposals from Cities for $5B Campus with up to 50K Jobs, 'Full Equal' to Seattle Operations," GeekWire, last updated September 7, 2017, https://www.geekwire.com/2017/amazon-build-second-hq-outside-seattle-seeks-proposals-cities-5b-campus-50k-jobs.

9   "2019 State and Local Annual IT Spending," GeekWire, accessed September 24, 2019, https://www.govtech.com/navigator/numbers/state--2019local-annual-it-spending_132.html.

10   "Procurement 101," Code for America, accessed September 24, 2019, https://www.codeforamerica.org/how-tos/procurement-101.

11   "Sidewalk Labs—Home," Sidewalk Labs, accessed September 24, 2019, https://www.sidewalklabs.com.

12   "Textio Hire," Textio, accessed September 24, 2019, https://textio.com/products.

13   "CityStream: Open Data & Transparency," City of Seattle, last updated November 30, 2017, http://www.seattlechannel.org/CityStream/segments?videoid=x85511.

14   "The White House Is Wooing Tech Workers to Do Tours of Duty in Government," Washington Post, last updated October 22, 2018, https://www.washingtonpost.com/technology/2018/10/22/white-house-is-wooing-tech-workers-do-tours-duty-government.

15   "A fireside chat with Matt Cutts, USDS Administrator, and Satya Nadella, Microsoft CEO: Civic Service Leave," U.S. Digital Service, last updated August 28, 2018, https://medium.com/the-u-s-digital-service/a-fireside-chat-with-matt-cutts-usds-administrator-and-satya-nadella-microsoft-ceo-civic-3bcaad68680e.

16 "Experteering: A New Way for Tableau Employees to Make a Difference in the World," Tableau, last updated April 18, 2019, https://www.tableau.com/about/blog/2019/4/experteering-new-way-tableau-employees-make-difference-world-105920.

17 "The Future of Work in Figures," OECD, accessed October 25, 2019, https://www.oecd.org/employment/future-of-work/Future-of-work-infographic-web-full-size.pdf.

18 "John F. Kennedy Moon Speech - Rice Stadium," NASA, accessed October 25, 2019, https://er.jsc.nasa.gov/seh/ricetalk.htm.

19 "Microsoft Corporation: Employee Count from 2005 to 2019," Statista, accessed October 25, 2019, https://www.statista.com/statistics/273475/number-of-employees-at-the-microsoft-corporation-since-2005.

20 "Microsoft Hits $1 Trillion Market Value for First Time," The Wall Street Journal, last updated April 25, 2019, https://www.wsj.com/articles/microsoft-hits-1-trillion-market-value-for-first-time-11556201153.

21 Satya Nadella, Greg Shaw, and Jill Tracie Nichols, *Hit Refresh: The Quest to Rediscover Microsoft's Soul and Imagine a Better Future for Everyone* (New York: Harper Collins, 2017).

EPILOGUE

In this book I have shared some ideas about how local governments could benefit from an infusion of technological talent. I've also shared examples of how civil servants are making progress toward improving how local governments can use data and technology more effectively—these efforts are being undertaken in conjunction with civic technologists, public-interest technologists, academics, and philanthropic organizations. Much work remains to be done, and new challenges driven by the rapid advancement of AI and automation are looming. The need for more technologists to join in these efforts and serve in their state and local governments is growing.

As this book is a call to action, I thought it might be helpful to end by sharing some thoughts on how I view my own contribution while serving within local government for two years. I also share insights into some of the events I witnessed and the people I encountered throughout my life that helped inspire me to join the public service. Because the hope is that many of you reading this book may eventually follow in my footsteps, and those of the many other technologists who have served in government, these insights and reflections will hopefully prove useful.

REFLECTIONS ON MY LOCAL GOVERNMENT SERVICE

When I first entered local government, I really didn't know what to expect or how I might have impact. Through initial conversations with staff from across each government department, as well as looking at what similar-sized governments across the United States were doing, I quickly developed a sense of how I could best achieve some lasting changes that others could later build upon. My impact was split into two distinct phases.

Year one was dedicated to addressing basic infrastructural needs that would be required in order to later make the more significant changes that I had in mind. It was hard to take that first year to do that basic but critical work, but it didn't mean that all the work needed to be "under the hood." I knew it was important for others to see changes that showed we were able to drive improvements in some highly visible areas. Our open data portal was the gateway to the data we were sharing with the world, and it was badly in need of a new design. Creating a better first impression was a great place to start, and we were able to roll out a modern and more responsive experience for users of our open data within a matter of months. It was a signal that positive changes could happen quickly, and the encouraging feedback we received acted as an incentive for the team to keep driving toward those other changes we wished to make. Later the internal infrastructure investments began to pay dividends, and we saw a significant growth in the volume of data flowing onto our open data platform. Communicating about both the external-facing and internal-facing work streams was another key aspect of what we did in year one. One important pillar of that communication effort was to create and publish a strategic plan early in my tenure. This acted as a 'north star' for the open data team and other city staff who interacted with the open data program, and it also gave the public who interacted with the open data platform a clear insight into the work being done on their behalf complete with requests for feedback and ideas. Being held accountable in such an open way is a great way to enable meaningful impact.

Year two was when we were able to shift gears somewhat and focus on some of the tougher problems we needed to address, such as data quality and data governance. I knew these were areas where it would take several years of hard work to get to an optimal state, and I also knew that it was likely that I might not be around to complete the task. We needed to develop new skillsets within the team in order to be able to build and maintain this new set of capabilities. This included adding some new people to the team, having interns assist with some of the projects, and leveraging the data science expertise of others across the organization. Essentially, year two was about figuring out how to scale what we were doing—deliver larger datasets with high quality; updated frequently via automation; and targeted at scenarios that would unlock real value for private-sector companies, researchers, students and teachers, and app developers, as well as the general public.

Even though my tenure in local government was fairly short, about two years, I am proud of what I was able to achieve in that time. Aside from the tangible deliverables referenced earlier, I am pleased that I was able to contribute to the development of a new culture within my local government, such as sharing new ways of thinking and approaches to how we can leverage technology and data to make a real difference, in relatively short amounts of time, and by spending less of our taxpayers' money. I am immensely grateful for the opportunities I was given and the freedom to challenge the status quo, incredibly thankful for the sheer volume of things I learned from so many amazingly talented public servants, and for the chance to serve something greater than myself. Not a day goes by where I don't miss the nobility of the work of government, and I will serve again at some point in my career.

BEING INSPIRED TO SERVE

Inspiration plays a huge part in any major decision; it acts as a North Star that can guide you to your ultimate destination. It can also help give you the courage to make decisions that may seem on the face of it to be counterintuitive—for example, why I chose to leave an established career in the private sector to serve in my local government. The question of why this scenario would appear to be counterintuitive is also a valid one, but that is a topic for a different book.

What inspired me to want to work in government? As it turns out, many things and many people. Like many of us who live in the United States, I didn't grow up here. I grew up in Ireland and emigrated to the United States when I was twenty-nine years old. As a child and then a young adult, I remember being fascinated with the complex political situations of the time, especially when it came to The Troubles in Northern Ireland. I watched with fascination as the governments of Ireland and the United Kingdom, along with local political leaders in Northern Ireland, struggled for decades to create the conditions for a lasting political settlement and a permanent stop to the killing and terrorism that had plagued our countries. Those herculean efforts eventually resulted in the Good Friday Agreement, which came into effect in April 1998. In the years that followed I saw how those peace dividends resulted in the transformation of a whole society, and it taught me about the power of government and the political process to effect positive changes in the lives of millions of people. I will also admit that I was quite envious of the senior aides who accompanied those courageous leaders and who played a key supporting role in those momentous achievements. Someday, I thought to myself, I want to be in a role like that and to have that kind of impact. A seed had been planted in my mind.

In my early twenties, I remember being quite frustrated with how certain things were done in my native land and how timely access to some essential public services required lobbying local politicians, which seemed fundamentally wrong to me. I knew there had to be a better way. In 2002 I wrote to the Irish minister of health to express my frustrations with the provision of certain health services. I was surprised when I received a reply directly from the minister. In addition to informing me of coming improvements to the system that would alleviate the delays I had complained about, he noted how impressed he was with my correspondence and that I should consider joining in the effort to improve government at some point in my career. Another seed was planted.

Throughout my education, both in Ireland and the United States, I have been fortunate to have had some amazing teachers and professors who have inspired me with their passion for public service. Some have acted as mentors during my career pivot into public service. I am very fortunate to be able to avail myself of their advice, even though I have been a working professional for over twenty years. Their passion for education and service instilled in me a deep desire to give back through teaching, writing, and mentoring and to realize the importance of lifelong learning. It's not widely understood that public universities are part of the overall public service ecosystem, providing current and future generations with the skills and connections to have successful careers in the public sector. Our public education institutions play an additional role when it comes to inspiration, and that is to help reinforce the decision to perform public service. Whenever I can reconnect with my alma mater, speak with students, or give a guest lecture, I come away inspired and recommitted to my work. Those connections with current and future generations of public servants can be vital sources of inspiration when working through difficult challenges in your local government service. A sizeable portion of this book was written in the library at the university where I earned my master's degree in policy studies. It was where I would go to be inspired when struggling with a topic or a chapter.

Like a lot of people who have worked in government, one of my inspirations was the TV show *The West Wing*. I was living in Ireland when the first four seasons were originally aired, and it added to my intense desire to live in the United States someday and to work in the government there. Fast-forward many years later, and having served in municipal government in the United States, repeated viewings of *The West Wing* on Netflix have continued to inspire me to want to use my talents and energies to help improve how our government provides services to the public. President Bartlet's catchphrase "OK, what's next?" is one that I've frequently used as I navigate my own career journey.

Then, there is JFK. I will admit to having a real bias of affection toward President John Fitzgerald Kennedy, partially because his great-grandfather emigrated from the same County Wexford in the southeast corner of Ireland where I grew up, and where the Kennedy family maintain strong connections to this day. Whenever I find myself in Washington, DC, I make a point of heading across the Potomac to visit his grave, gaze into the eternal flame, and reflect on the power of his words and achievements in his roughly 1,000 days in office. While Presidents Abraham Lincoln and Thomas Jefferson will remain untouched in their abilities as the creators of some of the most inspiring language ever written, President Kennedy is arguably the president in more modern times who came closest to having a similar impact. He eloquently described the role of government and the positive impact of public service in our lives. From his iconic call to patriotic action in his inaugural address, to his ability to align the vast resources of the federal government around the singular mission of landing a man on the Moon and returning him safely to the Earth, President Kennedy created phrases that still resonate as clearly today as they did almost sixty years ago. They certainly continue to inspire me.

Reflect on what is inspiring you to read this book and to consider a career in public service. Make sure to use that inspiration as fuel for your journey. And best of all, perhaps someday you'll be providing that inspiration for aspiring public-sector technologists and asking them to think about what they, too, can do.

ABOUT THE AUTHOR

David Doyle is a public interest technologist, with experience in both the public and private sectors. Between 2016 and 2018, David served as the City of Seattle's Open Data Manager and helped develop that program into a recognized leader in the US. After his local government service, he continues to act as a thought leader on topics related to open data, improving government, and how both public and private sector organizations can leverage the power of their data for social good.

Previously, David worked at Microsoft for 18 years where he led quality engineering teams focused on delivering Windows in over 100 languages, and a data analytics team that created insights used to improve the experience of millions of Windows customers worldwide.

David holds master's degrees in both Public Policy and Technology Management, and a bachelor's degree in Applied Sciences (Computer Science and Physics). He lives in Redmond, WA with his daughter Chandler.

https://www.askwhatyoucando.com
https://medium.com/@daithioduill
https://twitter.com/daithioduill
https://www.linkedin.com/in/davdoy

INDEX

Made in the USA
Middletown, DE
30 November 2022

16028965R00191